CAMBRIDGE PAPERS IN SOCIAL ANTHROPOLOGY

No. 6

COUNCILS IN ACTION

T0371574

CAMBRIDGE PAPERS IN
SOCIAL ANTHROPOLOGY

COUNCILS IN ACTION

EDITED BY
AUDREY RICHARDS
AND
ADAM KUPER

CAMBRIDGE
AT THE UNIVERSITY PRESS
1971

CAMBRIDGE UNIVERSITY PRESS
Cambridge, New York, Melbourne, Madrid, Cape Town, Singapore, São Paulo, Delhi

Cambridge University Press
The Edinburgh Building, Cambridge CB2 8RU, UK

Published in the United States of America by Cambridge University Press, New York

www.cambridge.org
Information on this title: www.cambridge.org/9780521113410

First published 1971
This digitally printed version 2009

A catalogue record for this publication is available from the British Library

Library of Congress Catalogue Card Number: 75-171675

ISBN 978-0-521-08240-2 hardback
ISBN 978-0-521-11341-0 paperback

CONTENTS

CONTRIBUTORS TO THIS ISSUE

R.G. Abrahams. Lecturer in social anthropology at the University of Cambridge, where he took his B.A. (1957) and Ph.D. (1962). He has done fieldwork among the Nyamwezi of Tanzania and the Labwor of Uganda, and is the author of *The Political Organization of Unyamwezi* (1967) and various papers.

Maurice Bloch. A graduate of the London School of Economics, where he is now a lecturer, Dr Bloch took his Ph.D. at Cambridge in 1967. He did fieldwork among the Merina of Madagascar, and is the author of *Placing the Dead* (1971) and a number of papers, listed elsewhere in this volume.

G. I. Jones. Lecturer in social anthropology, University of Cambridge, author of *Basutoland Medicine Murder* (1951), *Report on the Position of Chiefs in Eastern Nigeria* (1957), *The Trading States of the Oil Rivers* (1963), and various papers.

Adam Kuper. A graduate of the University of the Witwatersrand, he took his Ph.D. at Cambridge in 1966. Recently on the staff of Makerere University, Kampala, he is currently a lecturer at University College, London. Has done fieldwork in Botswana, and is the author of *Kalahari Village Politics: An African Democracy* (1970) and various papers.

Audrey Richards. Formerly Smuts Reader in Social Anthropology and Director of the Cambridge University Centre of African Studies. Her numerous publications include *Hunger and Work in a Savage Tribe* (1932); *Land Labour and Diet in Northern Rhodesia* (1939); *Bemba Marriage and Modern Economic Conditions* (1940); *Chisungu* (1956); *The Changing Structure of a Ganda Village* (1966); *Multicultural States of East Africa* (1969).

A.F. Robertson. Took his Ph.D. at Edinburgh in 1967, and has since held a research fellowship at the Cambridge University Centre of African Studies: fieldwork in Buganda and recently a study of government and politics in Ahafo, Ghana.

Paul Spencer. Took an engineering degree at Cambridge before turning to anthropology. Did fieldwork among the Samburu and Rendile in East Africa and received his D.Phil. at Oxford in 1960. Has since been a member of the Tavistock Institute. Studied local government in Coventry, and was subsequently seconded to the Royal Commission on Local Government. Now working on aspects of the Health Service. He is the author of *The Samburu* and various papers.

INTRODUCTION:

THE NATURE OF THE PROBLEM

By Audrey Richards

By tradition the volumes in this series consist of a number of essays in which a single topic is discussed in the light of anthropological field data. The subject selected for this volume is the machinery by which group decisions are reached in a number of different societies – decisions which may be political, judicial, economic, religious or may indeed refer to any other sphere of interest in which joint activities are carried out.

We limit ourselves as far as possible to the institutionalised processes of joint discussion as distinct from the informal arguments which take place over and above the debates of the recognised deliberative bodies for which we use the term 'council'; although we make some exception in the case of societies in which extra-conciliar discussions, secret meetings of pressure groups, lobbying or attempts at the 'squaring' of important individuals, definitely form part of the recognised council procedure.

Councils then, according to our limitations, are governed by conventions and persist in time, for that is what is generally meant by an institutionalised group. However it is obviously difficult to draw hard and fast lines, as we shall explain. For this reason we have adopted three main criteria to distinguish the bodies we are considering.

By a council we mean first a gathering of people of which the membership is limited by the rules of the society either to particular categories such as men rather than women, or old people rather than young; to persons of a given status, such as men of one rank rather than another as in the House of Lords; to members of a social group such as a clan, or a village, or even to the widest political unit such as a tribe; or alternatively to the residents in a territory, since non-members of the tribe may be allowed to participate in a tribal council as are Herero and some other minorities in the case of a Tswana *pitso*. The council may also be limited to particular individuals chosen in accepted ways, by election or nomination, for instance. We give reasons later for suggesting that this last limitation of council membership is much less common in the societies with which anthropologists usually deal, than in our own.

1

Secondly, councils, in our sense of the term, are usually, though not invariably, held in one place, whether this be a town hall or a spot under a particular tree. It is of course true that in many African societies decisions of a judicial type can be reached at any spot desired by the litigants. People may take a dispute for arbitration to any man they respect, and assemble for the purpose at his house. It is true also that this informal process of arbitration may continue whether or not there are established judicial courts in the same society or not. But it is arguable that a court or council has not become an institution unless it meets very generally in the same place, or is expected to do so.[1] When this place is a building, it easily becomes symbolic of the political activity associated with it. A picture of the British Houses of Parliament is used in this way. It used to be flashed on television screens to illustrate the concepts of democratic government which the people of the United Kingdom believed at the time to be their great contribution to the conduct of the political affairs of the world.

Thirdly, a council, as we use the term, is a body which accepts a series of conventions governing the behaviour of its members. We instance formal openings of meetings by a sovereign or authority; religious ritual such as the asking of the blessings of a deity or the pouring of libations; fixed seating arrangements reflecting party affiliations and office as in our own parliament in which members are in fact described by their seating as being 'front' or 'back benchers'; or groupings reflecting age distinctions or class or lineage allegiance in some other societies. The order of speaking may also be regulated and special phraseology used, either in the form of terms of address, conventions or rhetoric, or approved modes of speech. We ourselves talk of language as being 'parliamentary' or 'unparliamentary'. The Bemba, as we shall see, adopt in their tribal council special linguistic usages and an allusive turn of speech. It is in fact these conventions which mainly distinguish a council, as we are using the term, from any other gathering of people exchanging views or news. In a Bemba village those sitting eating, gossiping or mending their hunting nets in the men's shelter, change their behaviour when asked to decide a case or to arrange some important activity, and they become for the moment a village community 'in council'.

These then are the three criteria which we use to distinguish what we call councils from other gatherings which meet to reach a group decision. But, as we said earlier, the line is inevitably a very difficult one to draw. Councils, according to our usage, normally persist in time, and are governed by accepted conventions and can be clearly contrasted with groupings which arise and function spontaneously and then disappear once a necessary decision or set of decisions has been reached. But in many cases informal groups, constituted ad hoc, follow the pattern of decision-making current in that society. In England, for instance, committees spring into being to organise the most ephemeral activities such as a village fancy dress dance or a fete. They then immediately proceed to elect chairmen, secretaries and treasurers and often use the formal phraseology typical of institutionalised councils.

In other words the conciliar pattern for that particular society is adopted.

We have referred to the process by which groups become councils, so to speak, by the adoption of conciliar behaviour, as do Bemba villagers sitting in their shelter on occasion. Even a group as loosely organised as the body of kinsmen at an English middle class funeral may be said to become 'a family in council' when seats are taken for the solicitor to read the will. Expressions then become serious; malicious comments, anecdotes or slang are felt to be inappropriate and views tend to be given in some kind of order of seniority or of descent from different siblings.

Moreover there are societies in which important and recurrent negotiations may be carried out by groups which do not persist in time as regular councils, but which come into being when required and which then follow a traditional procedure during the period of deliberations. Discussions which preface a recurrent activity like marrying and giving in marriage are a case in point. Abrahams shows that among the Labwor, for instance, marriage negotiations involve two loosely organised groups of lineage members, which follow certain recognised conventions of deliberation. Although such gatherings differ greatly from formal meetings of bodies with fixed membership with prescribed 'terms of reference', and defined methods of reaching and recording decisions, such as those of an English borough council or a university senate, yet we have felt it important to include in our volume an account of some deliberations which fall into this intermediate field between the institutionalised council and the debates of an ephemeral group gathered in argument.

We define, as will be clear, by composition and procedure, that is to say by council structure and by behaviour patterns, rather than by the types of issue under discussion. This practice has proved convenient in the case of the wide range of societies covered by these essays. Many traditional African councils deal with all sorts of issues in the same day. A group of elders may, for instance, settle a dispute between two litigants, impose a fine on an offender, arrange for the repair of a bridge over a local stream and discuss the succession to a local village headmanship; and this all in one day. We have therefore found it difficult in some cases even to distinguish clearly between judicial bodies or 'courts', and deliberative assemblies making administrative decisions in the political, economic or military field. British colonial governments have generally been in favour of separating the judiciary from the executive and have done so early in the history of a colony in some cases. In other territories however the division was not made until a year or two before the Independence of the territory was reached. We use the term council therefore for a body which discusses a variety of issues, judicial, or executive, and refer in some cases to multi-purpose councils when some distinction is required.[2] We realise also that apart from the expressed purposes of a meeting there are a number of by-products, so to speak, of such attempts to reach decisions by joint discussion. A meeting may be the occasion for a struggle for power between two individuals, or two or more groups; the assertion of the authority of the 'establishment'; or the issuing of orders to inferior authorities who have not taken any part in the reaching of the decision in question; in fact in a whole range of political as distinct from government or administrative spheres of interest to follow M. G. Smith's usage.[3] The most important result of long discussion may be the communication of knowledge or the explanation of a policy rather than the reaching of a particular decision.

Few comparative studies of council structures, functions and procedures have been made by anthropologists to date, though students of the subject are grateful for Bailey's pioneer work published in 1965 and discussed later by Kuper. Ethnographers of course attend council meetings in areas where these are prominent features of the political and judicial life. Indeed such meetings are often the most striking manifestations of the political structure, values, and activities of the society in question. The existence of a hierarchy of councils such as village, district or tribal councils, or of a federation of town councils as among the Akan peoples may give a picture of what Radcliffe-Brown used occasionally to call the 'total social structure' of a society. This is specially the case where a colonial power has given definition and permanence to the situation by 'recognising' traditional councils, or instituting new ones with statutory powers. Anthropologists working in such areas commonly describe the constitution of these councils, their relationship to each other, and the processes by which judicial cases may be sent on appeal from one court to another, or the administrative decisions of a higher council transmitted to a lower. We describe the conciliar structure of our chosen societies in all the essays published here.

Ethnographers also use their detailed observations of individual council meetings as indices of the accepted principles of social structure and of the tensions which sometimes underlie these. The conventions governing seating, procedure or order of speaking reflect the social hierarchies, the divisions, the equalities and inequalities of status as surely as does the behaviour of the participants in some great religious rite. The field-worker who is familiar with the formal social structure of his society will recognise at once why certain members of the council sit together. They will be perhaps members of a lineage, of a royal line, or represent grades of a chiefly hierarchy. Men of client or slave status may also sit separately. But equally well the ethnographer may become aware of structural principles which he had not previously understood, by observing the grouping at a council meeting, as again he so often does at a religious rite. I myself for instance became conscious for the first time that the *bakabilo*, or liturgical specialists at the Bemba royal capital, were divided into groups according to their relationship to the king, or the order of arrival of their ancestors in the country, when I saw them seated, both at council meetings and on occasions of religious ritual. Similarly in Buganda in 1952, I was first made aware of the great distinction in status between the land-owners and their tenants by the way in which the parish chiefs introduced the land-owning members of the local council and their deputies in order of precedence, and then shouted to the tenants to stand up in an undifferentiated mass.

4

Council meetings also provide an index of the tensions and conflicts underlying the accepted rules of social structure. There may be changing alliances between one group and another, explosive utterances or again special devices to prevent explosive and perhaps disruptive utterances, or special arrangements to forestall overt criticism of established authorities as in the case of the Bemba tribal council. Examples of council conventions expressing structural principles are given in these essays as well as accounts of inter-group hostility expressed or concealed by them.

Lastly council meetings have been used as indices of a people's activities, interests and values. The listing of the number and type of issues discussed during a period such as a year is a useful gauge of a council's concerns. Kuper attended all the meetings of a Kgalagari council and lists the topics discussed there during his year of residence. Robertson gives the same type of information from the Akan. A number of other anthropologists and students of African law have analysed written records of court cases or council meetings where such records had been introduced by colonial governments. But written records are often sketchy and sometimes give nothing but the final decisions reached on an issue. Furthermore in an area under colonial rule the minutes rarely made mention of traditional issues or 'things which the European would not understand'. Nevertheless, however incomplete such data may be, the mere listing of the issues handled by a council in a given period has been valuable. Schapera's publications based on the records of Tswana courts and council meetings are notable in this respect.[4]

Finally the expression of political and moral values may be made in a very explicit fashion at courts and councils and often according to traditional linguistic usages. In fact such a public expression of the group ethos may be one of the main purposes of a meeting. The Great Council *(lukiiko)* of the Buganda kingdom originated, for instance in a gathering of chiefs and notables who greeted the king in order of precedence crying *'Osinze'* ('You have conquered, or shown yourself to be paramount').[5] This conventional greeting expressed the subjects' recognition of the unchallenged position of a warrior king and it also reflected the administrative hierarchy of the kingdom. Business was no doubt also conducted, but Apolo Kagwa, our informant, does not discuss such practical issues at all. The duty of warriors to fight for their people may be formally proclaimed after a decision to make war; or the obligation of commoners to bring tribute to nobles or chiefs may be expressed at the end of an economic discussion. After debates over the succession to an office, councillors may announce in formal language the obligations of the new authority to behave in a prescribed way. Our own politicians climb to unusual heights of rhetoric on important occasions such as a declaration of war or the death of a sovereign. Judges in most societies defend their decisions by proclaiming the moral rules on which they believe themselves to be acting.[6] Such formal pronouncements may reinforce social obligations by constant repetition, teach the young, inspire to action, implicate a body of councillors in a decision or act as a defence for a judgment. They certainly provide the ethnographer with useful statements of political and social values. We give some such statements in our essays but I think none of us set out to collect them methodically.

In brief, anthropologists have used observations made at council or court meetings mainly for the information so provided on the political structure and interests ·of the society itself. There are however two types of investigation they have hardly undertaken as yet. The first is a study of the council mechanism as a means of achieving results, say in linking the sections of a segmentary society together by means of some form of federal council; in reducing tensions and disturbances through joint discussion and pronouncement of a group judgment; in allocating tribal or national resources, its tribute or its taxes; in organising an activity such as a war expedition; or in legislating or planning for the future. These are results achieved in some societies by the direct command of a superior authority with the order enforced by his agents, his administrators or police. In other societies judgment may be given, or activities planned, after joint discussion. In the majority there is perhaps a mixture of the two methods. This is a type of study which is highly relevant to current debates on the 'participation' of members of the community in political decisions at the central or the local level, in local government, industry or university affairs. The wide range of conciliar practices with which as a group they are familiar, should enable anthropologists to make an important contribution to these topics.

We do not pretend to have exploited this material to the full in our essays. The work needs a good deal of organisation since it cannot reasonably be undertaken by a student unfamiliar with the structure and activities of the society concerned and also its administrative history. It may therefore have to be postponed until a late stage in ethnographic work, until a second or third expedition to the area perhaps.[7] We hope however that we have at least illustrated some of the possibilities of functional studies of this type carried out on a comparative scale.

The second type of investigation which should prove rewarding is a detailed and systematic investigation of conciliar behaviour. The use of special linguistic forms in council meetings is one such topic of study. Do traditional phrases or rhetorical utterances give validity to a decision reached at a meeting? Do they add authority, commit the speakers to support of a measure, or even have power of their own like some magic formula?[8] Does a formal statement of a fact already known constitute a public recognition of that fact?

Again there is the difficulty of expressing open hostility in a meeting of persons permanently linked by joint residence, kinship, clientship or some such enduring tie. How is violent opposition between one individual or group and another concealed, if this is thought to be necessary? How is a consensus seen to be reached whether by voting, or by judgment of a chairman or chief? These are important questions discussed by Bailey. What extra-conciliar activities are used to forestall a disruptive hostility or find peaceful solutions after a quarrel? The meeting of Ibo elders after a stormy debate by lineage members is a mechanism of this type.

Another set of conventions governs the expression of the relations between an accepted authority such as a king, a chief or even a chairman, and the members of the council he directs. A Bemba king was thought to have divine attributes and therefore could not be publicly opposed. He sat apart from his councillors, while a 'messenger' carried 'the words' from the advisors to the authority and back again. The exclusion of the king from the council or parliament is in fact a common device by which subjects can control a situation while the authority of the ruler is maintained. Akan chiefs in traditional councils walk out of debates on contentious issues, waiting to see what opinions are expressed and by whom. Other African monarchs are so powerful that their councils meet only to be told their monarch's decisions. The council of the Mukama of Ruanda seems to have been of this type. Even in our society committees tend to want a chairman strong enough to 'get things done', but not so strong as to make them feel impotent and unable to voice their views. The success of a committee meeting often depends on the skill and patience of some intermediary between an authoritarian chairman and the different members of the group such as an experienced secretary, who may act in a somewhat similar fashion to the traditional messenger among the Bemba.

There are many difficulties in making the systematic observations of council behaviour which would be necessary in order to get answers to such questions and it is for this reason, we hazard the guess, that so few anthropologists have concentrated on a study of this kind.

The recording of council debates is difficult. Written records are rarely full enough to be of much service in the case of most of the societies we describe here. Meetings in the village as distinct from those at a chiefdom or tribal level are usually not recorded at all. They do not in any case give any idea of the degree of hostility or boredom which may be expressed at the meeting itself, or the use of such conventions as deliberately blank expressions, by which the disapproval of councillors may be indicated even in a very authoritarian society.

Many anthropologists did their work in the days before recording machines were readily available. Some still find their own notes plus those of members of the society more useful. Bohannan worked in this way, as did Kuper and Robertson.

Then there are of course linguistic difficulties in the case of most ethnographic field-work. The observer has to be very fluent in a language to be able to follow rapid exchanges of view or quarrels. Much discussion in African societies is phrased in allusive terms and a grammar book knowledge of the language is then not enough. Bemba, as we shall see, support their arguments with reference to the crimes and virtues of dead kings and by proverbs with rich historic overtones. Sometimes they use archaic language in order not to be understood. Robertson attended meetings of a Ghanaian town council conducted in English, but also had difficulties with allusive turns of speech.

Finally of course this type of field observation is time consuming to a degree. It is necessary to attend meetings constantly before the patterns of conciliar behaviour become clear. Where meetings take place regularly it might be necessary to undertake this work to the exclusion of other observations, and to undertake it in the very late stage of an ethnographer's apprenticeship.

We have not all of us been able to work in this way as our notes show, but we think that a clear description of the observational problems involved in studying conciliar activities will itself be of value. We regard our work as an experiment which may be instructive to others rather than as a perfect example of how such work should be done.

The history of the book

Seven council systems are described in this volume and five of these occur in African societies. This is really fortuitous. Any ethnographer who has travelled in Africa is impressed by the striking differences in the conciliar procedure in different parts of Africa. My own experience came from working in the Bemba country of Northern Zambia, in Makapanstad, capital village of a group of Kgatla living not far from Pretoria, in Buganda and south Ghana, where I had the chance to attend a meeting of a divisional council of chiefs on the Akuapim ridge in 1963. African nationalists sometimes speak nostalgically of the democracy of the past when affairs were settled by 'a group of old men sitting under a tree', but this view certainly does not do justice to the complication of the decision-making procedures to be found in the continent; to their great variety, and to their vitality even at the present time. The relation between the council type and the political structure and activities of African peoples seemed to us to form a fascinating field for study.

The clash of viewpoints between the then colonial administrators and those of the African societies they administered, also threw up new points of comparative interest. Both types of authority, European and African, had obviously different ideas as to how a local council should be composed and what it should do.

The traditional African societies were without writing. For this reason decisions reached by a council could only be passed on to the rest of the community by the word of mouth of those who had attended the meeting. Hence the importance of large gatherings and lengthy discussions, so that as many people as possible came to understand what was going on. Senior men from different districts tended to come with junior kinsmen, who learnt the job of government in this way. Again, there were no written records of legislative decisions taken, nor of judgments given in court cases. It was therefore essential to have witnesses of an arbitration case or a criminal action. The young men and boys who followed an important man to a court-council meeting might subsequently prove invaluable witnesses of a transaction that had taken place in their youth. I refer later to a Bemba case with great political significance which was held up for two days while an infirm old man was fetched in a litter from his village to give evidence about an event which had taken place when he was young.

The mechanisms for enforcing political or judicial decisions were often most inadequate in traditional African societies. Even where a central authority such as a king or a chief existed, the use of police or any equivalent personnel was most uncommon and royal messengers tended to be scarce. Hence it was useful that those who attended council meetings should be considered bound by the decisions taken there, and it was important to have as wide a representation from the countryside as possible. Councillors were informed of the chief's wishes, but he could have no guarantee that he would be obeyed, unless he could see that his sub-chiefs and headmen were willing to carry out his decisions. Even among the Bemba, who thought it wrong to criticise a chief directly, councillors could assume faces that were said to be 'dark', that is to say expressionless and in this way they showed that they were unwilling to co-operate. In a segmentary society without any centralised government, a decision had to be supported by senior lineage heads at a council meeting if there was to be a chance that it would be put into force. Kuper shows that attendance at a Kgalagari council meeting put councillors under an obligation to apply a measure there agreed upon.

Again in the absence of written charters or historic documents, the public recitation of ancestral claims to office, historic precedents for political action, the formal taking of oaths of allegiance were important features of council procedure and had to be constantly repeated. By such means people living in small remote villages may well have become aware for the first time of their membership of a larger group when they were summoned to a central council meeting. In a somewhat similar way Durkheim would have us believe that participation in a great religious rite made men conscious of the power of the society to which they belonged. Bemba put this concretely by saying 'When people come to the capital they understand who is their chief' or 'When a young man listens to the old men holding a council he begins to understand the things of the past'.

Colonial administrators, in contrast, were not unnaturally impatient of large meetings which slowed down procedure and held up the type of discussions which they felt to be the proper tasks of local government councils. As time went on they began to try to stream-line the procedure by fixing the personnel of councils, whether by nomination or election. The new activities which local government councils were to undertake also demanded more specialised knowledge and a European-type education. Hence the efforts of colonial administrations during the thirties and forties to introduce new elements into traditional councils such as teachers and members of welfare services, and to set up small specialist sub-committees such as finance and education committees.

The traditional councils had, as we have stressed, multiple functions, and this was natural in types of society in which most authorities, family or lineage heads, village headmen, and chiefs had multiple functions as leaders of kinship groups, judges, economic or military leaders or ritual specialists.[9] British colonial authorities, in contrast, tried to define very carefully the powers of the different councils they 'recognised' and to assign different duties to each level of council, village, district or tribe, and as we have indicated they also tried in time to separate judicial courts from local government bodies. The allocation of annual budgets and sometimes rate-raising powers to the most important councils in a tribal area or a town, made the definition of each body's powers even more exact.

The priorities of both types of administration were also different. Colonial officers judged the success of a local council in terms of the welfare activities it undertook, the speed with which it acted, and its skill and probity in handling its budget. The traditional council seems to have put first its duty to settle disputes and it must be remembered that small communities easily break up if there is unresolved enmity among their members.[10] The preservation of charters of office and lines of descent may well prove to be the next most important object of discussion in societies in which legitimate authority is usually based on descent or fictions of descent. Much of the time of traditional councils seems to have been given to discussing succession to office and in preserving past political values rather than in undertaking new activities. Legislation, in the sense of making new codes of conduct for the group, was rarer, and some anthropologists question whether traditional councils carried out this function at all, since the conditions of life in an isolated society rarely required change.[11] Planning, in the modern sense of the term, that is to say long-distance planning, was probably unknown. Executive decisions as to the conduct of traditional activities, such as economic or military undertakings, must have been made at the level of the local community in societies in which centralised government was weak.

As to participation, it is worth remembering that in the traditional system, the leaders of different sections of the community or different areas discuss measures which they themselves are going to carry out, together with their supporters, their younger relatives or fellow villagers. According to British local government, in contrast, those who make policy decisions, mainly by raising rates and allocating funds, do not themselves carry out these decisions, and this work is in the hands of executive officers and specialists who have responsibility for doing so.

The right of attending meetings in most traditional societies depends, not on the choice of the community as a whole, but on hereditary descent, membership of a kinship, territorial or occupational group, and usually on account of age and status in that group. By this means young men are committed to the system in that they will eventually acquire positions of authority in it by the mere fact of continuing to live, and so in time becoming 'elders' in a society which honours age. [12]

It is thus that two aspects of comparative field-work occur to the ethnographer in the field. One is the contrast between the type of council system found useful in a society which is pre-literate, without a strong centralised government, facing few challenges to change, and not consciously desiring change, and that of a literate society with a central government, a highly developed bureaucracy in charge of

10

specialised social services, and constantly facing change. The second type of comparison is between the conciliar systems of a variety of types of political structure in traditional Africa, in a strong or a weak monarchy for instance, in a federation of chiefdoms or segmentary societies of different types, and in large towns.

Such a programme of comparative research would have taken more years than I had available, but in 1965 Kuper returned from Africa with some excellent material on Kgalagari councils and under the stimulus of his enthusiasm we held a seminar on the subject at the Cambridge Centre of African Studies. Naturally, most, though not all, of those who took part were specialising in African ethnography and hence the concentration on African material in this volume. Our talks were of a very exploratory kind. None of us, except Kuper, had made any systematic observations of council procedure in the field and therefore much of the material we present, including my own, was based on impressions. We believe however that we raise subjects of importance for future research workers even if we have not been able to frame any clear-cut hypotheses.

In the event only three members of the seminar were able to contribute essays to the book, Bloch, Kuper and myself.[13] All the contributors have however had the same comparative point of view. We invited Spencer to give us a paper on the working of an English borough council since it was the British model of local government which was adopted in most of the African societies here described.

One of our difficulties in undertaking any type of comparative work has been the length of time our societies had been in contact with British, or in one case, French authorities. The contrast between the traditional and the post-colonial council system was usually blurred. The writers of these essays have obviously concentrated on the description and analysis of the councils which they saw in operation, but there is no doubt that there is considerable interest in such general points of comparison as I have been listing, such as those between pre-literate and post-literate societies, and it is for this reason that some of us have tried to give some account of historical reconstruction of the pre-colonial days. For instance Jones was able to describe clearly the traditional council system of the Ibo as well as the various stages in its adaptation to modern conditions. Bloch has given us rich historical material on the development of the Merina; and I myself arrived in Bemba country only two years after a new court-council system had been set up. Yet in most of the essays it is difficult to disentangle the introduced British and French ideas from those of the people themselves. A number of compromises is everywhere apparent. The traditional council may be given formal recognition and asked to carry out new tasks of local government as among the Bemba (pp.126ff), or a new local government organ may be established, which is responsible for modern social services, sometimes following British council procedure and sometimes with traditional ceremonies incorporated, as when libations are poured to ancestral spirits before or during an Akan council. There may also be a recognition of both types of council, traditional and modern, each with its own sphere of interest as Robertson described in the case of the same Ghanaian town. The survival value of council structures or council procedures under present day conditions is itself an index of their functional value at the present time.

Notes

[1] Mair, in a survey of the beginnings of government, suggests that the provision of a place where people know that disputes can be publically discussed is one such step. She considers that one of the chief functions of an Anuak headman is the provision of such a place outside his homestead gate (Mair, 1962: 71).

[2] It will be remembered that P. Bohannan takes another course and uses the vernacular term *jir* with a qualifying adjective, e.g. a market *jir*, a village *jir*, or a family *jir* (1957).

[3] Set out in M. G. Smith, 1960, ch.2, and in Smith, 1956.

[4] See Schapera, 1943; 1947; 1970; Fallers, 1969: 87-9.

[5] Kagwa, 1952 edition, ch.12.

[6] Schapera has published a list of legal maxims heard in Tswana courts (1966).

[7] P. Bohannan came to the same conclusion, i.e. that courts and councils must be studied at a late stage in field-work (Bohannan, 1957: vi).

[8] Oaths used in court or councils meetings are certainly thought to call supernatural power into play.

[9] Multiplex relations in Gluckman's sense of the word.

[10] See also Mair's statement about East African societies 'We shall also find that judging cases is thought of as the first duty of a ruler' (Mair, 1962: 71).

[11] R. E. Bradbury writes of the Yoruba 'It would be wrong to say that the elders had no legislative functions... Nevertheless, the emphasis in their authority, was on the conservation of that code as it had been handed down to them from the original elders' (Bradbury, 1969: 19).

[12] Bradbury, 1969: 18.

[13] I. Nzimiro a member of the seminar prepared a paper on Ibo councils but owing to the troubles in Nigeria it was too late for publication. A. F. Robertson subsequently engaged in a special study of the council system of one Ghanaian town and his results are published here.

INTRODUCTION:

COUNCIL STRUCTURE AND DECISION-MAKING

By Adam Kuper

The council and the social structure

Richards has indicated some general problems in the comparative study of councils. I shall try to sketch some of the issues which emerge from recent studies, including those published here. Bailey's stimulating paper on decisions made in councils (Bailey, 1965) may serve as a starting-point. It provided a focus for many of our discussions in the 1965 seminars, and his characterization of elite and arena councils provides one of the few analytic tools which we have all used, to a greater or lesser extent. Bailey wrote:

'Elite councils are those which are, or consider themselves to be (whether they admit it openly or not), a ruling oligarchy. The dominant cleavage in such a group is between the elite council (including, where appropriate, the minority from which it is recruited) and the public: that is to say the dominant cleavage is horizontal. The opposite kind of council is the arena council. These exist in groups in which the dominant cleavages are vertical. The council is not so much a corporate body with interests against its public, but an arena in which the representatives of segments in the public come into conflict with one another.' (Bailey, 1965: 10).

For Bailey the classification is a necessary preliminary to predicting decision-making techniques. This is a problem to which I shall return. However, the two types of council are so widely dispersed and yet so easily recognized that it is worth considering this brief set of structural criteria in its own right, and asking questions about the kinds of political system, and the characteristic social or ecological conditions, that are associated with each type of council.

Several features characterize elite and arena councils, aside from the diagnostic feature, the relationship of the council to its public. An elite council is typically small and has a fixed membership. The council members often have specialized political roles – specialized in the sense that their area of competence is precisely delimited; and also in the sense that each member may be an expert in a particular, relevant field. Not all elite councils are either specialized or expert: but councils which do have special and limited responsibilities, or are composed of experts, will tend to be elite councils.

13

An elite council may have the authority to promulgate decisions, or it may be advisory to another political authority. However, where it has the power to make authoritative decisions, it must have sanctions at its disposal which are largely independent of popular support.

It is obvious, then, that elite councils are adapted to political systems in which there is effective centralization of power, and also a fairly high level of political role differentiation. Elite councils will therefore be found in states or in modern corporations. In a highly differentiated society or a bureaucratic organization, elite councils may function effectively at almost every level. Tribal states are often exceptions to this rule, since in practice the state apparatus hardly penetrates community political organization at the village level. The ruling class is content to allow the day-to-day affairs of the peasantry to be regulated on a parochial basis, and political role differentiation in the political sub-system of the community is slight. Thus one does not find elite councils at this level.

It is probably worth-while to distinguish between two forms of the arena council. First there is the community-in-council, or assembly, described in several papers in this volume. As Bloch defines the paradigmatic case of the Merina *fokon'-olona:* 'The *fokon'olona* council is the *fokon'olona* (i.e. the community) doing something'. (Parentheses added.)

Councils of this type are associated with strong community life. All full members of the political community have the right to attend and participate in meetings, although the actual turn-out may fluctuate widely, depending on the issue under discussion. Such councils naturally have a wide sphere of competence – the total field of public, or community activity. However, they do not normally dispose of sanctions aside from their built-in reliance on public opinion.

In contrast, arena councils which are distinct from their public usually have more strictly delimited spheres of competence, and command more specific sanctions. By definition, of course, membership is more strictly limited. In some cases such arena councils may develop attributes of elite councils. This is a common feature of modern parliaments. Once again, tribal states are somewhat unusual, for they seldom have arena councils at the higher levels of government. Where they do, as for example among some of the Southern Bantu peoples, the councils usually have little power or initiative.

Bailey was reluctant to recognize the community-in-council as an arena council. Discussing traditional *panchayats* in India, he remarks that they were often 'merely arenas in which the players scored points off one another in what was literally a game of politics', and asks:

'Are they, then, arena councils? Certainly opposing points of view are given an airing. Yet they are not arena councils because the members are not steered by cleavages in the public: members are not, so to speak, constantly looking over their shoulder to see what their constituents will think of them' (Bailey, 1965: 16).

This is not persuasive. All arena councils, including communities-in-council, develop within themselves decision-making elites. These elites are made up of spokesmen for the interest groups within the broader political reference group: and it makes little difference if this 'public' is actually sitting in on the meeting or not. The community-in-council is best seen as a structural variant of the arena council.

It is rewarding to look beyond the purely political determinants of council structure. For example, the principles by which membership of any council is fixed must be directly related to the forms of social differentiation in the society. More specifically, if there is any notion of representation, it must relate to the principles of segmentation at the appropriate level of the society. This may be a two-way relationship, as several of the studies published here demonstrate – that is to say, social status may be affected by performance in council.

The question of representation arises by definition where there is an arena council. I have suggested that this is true equally of Bailey's arena council and of the community-in-council, or assembly, where certain members are regarded as spokesmen for groupings within the council itself. Nonetheless, the principle of representation may be implicit and informal. For example, the Kgalagari village council acts on the assumption that the leading members of the major communal divisions must participate in the formulation of any public decision. However, this is not the ideological picture, and I established the rule only after prolonged observation. It finally became clear that the rule of representation existed, and that one could trace its influence in all council meetings; but there was no explicit rule nor any ideology backing the practice.

Even within tribal societies the principle of representation may vary at different levels of organization. Jones describes how among the Ibo each level of segmentation generates its appropriate form of representation. There is lineage representation in village councils, and village representation in town councils. The Arusha are a more complex case. They have two alternative series of councils, one associated with the age-sets, the other with the lineages; and each series of councils is naturally constructed on its own representative basis – age-set or lineage membership. This creates a situation which the Arusha politician can manipulate in the most complex fashion (Gulliver, 1963).

In more differentiated societies, various classes and functional groupings may be represented. Robertson provides a fascinating account of the way in which various interest groups (women, strangers, elders, guilds, etc.) are represented in Ghanaian town committees. Comparative material of this kind – together with historical studies – point up the revolutionary nature of representation in modern democracies, based on territorial or proportional principles.

Factional behaviour – alliances of council members on particular issues – is relevant here. There is already a large anthropological literature on factions, and this is not the place to survey the whole field. However, it should be stressed that the literature, which has been written largely by Indianists, tends to concentrate upon the exigencies of political strategy, assumed to set similar constraints in all political systems. Taken together with the peculiarities of the Indian material, this has led to an emphasis upon the personal and temporary nature of factions which must seem exaggerated to the Africanist. In many African arena councils, and in particular at the community level, factions are fairly stable. They may be seen as the political dimension of the segmentary pattern of the society. (Alliances between factions, however, are determined rather by tactical considerations.)

The geographical, technological and economic bases of societies also set limits to the possibilities of council organization. Given a simple technology, and more particularly poor means of communication, councils can operate efficiently and on a regular basis only at the level of the local community. An exception to this would be the elite council whose members are attached to a central court.

The force of these material circumstances may be deduced from the situation of the dispersed and semi-nomadic pastoral societies of Eastern Africa, which lack formal councils. In these societies decisions are made in ad hoc groups brought together by men of influence. Equally, in what Richards has called Africa's 'pedestrian states', where all communication between the local community and the centre was by messenger, no significant arena councils developed to cover the whole state. An exception which proves the rule is the Tswana *lekgotla,* which has always been extremely important since the majority of the tribe, and certainly the more important segments, live in the large capital town (see Schapera, 1956: 65).

Advances in communications may permit the establishment of centralized arena councils, representing widely dispersed populations. However, the new modes of communication have imposed their own constraints on council behaviour. Spencer's analysis of the relationship of an English town council to the press brings this out very clearly. This is, of course, a live issue in British politics, where television coverage of parliament was recently disallowed.

Finally, the form of economic activity may influence council structure and behaviour. For one thing, the exigencies of economic organization may necessitate a particular form of decision-making. Barnes has suggested that the conditions of Norwegian fishing are such that there must be a captain with authority to make snap decisions that are obeyed without question. A council of any sort would be unworkable in this situation (Barnes, 1954). Bloch's paper illustrates by way of contrast how the need for co-operative activity in rice growing among the Merina is met through a council system, and Richards gives an account in her chapter of the economic needs of the Bemba in relation to decision-making.

Further, at a more general level, the degree of economic specialization is usually covariant with the degree of political role differentiation. Thus if my earlier argument is correct, a fairly well-developed division of labour will usually be found in societies which have elite councils. And as economic specialization develops, new interest-groups emerge, which demand representation in the councils.

16

Decision-making in councils

Bailey, however, was not interested in classification for its own sake. He distinguished elite and arena councils because he was interested in predicting the circumstances under which councils would reach decisions by consensus or by majority vote. He set up a model in which he opposed two ideal types:

A	B
Councils lean towards consensus when they have one of the following characteristics:	Councils proceed readily to majority voting when they are
(1) an administrative function, especially when they lack sanctions, or	(1) policy-making, or
(2) an elite position in opposition to their public, or	(2) arena councils, or
(3) concern with external relationships.	(3) concerned with internal relationships.

(Bailey, 1965: 13)

In other words, three variables must be taken into account if one is to predict this range of council behaviour — (1) the council's task; (2) its relationship to its public; and (3) its relationship to the external political environment. It should be noted that these variables may change for a single council during one meeting: several examples will be found in the case studies. The main point to grasp, however, is this: Bailey contends that these three variables are sufficient to explain (and predict) the conciliar decision-making processes. Although our studies have forced us to amend aspects of Bailey's formulation, we accept this basic discovery.

I shall begin by suggesting some alterations to this model, which allow one to predict a greater range of decision-making processes.

First of all, decisions taken by majority vote cannot be so neatly opposed to decisions reached by a consensus. What indeed precisely constitutes a decision by consensus? The pattern of a straw vote followed by a second, official, recorded, unanimous vote poses an obvious difficulty here. There are other problematic cases too. In many arena councils — perhaps particularly in Africa — people often 'vote with their feet', avoiding a meeting, or even walking out, if they find themselves in the minority. Robertson describes such scenes in his paper in this volume. If the council then reaches a decision can one call it a consensual decision or a decision by majority vote?

More fundamentally, Bailey's concern with two widespread techniques of conciliar decision-making has led him to neglect an extremely significant and perhaps equally widespread kind of conciliar activity — the failure to take a decision, or the formulation of a merely ceremonial decision, or a decision which is ambiguous. I have remarked the grounds he gave for ignoring the traditional *panchayat,* but a study of this council would have forced him to consider these very interesting problems. I shall return to this issue, but I would stress here that

17

councils may continue in active existence even though they are very bad at making decisions by any means (see Barnes, 1954 and Block below 4).

The issues Bailey takes into consideration, administrative or executive v. policy-making, are at once too broad to serve as useful indices, and too narrow, since they exclude important types of conciliar issues. For example, many tribal councils deal not only with strictly political matters, but also with legal and ritual affairs. These activities impose a logic of their own on the decision-making process. There is a rich literature on the judicial process, and if we know less about decision-making on ritual matters, Richards' paper in the present volume constitutes an important enlargement of our knowledge. It is already apparent, however, that when a council deals with matters of law or ritual the members refer explicitly to general principles, recognized by everybody as binding, and, often, to precedents which may have the force of law. Moreover in many legal systems the court is structurally opposed to the litigants. These factors facilitate consensual agreement.

There is more to be said about the internal logic of issues. Barnes noted in his Norwegian study that while committees may be left to sidestep some problems, there are other issues which demand a decision one way or the other. If there is a division of opinion, then the chairman may be forced to demand a vote, even at the risk of bruising multiplex relationships. He recorded that:

'On one occasion I observed, when an unusually controversial matter was up for discussion and three members had, one after the other, spoken briefly to say that they were related to the parties in the case and therefore could not take part in the discussion, the mayor intervened to point out that the council members were probably all related in one way or another to the parties concerned, but that nevertheless they must come to a decision' (Barnes, 1954: 52).

A much more fundamental constraint is at work here than that imposed by the inner logic of what Bailey rather nebulously distinguished as 'administrative' or 'executive' and 'policy-making' functions. The constraint is simply that sometimes the costs of not making a decision are so high that they override the pains of dividing a council or community that is very closely-knit, or that lacks convenient sanctions. (At times in his argument Bailey seems to equate administrative or executive functions with the need to take urgent decisions, and hence with a tendency to resort to voting (Bailey, 1965: 9 and 14).)

Urgency, even apparent necessity, may, however, be insufficient. When I lived among the Kgalagari in the terrible drought year of 1964 I was continually upset by their inability to take certain decisions – seemingly quite straightforward – which would have guaranteed their water supplies. When I returned to the Kalahari in 1966–7 I found them dealing with this and similar problems far more efficiently. This was because in the meantime the newly-created District Councillor had become a more or less official chairman of the village council. The District Councillor had an external power base (like the Norwegian mayor), and so was in a comparatively strong position to force the council to make a decision, and to direct the decision-making process (see Kuper, 1970: chs. 3 and 7).

As this example shows, one must also reconsider the forms of relationship which may exist between the council, its public, and the external political environment. The neatness of the opposition between elite and arena councils must not be allowed to obscure the subtleties of lines of support and demand. The Kgalagari *lekgota* is structurally opposed to the District Administration, but its new and powerful chairman derives the support he needs precisely from his position in the District Council.

This is an important point, which must be developed. It is not as obvious as it may seem, that members of an elite council will tend to present a common front because the council is structurally in opposition to its public. In some cases members of an elite council will ignore this structural opposition, to the fury of their colleagues, and reveal to members of the public that they differed with the majority, or with the leadership, on a particular issue. A member of the British cabinet, to take one example, may put it about that he is standing up to the majority on some issue, in order to strengthen his position with elements of his party — and perhaps later, as a consequence, acquire greater influence in the cabinet. Or, to cite a rather different kind of example, a member of the United States Supreme Court may enter a dissenting judgment based on his personal reading of the law. Professional integrity here overrides the corporate interests of the court, which may fall in public esteem — as it has at times — when too many issues are resolved by a close and public vote.

Nor is it necessarily the case that an arena council which lacks effective sanctions must negotiate a compromise which will command a consensus; and that where the council does have some power its members will necessarily divide since each is steered by 'the heavy rudder of those whose interests he represents. . .' (Bailey, 1965: 10). This is to neglect the fact that many councils simply fail to reach any decision. But it also ignores the fact — which emerges quite clearly from our studies — that every council contains within itself a decision-making elite. This elite provides an element of unified command, and its members will rise at times above conflicting interests to formulate a policy 'in the public interest', or in their own interests as leaders, which is not necessarily a compromise between the competing factions; nor a majority decision in which some persistent minority is overridden. One might say that within every arena council there are the makings of an elite council, and that this central tendency may be strong enough to introduce a bias towards consensus.

Jones tells us that when an Ibo town council fails to reach a decision, or breaks up in disorder, influential members meet, agree on a solution to the problem, and go home to convert the members of their segments. Robertson describes how Ghanaian councils are in the same way guided through dissension by a caucus of influential men. They retire in the course of acrimonious meetings to consider a line of action away from the factional heat of the meeting itself, then return as an

19

irresistible pressure group.

A final consideration of some importance is the time factor: councils persist in time. It may therefore be worthwhile to yield a point now in the hope of winning a point later. The compromises may not be on particular issues, but may appear only in the context of a series of decisions.

These criticisms of Bailey's model are not meant to invalidate it, but rather to improve it. Bailey was quite right to point out that if we want to understand why a particular sort of decision-making process occurs we must fasten on the immediate situational determinants, and these I believe he identified correctly — the structure of the council, the nature of its task and resources, and the relationship of the council to its political environment (the lines of support and demand).

Bloch, in his contribution to this volume, takes issue with Bailey and with this whole approach to the study of decision-making processes. Bloch is concerned with the great differences he observed in the operation of councils of men and councils of women among the Merina, and he considers that:

'such factors as the type of issues considered, or the type of the council, are not sufficient to explain why a particular process of decision-making is used. More significant is the accepted way for men and women to behave and argue. This is not limited to behaviour in councils and ultimately links up with the way the sexes are educated and the beliefs held about their respective natures.'

In short, he believes that 'The functional sociological pressures can only be seen to operate within the historico-cultural framework'.

If Bloch is correct it will be futile to look for general situational determinants of council behaviour. On this sort of argument, each council will necessarily exhibit idiosyncratic patterns of behaviour. However, I do not believe that it is necessary to retreat to such a particularistic position. Bloch's data can be explained in terms of the general principles we have adduced, and without falling back for explanations on the peculiar etiquette of Merina men and women.

As Bloch shows, the male-dominated village council is structurally opposed to the government in much of its business, and it is often concerned with trivia. When it acts as a court, the type of issue imposes its own constraints. The councils of the Merina women, on the contrary, are concerned with internal relationships and critical economic decisions. This is particularly true of the councils concerned with the transplantation of rice seedlings, but even the Red Cross committees — on which Bloch has less information — must choose officers.

By Bailey's most plausible rule, the village councils will tend to consensus when they are structurally opposed to the government. I have suggested further that where trivial issues are concerned councils will avoid divisions. The presence of an elite group within the council, as Bloch stresses, also facilitates consensus. Finally, in the case of the courts, the Merina are merely another instance of a universal tendency to settle legal disputes by consensus, if it is possible to isolate the parties from the dominating body of the court (see pp.23ff).

The women, on the other hand, are concerned mainly with internal relationships, and so they will tend to divide. Since they usually have urgent matters to settle it is not remarkable that they resort to voting. It seems unnecessary therefore to invoke special cultural factors to explain the characteristic decision-making processes.

Of course, the etiquette of the council is a peculiar cultural product, and Bloch goes on to argue that Bailey is making a grave mistake in ignoring the cultural modes in favour of what he considers to be the substance of the behaviour. I sympathize with Bloch here. Bailey tends to exaggerate the antithesis between symbolic and substantive behaviour, all emphasis being placed on the latter. However, I do believe that a concern for cultural peculiarities should not obscure structural regularities. Perhaps Bloch agrees. In any case, the reader can settle these questions in his own mind by studying Bloch's paper.

Unauthoritative decisions

An interesting test of the value of isolating this small set of variables is presented by the range of decisions Bailey ignored — the ineffectual or unauthoritative decisions which are in fact very common. I would isolate three categories of unauthoritative decisions. First there are the out-and-out failures to reach any resolution. The council debates a matter, often at length, but finally the matter is dropped, or postponed indefinitely, or the meeting breaks up in frustration. This is characteristic of arena councils lacking effective sanctions, particularly when faced with a matter which is not very urgent, or when they lack a strong chairman with an external power base.

The other types of unauthoritative decisions are more complex and more interesting. The second type, the ceremonial decision, presents itself as a decision when it is not one in the full sense. For example, in British town councils, as Spencer shows, decisions are not normally made on the floor of the chamber. The effective decision is taken before the assembly meets by the caucus of the governing party. The formal debate and vote is a ceremonial affair. It has various functions — but they do not include decision-taking. Frankenberg has described another picturesque example. Welsh villagers often make decisions which they know will not be implemented because a higher authority will immediately overrule them (see Frankenberg, 1957).

Thirdly, there is the ambiguous decision, the decision which is open to at least two reasonable but conflicting interpretations. I leave to one side what might be called self-regulating ambiguity. A decision is ambiguously phrased, or fails to deal with unforeseen factors, and no action is possible until the council has once more debated the matter and issued a clearer statement of its meaning. My concern is with functionally ambiguous decisions. I could cite well-known examples — the Congo resolutions of the United Nations, or the laws concerning the desegregation of schools passed by the United States Congress. However, there is a good example in this volume, again in Bloch's chapter on the Merina.

The etiquette demands that in the male *kabary* a speaker should not be directly contradicted. Bloch reports how in the course of a debate about a work-party two men suggested, without openly contradicting the other, two different days on which the job should be done. When the meeting broke up it was not clear which day had been chosen. The villagers had to keep an eye open on each of the days to see when a number of their neighbours would in fact turn up, so as to know when to report for duty themselves.

The first explanation which might suggest itself is that ambiguous decisions will be favoured by arena councils which lack sanctions. Failing a compromise they may formulate an ambiguous decision because it will mean all things to all men. This is, of course, the advantage of the ambiguous decision, but when one recalls the long record of ambiguous decisions passed by the U.S. Congress it is apparent that even powerful arena councils, faced with urgent problems, may choose this easy way out of trouble.

The position may be clarified by a consideration of that other type of unauthoritative decision, the ceremonial decision. The English town council debates heatedly and votes, although the decision has effectively been taken before the meeting begins. The Welsh villagers debate and formulate a decision, knowing that it will be overruled by external authorities. In both these cases public conflict is being deliberately dramatized, perhaps without reference to the issue formally before the council. In the English town council the motive is to demonstrate to the public, through press reports of the debate, that the parties are truly divided, in the hope of gaining votes at a future election.

Where an ambiguous decision is formulated the contrary occurs – public dissension is minimized, conflicts are apparently resolved. However, as with the ceremonial decision, a decision is only apparently being made. If action is to follow an effective decision must be made elsewhere. Hence the drama of the Merina work-party: people decide when to work by seeing how much effective support each proposal commands. This support is demonstrated by attendance at the worksite, not by an open division in the council, and so face-to-face disagreements are avoided. In the United States, the effective decision can be left to the executive or to the courts. In the case of the United Nations, it appeared for some time that the effective decisions would be made in the office of the Secretary-General. This has been nicely pointed out by Conor Cruise O'Brien. He writes that on appointment as Representative-Designate of the U.N. in Katanga:

'... my own task, as I supposed, was relatively simple for, in the last analysis, all I had to do – apart from reporting and advising – was to apply the resolutions *as interpreted by the Secretary-General.* I did not, it is true, feel personally very happy about the wide spans of ambiguity, the underlying contradictions, in the resolutions which we were supposed to implement. I knew, however, that to Mr Hammarskjold such ambiguities were the breath of his nostrils, the medium in which he had his being. The greater the ambiguity in a Security Council decision, the wider was the Secretary-General's margin of interpretation. Through ambiguities resolved, through margins skilfully used, the office of the Secretary-General had grown in stature and authority far beyond what the framers of the charter seem to have envisaged at San Francisco. This was quite widely recognized; someone, I know not who, had even jested that the motto of the Secretary-General ought to be *Per Ambigua ad Astra'* (O'Brien, 1962: 47).

Ambiguous decisions, then, like ceremonial decisions, presuppose the existence of an effective decision-making institution outside the council. Given that, the council meeting can be used to maximize appearances of conflict or appearances of unanimity, depending on the nature of the game — depending, that is, on the relationship between the members of the council and their publics, and on the nature of the issue.

Decision-making in courts

As Richards has remarked, most African councils, and many councils in traditional monarchies, move easily from political to judicial matters and back again. There is much valuable anthropological discussion of the judicial process, but most writers deal with it in isolation from political decision-making. However, in line with the argument so far, it may be illuminating to juxtapose them; and to ask what situational determinants are peculiar to councils acting as courts.

By a court I mean a council which is considering a conflict not in political terms but in legal terms. This involves isolating the parties, opposing them structurally to the court, and relating the principles behind their dispute to the law or precedent which can then guide the judgment. These guiding principles may be strictly jural, but in some courts, particularly familial or lineage moots, the principles may be primarily moral.

The crucial feature of the court, for my present purposes, is that it is structurally opposed to the parties. I would contrast this with those situations where a conflict is dealt with through the confrontation of two negotiating blocks in an arena, the 'court' (perhaps reduced to a symbolic leopard-skin chief) merely holding the ring. That is a political, not a judicial, mode of dispute settlement (see Abrahams' paper).

How does the structural relationship of court and parties influence the decision-making process? Gluckman has advanced a hypothesis which is directly relevant here. He argues that when the Lozi *kuta* is faced with a legal action between two parties who are bound 'in permanent multiplex relationships', it 'tends to be conciliating; it strives to effect a compromise acceptable to, and accepted by, all the parties' (Gluckman, 1955: 21). This is because the authorities are concerned to maintain the web of multiplex relationships within which the parties live. In other words, Gluckman is arguing that the court's behaviour ('compromise and conciliation') is determined by the relationship between the parties. Can this analysis be generalized?

The Kgalagari, who speak a related language and live in the same broad region as the Lozi, behave differently in their courts. Far from trying above all for compromise and conciliation, the Kgalagari court imposes the law in a comparatively legalistic and inflexible fashion, although an attempt is then made to reconcile the losing party to the judgment. And yet the Kgalagari court normally deals with villagers who are locked in durable and multi-faceted relationships. It seems, then, that Gluckman's hypothesis cannot be extended even to cover this culturally cognate tribe.

However, Gluckman's hypothesis can be modified to cover both the Lozi and the Kgalagari cases if one considers also the relationship of the court to the parties, and the sanctions at the court's disposal. One might make a distinction rather like that between elite councils, assemblies, and high-level arena councils.

The Lozi courts with which Gluckman dealt were elite councils, highly-placed within a state organization. The court had specific sanctions at its disposal, and its members were normally detached from the parties to a dispute. The Kgalagari court is a community-level arena council, and all adult male villagers are council members. In practically all cases at least one of the parties to a law-suit is normally a council member (though litigants are excluded from membership of the court when their own case is under consideration). Its primary sanctions are those of public opinion.

It seems to me that the crucial problem facing these courts is to maintain their structural distance from the parties. If this collapses the court becomes an arena council dealing with a political issue, with all the limitations that this implies. (This may be judged with reference to the typical dispute-settling procedures of the Arusha (Gulliver, 1963), and to some Tiv institutions, such as the 'Inquest' (L. Bohannan, 1958: 56).) The Lozi court is safe enough, for the standing of the judges is bolstered by the total Lozi state, powerful and hierarchical. Therefore, particularly where the judges are in fact virtual strangers to the litigants, they can afford to suspend purely legal considerations in favour of specific social concerns. The Kgalagari court, however, is severely threatened by the potential politicization of the case: it is too close to the parties: and it protects itself by the apotheosis of the law. Significantly, the Kgalagari courts were seldom capable of settling cases involving headmen.

Lozi (A)			Kgalagari (A)		
	C			C	
−		−	+		+
P	+	P	P	+	P

I am arguing, then, that the behaviour of the court is influenced by the relationship between the court and the parties. If one adds to this the relationship which Gluckman isolated, between the parties themselves, it is possible to construct a model which will predict court behaviour. In the foregoing diagram, C = Court and P = Party. A positive sign indicates a close personal bond, a negative sign its absence. This may be phrased as an opposition between relationships of status and of contract.

In the case of Lozi (A) the court is in a position to impose a compromise settlement in the interests of reconciling the parties. In the second case the court must rely on the strict application of an objective code in order to maintain a necessary structural distance from the parties, even if it cannot then give priority to the reconciliation of the parties with each other.

But Gluckman noted that 'reconciliation is not an ultimate, almost mystical value of Lozi courts. . . Matters of property-rights, contract or injury in permanent multiplex relationships require reconciliation: the same matters between strangers do not' (Gluckman, 1955: 55). So if the relationship between the parties is altered, one finds the court behaving differently. This yields a third situation, in which the court behaves like the paradigmatic Kgalagari court.

Lozi (B)

C

$-$ $-$

P $-$ P

There are several other logical possibilities, but only one which, I think, occurs in practice. This is when the court is connected to one party only, as shown in the third diagram.

Kgalagari (B)

C

$+$ $-$

P $\pm$ P

I call this situation Kgalagari (B) because I have witnessed several trials where a citizen is embroiled with an outsider, usually a Bushman. Naturally enough the court in such cases is inclined to be biased, though it still relies on a legalistic idiom which masks the bias, and may even mitigate its effect.

Anyone who finds this analysis even remotely persuasive must now consider a rather different hypothesis advanced by Fallers in his masterly new monograph on Soga law. Fallers writes:

'There is, I think, a continuum here from the less to the more legalistic legal subculture. To what, outside the various subcultures themselves, may these differences be related? I suggested earlier that the necessity for the legal process to oversimplify moral situations required that the judges enjoy substantial respect and authority to allow them to handle the resulting strain between law and morality. My analysis has, I think, shown that in Busoga, where litigation and adjudication are relatively legalistic, the bench does indeed enjoy such respect and authority' (Fallers, 1969: 328-9).

But Fallers immediately finds himself up against the fact that the Lozi proceedings Gluckman reported are less legalistic than are those of the Soga. He does not attempt to relate this to the different degree of authority and respect enjoyed by Lozi and Soga judges, as his hypothesis demands. Instead he invokes new variables, the fact that the Lozi *kuta* also has non-judicial functions, and the plural nature of the Lozi state.

In my view Fallers' first shot at an explanation was more persuasive. Then he was concerned with the structural relationship between court and parties (which he expressed in terms of the social distance between litigants and judges). His failure, however, is the opposite of Gluckman's: where Gluckman ignored the relationship between court and parties, Fallers ignored the relationship between the parties themselves in formulating his hypothesis.

The Soga courts Fallers dealt with should be compared with Lozi (B), and not with Lozi (A) as Fallers did, because among the Soga cases involving people in ascribed personal relationships are dealt with outside the formal court structure, in the informal moots. Like Lozi (B) courts the Soga courts are legalistic, as predicted by the model.

What then of those Soga cases which involve parties bound in multiplex relationships, and are dealt with in the moots? This is a Kgalagari (A) situation, and so once again one expects the moot to behave in a strictly legalistic fashion. Fallers does not give enough material on the moots to test this idea, but he does drop at least one tantalizing hint – 'The same language and gesture of litigation and adjudication are used throughout the hierarchy of tribunals, from the family to the highest courts' (Fallers, 1969: 26). If these moots are legalistic this is in clear contradiction to Fallers' own hypothesis.

My argument is, of course, not conclusive. At least one would also have to consider the special case of the moot in the domestic domain in many societies, which is characteristically moral and concerned with the maintenance of non-contractual relationships. However, the point I wish to make is simply that the variables which must be isolated to explain council behaviour in general must all be brought into play to explain the behaviour of courts. My argument illustrates the significance of the complex bonds which link the council with its public; and demonstrates something of the constraints imposed by the type of issue with which a council is concerned. [1]

Conclusion

If we can generalize already about certain aspects of council structure and performance, a number of interesting questions remain unresolved. Spencer raised one such question in correspondence with the editors – why do some councils proceed with great pomp and formality, while others are comparatively informal? Is this a function of the complexity of the council's business, or of its structure, or is it related to the extent to which council members are divided? One begins to look for more comparative material, then recalls Richards' observation that dominant modes of council procedure, like the parliamentary and committee modes in Britain, tend to impose themselves on councils at all levels. Which leads one to ask when the committee mode will be adopted, and when the parliamentary... But although we may begin to understand the determinants of council behaviour, and even to chart some broad correlations between council types and political and social structures, we are still far (as Richards has stressed) from a comparative theory of council functions and of council development (if this can be achieved).

Nonetheless the material collected here makes further theoretical progress more likely, and I have no doubt that new problems and novel hypotheses will occur to anyone who studies these papers closely. They cover a variety of societies and council types. Bloch describes the Merina *fokon'olona,* pre-eminently a community-in-council, which continues in operation although it has been stripped of most decision-making functions. The value of this analysis is enhanced by the contrast he describes between the dominantly male *kabary* and the councils of the women. Jones and I describe arena councils in two of Africa's traditional democracies. Jones' description of Central Ibo councils is informed by his long experience as an administrator concerned with guiding conciliar development. His paper also provides new material on that common West African institution, the council which is integrated with a title-system.

By contrast to these democratic affairs, Richards describes a highly-specialized elite council in the Bemba state, distinguished by its aristocratic character. It is worth emphasizing, however, that the *bakabilo* do see themselves as guardians of the interests of the tribe, if necessary even against the paramount chief. Her analysis is also a major addition to the slim literature on decision-making on ritual matters. In addition, she outlines the structure of the other Bemba councils, and faces up to the vital question, when and why is a conciliar form of decision-making preferred to the simple order of chief or headman?

Two of the studies are concerned with modern local government councils, but Robertsons' report on the Ghanaian town council brings out the continuity of

27

classical African forms of council behaviour, notwithstanding the modernist assertion of the Chief of Mim that life is now mathematical.

Spencer's analysis of an English town council brings the other studies into a new focus. The British local government system was a most important model for the new councils in the ex-dependencies, and as Spencer so clearly shows, local government in England is intrinsically political, despite the illusions of the architects of the colonial councils, who wanted tamely administrative organs. But more important, the English town council is clearly constrained by the same sorts of pressures as councils in Africa, and Spencer's analysis greatly strengthens our case for a truly comparative approach to the study of councils. It also underlines the fact that even in modern bureaucratic societies, councils are not simply (or necessarily even primarily) decision-making bodies.

Finally, Abrahams describes decisions reached by negotiation outside the council context, and his data throws into relief, by contrast, the constraints and advantages of decision-making within a persisting institutional framework.

This volume will have served its purpose if it generates among anthropologists an interest in councils. This may help to redress the balance of political anthropology, which has been too much concerned with roles of leadership and too little with the widespread institutions of government by discussion. It may also bring to the current interest in decision-making processes a greater respect for institutional constraints. Such concerns should also extend the area of common discourse with political scientists.

Notes

[1] I am indebted to Mr T. Crump for the following note, in which he shows the way in which this model could be applied to judicial decision-making in Britain:

... I was drawing attention to the contrasting and originally separate and each in its sphere autonomous jurisdictions of the civil and ecclesiastical courts in England, which were finally only fused together by the Judicature Act, 1873, although the Chancery Court had not really been ecclesiastical since before the reformation.

The civil courts of the King's Bench represented the law common to the whole realm, and quite early on the characteristic action became one between *two* persons unrelated (and now in running down cases etc. unknown) to each other, for an award of damages which once paid liquidated the action, for which judgment was mandatory upon the court, which through the fountain-head of justice, the King, represented the people, who appeared also as jurors, in another sort of representation, with a role in maintaining 'peace', and in your interpretation being an 'arena council'.

The ecclesiastical courts represented a law which was more universal and less popular, and the characteristic action was one in which the parties were related to each other (two brothers contesting a will, or two spouses, a divorce), for an order (not for damages) which could be interim, or enduring but subject to periodical review *(vide* Dickens' *Bleak House,)*- and indeed, being discretionary, need not even be granted: the judge, or chancellor, represented not the King but the Bishop, a spiritual overseer, who was interested not so much in 'peace' as in 'conscience' of which he was the 'guardian', not troubled by jurors and often not by witnesses, and in your analysis an 'elite council'.

The civil courts thus correspond to Lozi (B), the ecclesiastical courts to Lozi (A).

DECISION-MAKING IN COUNCILS AMONG THE MERINA OF MADAGASCAR

By Maurice Bloch

The Merina inhabit the north part of the central plateau of Madagascar. They number approximately a million and a quarter, and live in extremely varied conditions from modern towns to remote villages where only a relatively simple technology is used to obtain the staple crop, rice. Other less important agricultural products such as manioc, sweet potatoes, taro, beans, voanzo, cattle, sheep and poultry are also produced. Certain cash crops, tomatoes, groundnuts, tobacco and onions are cultivated to differing extents in different parts. As varied as their means of livelihood and indeed standards of living are the racial origins of the Merina. All intermediates from typical Indonesian types to full Negroid types are found. Culturally the Merina are not sharply distinct from their neighbours. In fact, it is only their association with the Merina kingdom (overthrown by the French in 1896) which marks off the Merina as a people. This association with the past is of extreme value to the Merina and to the other Malagasy and is of great significance for their present day social organization. [1]

Although the ethnography of the area is surprisingly thin there is at least one feature of Merina society which has been written about ad nauseam; that is the *fokon'olona,* a word which has been variously translated as traditional community, village council, clan, clan council, commune, district council, traditional court, popular assembly, and in many other ways. As we shall see this lexicographical difficulty is significant in itself. It will be necessary to return to the meaning of the word, but at this stage it suffices to say that the word may mean a given territorial unit of one or more villages traditionally linked by a quasi-kinship tie; or it may mean the members of the above community gathered together in council. It is with this latter meaning that I am principally concerned when I discuss the literature and history of the institution.

Previous studies of the fokon'olona

Two questions arise when considering the literature on *Fokon'olona.* In the first place, why has this institution been given such disproportionate attention?

29

Secondly, why, if so much has already been written about it, is it still necessary to add to these accounts? Surprisingly, the same answers may be given to both these questions. The reason why so much has been written about the *fokon'olona* is the administrative and jural importance of this institution in colonial and independent Madagascar both for the government and the jurists; and also the notion of *folon'-olona* has been given great sentimental value by Malagasy and European writers. Neither of these motives for writing about the *fokon'olona* is ideal for obtaining sociological information on the institution. Consequently, too few of these writings are concerned with the *fokon'olona* as it works and too many have given descriptions of how it *should* work, either, when certain laws are enforced, or when its true nature is realized. I shall only review the literature briefly here, under main headings which correspond to the types of interest of writers on the *fokon'olona*, the administrative and jural writings, and what may be called the sentimental writings.

The administrative writings

Since the French hoped and tried to use the *fokon'olona* as the lowest echelon of their administrative structure many writers, especially French administrators, attempted to define the functions of the traditional *fokon'olona*. They then go on to suggest how this institution could be used in modern times to enforce law and order and, more recently, community development. Much of the work of these writers is historical. They sometimes base their work on written documents, sometimes on oral tradition which they often use uncritically.[2] Their emphasis is on the mode of recruitment to the *fokon'olona* and the role the institution played in enforcing the *status quo* in the past. Implied is the proposition that if the *fokon'-olona* was able to keep law and order for the Merina monarchs, it ought to be able to do the same for the French government. In other words, mixed with what is often of genuine historical interest is a proposal for colonialism on the cheap. Perhaps one of the best examples of work of this type is the book by G. Julien, *Institutions politiques et sociales de Madagascar.* This book tries to deduce the administrative structure of the Merina kingdom from the remembered orations, *kabary,* of the Merina kings, and then, for a later period, from written laws. In the same tradition and, in a largely derivative way, are the works of F. Arbrousset (1950) and P. Delteil (1931) which lay greater emphasis on the written conventions set up by the *fokon'olona* during the latter days of the Merina kingdom. Here too concern with the place of the *fokon'olona* in the overall system of government is dominant.

The more recent book by the anthropologist, G. Condominas, *Fokon'olona et Collectivités Rurales en Imerina* is in somewhat the same tradition, although the considerable sociological material it contains means that it will require special examination. (See pp.40ff). Nonetheless, it too is a study of the history and the function of the *fokon'olona* with a view to the evaluation of the use of the institution for certain community development projects: the C.A.R. *(Collectivités Authochtones Rurales)* and C.R.A.M. *(Collectivités Rurales Autochtones Modernisees)*. Condominas is, as far as I know, the only one of these writers who has observed the *fokon'olona* as it operates and who has used questionnaires for obtaining systematic information. However, the fact remains that the short time he stayed in any particular village (three weeks as a maximum) makes it unlikely that he can have observed the *fokon'olona* working normally, and indeed his work gives no evidence of this. This study, however, is a marked advance on what had gone before, since most intervening studies between this book and that of Julien are largely derivative from the earlier works and add surprisingly little to them. Condominas, by contrast with these writers, attempts to put the *fokon'olona* in a wider sociological context. He stresses the essential point that the *fokon'olona* is primarily a moral institution drawing cohesion from shared values, and that it cannot be considered only in terms of the administrative functions which it performs, a point which will be further illustrated. Although I find myself in disagreement with some of the points made by Condominas his contribution cannot be over-estimated, especially when we think how brief is the study on which this work is based. It furnished an orientation to my field study and underpins much of the argument here.

The jural writings

Closely linked to the 'administrative' writings on the *fokon'olona* are the jural ones. In fact the interest of the jurists in the *fokon'olona* springs from the fact that in a very vague form this institution was incorporated into the French system of government. This having been done its functions had to be judicially defined. The jurists have tended to concentrate on the written constitutions of the *fokon'olona* which were drawn up from 1860 onwards especially in the case of Tananarive. The impetus behind the writing down of these conventions in the form of a legal code is clearly a part of the attempts of the Merina court towards the end of the nineteenth century to fashion their administration and government on a European model. These conventions and other Merina written laws were naturally considered a useful base by the French government, and after it by the Malagasy government, for their own legislation. Thus, the study of the legal side of the *fokon'olona* became important to the French government and studies on this aspect of its work were consequently published. As an example we may mention again the work of Delteil (1931) and of jurists such as Pain (1910). A recent attempt to transform the traditional *fokon'olona* into a clearly defined legal institution is manifest in much legislation and in legal discussion in Madagascar today. Much of this activity is part of the general process of law-making and government, but a more general attitude can be seen in H. Raharijaona's article 'Le droit Malgache et les Conventions de *Fokon'olona*' (1965). The concern of the jurists with the *fokon'olona* is natural and sometimes praiseworthy. It must be seen as part of the attempt to give traditional authority for what is in fact largely new administrative legislation. However, the work of jurists is often of little use to the social anthropologist. There are two reasons for this. Like many writers on Madagascar, the authors we have been considering are often so eager to stress national unity that they close their eyes to the existing diversity in various parts of Madagascar. Secondly, it is often difficult to know where the observation of what *is* ends, and where suggestions as to what *should* be begins.

Sentimental writings

The third type of writings on the *fokon'olona* is the type I have described as 'sentimental'. Again these are not completely distinct from the two earlier types of writing. Here too, much of the emphasis is historical, but history of a vaguer kind, not clearly linked to any particular time. These works look back to an undocumented past when the institution of the *fokon'olona,* a kind of primitive democracy, enabled the finer sentiments of mutual help, respect for the family, and allegiance to an uncomplicated society to be expressed within a universally accepted framework. These writings are significant in that they often stress important aspects of the *fokon'olona* as it was, and also in that they represent a picture of the past which is relevant for the beliefs of many present-day Merina. Naturally, however, we may be somewhat sceptical about the idyllic quality of such a hazy institution. This type of writing is of two kinds, that produced by Europeans and that by Merina themselves. The source of the European sentimentality is perhaps less obvious than the Malagasy, but is still not far to seek. It is a late manifestation of a nostalgia for a natural society, a nostalgia which formed a particularly strong current of intellectual belief when these writers were working. An example of this type of writing can be found in some passages in the great work of Julien. Writings of this type by Malagasy are well represented in the journal *Fokon'olona*, which advocates a return to the golden days when European influence had not brought discord to the Merina people. Not only would these writers have us believe that the past was idyllic. So is the present-day working of the institution in their view; no conflicts arise, decisions are reached easily almost instinctively. Such writings are not totally devoid of value because of the information they sometimes produce, but they need to be treated with extreme caution. However, their great significance lies in the fact that they offer a particularly good guide to the kind of myth of a golden age which is fairly current in present-day Merina.

The purpose of this review of the literature is to show how in spite of all that has been written there is little which tells us how and whether decisions are reached by the *fokon'olona;* or to what specific social activities and categories of people the concept refers to in particular instances. The work of Condominas gives us most information on these topics, but I feel the material I have gathered here takes the enquiry further, in that it offers more information as well as a critique.

The history of the fokon'olona
The place of the *fokon'olona* at present cannot be fully understood without a certain historical perspective. Only by understanding what the word has meant can we understand what it now means. Secondly, as we have seen above, the interpretation of what the *fokon'olona* was in the past has been considered by all concerned as justification for what it *should* be. Thirdly, it is only in a historical context that many present features are readily understandable.

The history of Imerina falls into three parts. First, a period ending around 1800, for which our information only comes from oral traditions collected from 1850 on. These, however, tell us much which even the most critical historian could accept, supported as they are by the accounts of travellers, and striking remains, especially fortifications. Merina society at that time was a 'double' sort of society. There was a society of rice cultivators living in river valleys, where they built villages protected either by deep single moats or mud walls; and there were small groups of what may be called robber barons, who lived at the summit of the highest hills where they protected themselves by elaborate fortifications consisting of many parallel moats. The traditions recorded in the *Tantaran ny Andriana* and collected by R.P. Callet [3] make it quite clear that they lived in part by operating what could be called a 'protection racket' over the valley cultivators, and by pillaging the villages protected by their rivals. It seems clear that the life of these 'kings' and their 'kingdoms', as they are referred to in the literature, was 'nasty, brutish and short'.

What is relevant to our concern is this: the very impermanence of these petty principalities meant that they cannot have been an important part of the system by which the cultivators organized themselves among themselves. This is what I mean when I refer to the political system as double. There were on the one side the predatory rulers and their bands of followers, on the other the peasants and their organization. Clearly these two systems were linked. The rulers and their followers can be said to have lived off the peasant in two ways, by pillaging or taxation, and also because presumably the followers of these petty 'rulers' (if not the 'rulers' themselves) were most probably of peasant origin. In spite of this linkage it is clear that the two systems of organization were basically independent.

When the Merina refer to this period they call it the *fanzakana hova*, literally the government *(fanzakana)* of 'commoners' *(hova)*, by opposition to the *fanzakana andriana* [4] the government by 'aristocrats' *(andriana)* which followed it. By this comparison they underline the lack of authority and permanence of the earlier petty rulers (Condominas, 1960:37).

At the time of the *fanzakana hova* it seems that villagers reached political and judicial decisions when they met together. Sometimes one village only met together, sometimes several. This kind of meeting was and still is called *fokon'-olona*. The word here means both the council and the people for whom the council was making decisions. Since these two were potentially the same they are not terminologically distinguished. Obviously then, as now, problems of representation

33

must have arisen but we have no evidence of this for that period. We also have no direct evidence on the functions of the *fokon'olona* as a council at that period. It is however perfectly clear that this local council organization was the means whereby the cultivators organized themselves and the councils were not attached to any rulers. There is no tradition for the existence of political leaders at this level of government. Another fact can be deduced. The very impermanence of the robber baron 'kingdom' meant that little actual administration of their subjects can have gone on and evidence suggests that the *fokon'olona* was sovereign within its own territory. In other words, it can be said that by contrast with the present, the governmental functions of the council were very much more important. Indeed, we have direct evidence of this. The traditional origin of a *fokon'olona* council is recorded in Julien's work and this gives us an idea of the type of function this council was thought orginally to have had.[5]

'One of our ancestors one day said: "We must now agree together and become one body by a mutual undertaking which we shall mark by killing a bull and setting up a megalith. This undertaking will enable us to take action together when anybody is guilty of a misdeed like stealing manioc or chickens or sheep or cattle". They all agreed and they decided what the fines would be for the various misdeeds ... Then they shared the bull and they shared the price and its cranium was hung over the village gate.'[6]

The *fokon'olona* also had functions less directly concerned with the regulation of conflict and power within the community. It organized the kind of mutual aid which has won it the admiration of many subsequent writers. At life crises, times of great need, members of the *fokon'olona* had a moral obligation to help each other. In other words, certain residual rights over property and labour were held in common. This unity of the *fokon'olona* was expressed in kinship terms and indeed it seems likely that the *fokon'olona* originally was part of some kind of descending kindred or descent group (see p.40). Condominas rightly stresses the point that originally at least the *fokon'olona* was not an instrumental grouping but a moral one. As we shall see this aspect is still relevant today although in a very changed way.

Clearly our picture of the *fokon'olona* council in the early times just referred to, must be in great part a matter of guesswork; but it is a guess informed by what we know with much more certainty of the period immediately following.

Towards the end of the *fanzakana hova* there was a tendency for the petty dependencies of the robber barons to get bigger. This transformation seems to have been a result of the gradual introduction of firearms obtained mainly from European pirates and/or traders. Ultimately the whole of Imerina became unified under one ruler only to split up again. However, in the end the unifying tendency reached its peak when Ramboasalama (the healthy dog) managed to succeed a relative in the developing kingdom of Ambohimanga in 1787 when he took the name of Andrianampoinimerina. He first conquered the other petty kingdoms and in this way unified Imerina, a land about the size of an English county. As part of the unification of Imerina he moved his capital to Tananarive, which has since become a large town and the capital of Madagascar. Andrianampoinimerina still holds the place of a culture hero in Merina history. He is a kind of Charlemagne figure, remembered more for his wisdom than his aggression against his neighbours. Indeed there seems little reason to doubt his ability. In fact Andrianampoinimerina did not stop at the unification of Imerina, but began the spectacular territorial expansion which reached its peak after his reign, when nearly the whole of Madagascar fell to the control of the Merina monarchs.

The considerable achievement of unifying Imerina seems to have been due in great part to Andrianampoinimerina's personal charisma, but his greatest claim to fame is his attempt to put his kingdom on a permanent basis. He did this in two ways. First by initiating and organizing a large drainage project which transformed the marshes around Tananarive into fertile rice fields.[7] Of these a large part was kept and cultivated by the crown for financing the administration.[8] Secondly he organized the kingdom by establishing control over what had been up to then largely independent peasant communities. His first attempt along these lines was to try to define and delimit the powers of the *fokon'olona* council. This was to set a pattern which has gone on till the present day.

The pattern consists in the central government not openly trying to change or transform the *fokon'olona* council but restating from on high, as it were, the functions which it had had previously. The effect of this is to make it seem that the council operates as it does because it has been given permission by the central government and not because, as previously, it is an assembly of people regulating their own affairs. This definition of the powers of the councils is therefore an attempt to replace the source of power by which the council acts, to begin with at any rate, without changing the council itself to any extent. This profound 'constitutional' change is not therefore likely to come as a shock to the members of the *fokon'olona* since they appear to carry on much as before. It is only later, when the central government tries to enforce decisions which go against the will of the council, that the significance of the change implied in acting 'for the crown' instead of acting 'for the *fokon'olona*' is realized. Much of the subsequent history of Imerina can be understood in the light of the conflict which such an ambiguous transformation implies. This can be seen as part of a general principle noted by political anthropologists whereby the political functions of small groups whose source of power comes from *below* has to diminish as government centralization increases.[9]

Andrianampoinimerina did not stop at constitutional changes but also took advantage of the situation he had created to obtain taxation, whether in kind, in work, or in money.[10] As far as we can tell it seems that Andrianampoinimerina's personal charisma was sufficient to bring about the radical changes which he initiated. His laws and decrees were announced in large public assemblies in speeches *(kabary)*, a practice which continued till the collapse of the Merina kingdom. This type of public meeting allowed personal charisma to have a great effect.

If little of the traditional function of the *fokon'olona* was changed, Andrianampoinimerina did to a certain extent limit its powers in the judicial field. Characteristically he first stressed its traditional functions. He is reported by Julien as saying:

'If a quarrel should arise in a particular place then the neighbours living in the two or three neighbouring houses can form themselves into a court like I do . . . If this is not sufficient then the whole of the Fokon'olona should gather . . . and when both sides have accepted the decision of the Fokon'olona they will pay a tax to me and money or livestock to the Fokon'olona.' [11]

He also stressed the competence of the *fokon'olona* in such things as family law and as a registry of birth, death and transfers of property. Nonetheless relations between *fokon'olona* were to be regulated by the central government, and certain particularly heinous crimes, largely of a rebellious character, were to be dealt with by the king. [12]

Apart from its judicial duties the *fokon'olona* was to act as a co-ordinating body and to initiate certain communal activities. The most obvious of these was the upkeep of the major irrigation ditches, mutual help at life crises of members, and activities requiring village-wide cooperation like rice transplanting or tomb building. These obligations still exist to a large extent today. Andrianampoinimerina restated in his speeches these traditional functions of the *fokon'olona* but he also put it in such a way that much more important works like the drainage of marshes seemed to be part of the traditional duties of the *fokon'olona*. This was a precedent which his successors and the French both used and abused to obtain cheap labour.

Towards the end of his reign Andrianampoinimerina went further in his attempt to contain the *fokon'olona*. He sent out to each of them an official whom he called a *vadin-tany* (lit., a spouse of the earth), who was to represent him in the *fokon'*-*olona*. This implied three things. First, as the Merina kingdom had increased in size the *kabary* in Tananarive became insufficient and the *vadin-tany* had to repeat in their villages the speeches of the king. Second, these officials were given powers so that people who did not agree with the decisions of the *fokon'olona* could appeal to them. Third, the officials from the centre were to act as government spies.

These innovations of Andrianampoinimerina proved to be the basis of all subsequent changes to the *fokon'olona* as a governmental institution. The successors of Andrianampoinimerina tried therefore, on the one hand, to limit the power of the *fokon'olona,* and on the other, to give more power to their representatives in the village. As the personal popularity of Andrianampoinimerina was clearly not transferable to his successors, these attempts were resented and gradually were more and more resisted. This resistance seems to have been fairly successful, which is hardly surprising considering the few means at the government's disposal for enforcing its decisions. The presence of resistance is revealed by the fact that after only a few years it was felt that the *vadin-tany* had become so unpopular that they were ineffective. They were replaced by other officials with similar functions, but different titles, who in their turn were also replaced. In fact the continual sending out of new administrators at shorter and shorter intervals suggests that they were being put in a difficult position. The implicit contradiction between the existence of a body whose unity ultimately comes from below although it is being ruled from above came more and more to the fore as the other innovations of Andrianampoinimerina were also extended. The increase in the number of directives by *kabary*, and the use of the *fokon'olona* as a supply of cheap unremunerated labour were the most important of these. Successive governments reduced the rights of the *fokon'olona* and increased its duties. However, it seems difficult to see how the government could have hoped to enforce this type of rule and the *fokon'olona* retained a certain independence until the French conquest. Indeed it has been suggested that the continual opposition between the local councils and the central government may well account for the rapid collapse of the kingdom in the face of the French. [13]

The Merina government of this period was more and more influenced by European models. Missionaries and diplomats encouraged the Merina rulers to introduce such things as ministries, a standing army with European ranks, and European-type laws. Their success was in a way tremendous and the Merina kings, impressed by the superior technology of France and Britain, accepted foreign innovations with extraordinary willingness. However, this type of government implied a control of the country which was incompatible with a simple technology and little division of labour. In spite of ever increasing taxation of all kinds (forced labour, taxation in kind, taxation in money, and military service), the government did not have the ability to administer the immense kingdom which Andrianampoinimerina and his successors had conquered, a kingdom which spread over nearly the whole of Madagascar. As we saw, the successive Merina governments continually tried to increase the number and power of their administrators and garrisons but, since they were unable to pay their agents and soldiers these had to make themselves acceptable and therefore compromise with the local population. Consequently they rapidly proved ineffective as representatives of the central government. The contradiction between administration from above and political groupings based on agreement from below did not destroy the latter because the administration from above could not be fully effective.

In 1895 the French invaded the Merina kingdom and after a short attempt at a protectorate decided to administer Madagascar directly. It is then that a most ironical development took place. The man who had conquered Madagascar and who was to govern it until 1905 was General Gallieni. He was a man of liberal ideals who believed that each people ought to be governed according to its own laws. He employed lawyers, among them G.Julien, whose work is cited here, to publish the old laws of the Merina kings, and he then went on to enforce them, a thing which their originators had never had the means of doing. Gallieni's attempt was therefore principally designed to maintain as much of the *status quo* as possible. But in fact what he did was to introduce an entirely new type of government by giving teeth to an administration which had never had any. The effect of this on the *fokon'olona* was naturally radical. Gallieni was able to make it part of an administrative system in which power devolved from the top. Condominas makes the point very concisely by concluding that he made the *fokon'olona* council into merely 'a territorial administrative institution' thereby emptying it of its earlier character.[14] The *fokon'olona* council became, and has remained, a place where orders from the central government are received and then read out, and also an organization for collecting taxes. French and Malagasy governments have varied in the details of their policy towards these councils, but clearly, as we shall see, they have not been able to solve the basic contradiction between the conflicting sources of power which we have been referring to. Some politicians have tried and are still trying to revive the old *fokon'olona* and its 'traditional values', but this cannot be done by laws from above; indeed it cannot be done so long as the central government wants to use the *fokon'olona* for its own purposes.

The impossible position in which the *fokon'olona* is now situated can be understood if we look at its place in the wider administrative system of Malagasy administration as it was in 1964-6. This position is as follows. Madagascar is divided into six provinces which are each headed by government ministers. Each province is divided into a certain number of prefectures; each prefecture is divided into a certain number of sub-prefectures; and each sub-prefecture is divided into a certain number of cantons of around 5,000 inhabitants. The prefect, the sub-prefect, and the chief of the canton *(chef de canton)* are all government civil servants. The last-named official gets his wages in part from a fixed proportion of the taxes he manages to collect. Under the *chef de canton* are heads of *quartiers* (small districts) and under them headmen of 'villages'. These officials are entirely paid by a fixed proportion of the taxes they succeed in collecting.

Each administrative 'village'[15] has a *fokon'olona* and the 'village' headman's place is very similar to what the *vadin-tany's* role was intended to be. That is, he receives orders from the government in the forms of letters, or orders at briefings at communal headquarters, and he delivers these commands in the form of speeches at the *fokon'olona*. These meetings of the *fokon'olona* council are called to this day *kabary*. This shows clearly that the meeting of the *fokon'olona* is not normally an occasion for reaching decisions but for hearing them. As we shall see, very few decisions are made by the *fokon'olona* as a government council. The headman is the representative of the administration at the *fokon'olona*. He is in theory elected but in fact, in the cases on which I have information, he was nominated by the head of the canton. He is not normally a particularly important person and his position, on the one hand representing the government, and on the other representing the *fokon'*-

olona, is self-contradictory.[16]

Recently certain other officers have been created. There is now for each canton an elected mayor helped by one councillor from each 'village'. I was not lucky enough to witness the election of mayors and councillors, but it is fairly clear that government influence was very strong here too. The function of these people takes away still more of what was once a part of *fokon'olona* activities. Births, marriages and deaths should be recorded by the mayor, and he, with one other councillor, can take certain minor administrative decisions for which the sanction is a fine. Finally he has a right to arbitrate in disputes if the *fokon'olona* has been unable to make the parties reach a settlement. In the area where I was working there was tendency to by-pass the *fokon'olona* and to go straight to the mayor and councillors. This is part of what seems to be a general tendency away from submitting matters to the councils in favour of taking them for decision to important men.[17]

Finally, and parallel to these two systems, there is a third organization, that of the government party, the Parti Social Democrate (P.S.D.). This is a party organiza-tion of which the cells naturally parallel the administrative councils. Although Madagascar is not in theory a one party state only the P.S.D. operates openly in the countryside. This means that the distinction between party and government is not always clear, and in fact feed-back from the lower echelons of the administration to the governmental powers is more likely to occur through the P.S.D. than the *fokon'olona.* Legamble in a recent study entitled *Le Fokon'olona et le pouvoir*[18] makes this point clearly, although he might well be missing some further ambig-uities of the situation. He states: 'The main fact is the systematic twinning of the sections of the P.S.D. and the "mairies". A man who is a rural councillor is also a member of the local branch of the P.S.D. and this is not surprising. What is more surprising however is that in the mind of the councillors the two structures seem to be only one.'[19] Further, discussing the P.S.D.'s para-administrative functions, he emphasizes that 'The P.S.D. is in this way the information service and the means of psychological action of the government'.[20]

Clearly the *fokon'olona* today is only one of many administrative structures which carry out its traditional judicial, and social and political functions. What then if anything does the *fokon'olona* council do today? What is its place in the social structure? What does this concept, which many writers assume is at the very heart of Merina society, mean? To answer these questions we must look at the notion of *fokon'olona* in a wider context than we have done up to now, and we must not limit ourselves to the *fokon'olona* as a council which is part of the administration. First we must see how the word is used now in all its contexts.

The fokon'olona

Most government officials and indeed most writers on Madagascar mean by *fokon'olona* only the council as it manifests itself as a part of the administrative system of Madagascar. Nevertheless it is clear to many of them that the concept '*fokon'olona*' is not limited to this aspect. This point is usually made by referring to and discussing what is the 'real' or 'original' meaning of the word. Sometimes this becomes a clear attempt to discover through some kind of historical research what the institution of *fokon'olona* was in the past. Condominas is one of the writers who formulates the argument in this way. Because of the importance of his work the definition he offers is a good starting point to the always elusive attempt to circumscribe concepts. Condominas offers as an 'essential' definition of the *fokon'-olona* the following:

> 'The *fokon'olona* is a clan (or sometimes a lineage) of patrilineal patrilocal type which unites in a single territory *(Fokon'tany)* the descendants of a single ancestor *(razana)*, whose tomb constitutes the mystical pole where the group recovers its cohesion. It is this common descent which is expressed by the name of each *fokon'olona: teraka* or *zanaka* ("the child of . . ." "the descendant of . . .") followed by the name of the eponymous ancestor. The ancestor is at the very root of the *fokon'olona.*'[21]

Condominas adds to this definition the qualification that although he has described the 'real' *fokon'olona,* this is now obscured. 'The present day notion of *Fokon'-olona* is skewed. There is a tendency to emphasise the territorial and administrative aspect to the exclusion of everything else.'[22]

These definitions need further examination. Condominas, in the first passage quoted here, must be thinking of the past, not the present since, as he recognizes, the *fokon'olona* in any sense of the word as it is used now is not made up of kinsmen. Nonetheless Condominas is clearly equating the *fokon'olona* with a named kinship grouping which was, at least in the past, localized. The existence of such groupings is one of the most striking features of Merina ethnography, but the nature of these groups is somewhat complicated. Suffice it to say that ideally they are groups which are believed to have been endogamous in the past and can therefore be called *demes.*[23] However one point is clear to me. At no time in the past or now did any category or group of people which could be referred to by the word *fokon'olona* include all the members of a *deme.* The territory of a named *deme* always contained the territory of several unnamed *fokon'olona.*

There are yet other difficulties in Comdominas' definition. Not only are the *fokon'olona* and the *deme* different order groupings, they are also different in nature. The *deme* can be considered a descent group in that it has an ideology of descent and its members consider themselves descended from a named ancestor. It is, however, not patrilineal or unilineal, and any degree of corporateness it possesses is due to in-marriage rather than unilineal descent.[24] The *fokon'olona* is a territorial division of the *deme.* It therefore has an ideology of kinship since anyway all *deme* members are regarded as kinsmen, but it does not have an ideology of descent as the *fokon'olona* is seen as *just* a territorial division. There is no record or tradition of a time in the past when the *fokon'olona* had a specific ancestor, or when the ability to trace descent (through whatever line) established a claim to membership.

There is yet a third element referred to in Condominas' definition, and that is the tomb. Here again Condominas must be referring to the precolonial situation, but even with this proviso I find it difficult to accept his proposition. In all old villages there are a number of ancient tombs belonging to various families. This was also the case in the nineteenth century.[25] This means that there were several tomb groups within one *fokon'olona*. In other words, it seems to me that Condominas is merging three levels of division which are still clearly distinct. The named kinship groups *(demes)* and their territories are still well known and retain a certain significance to the present day. They include many villages. On the other hand the tomb groups[26] are below the level of the village, and there are always a number of them in one village. If the *fokon'olona* was, as it still is today (and this is assumed by Condominas), a group of people living in usually one but sometimes more (up to three) villages, and a kinship group, it follows that it represented an intermediary level between the tomb group and the *deme,* as Fig. 1 shows in a schematic way.

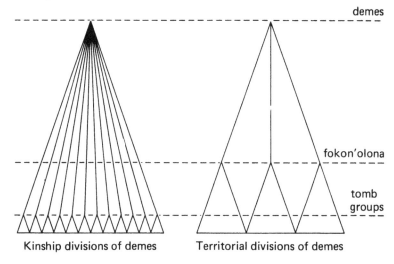

demes

fokon'olona

tomb groups

Kinship divisions of demes   Territorial divisions of demes

Fig. 1   Traditional divisions of Merina *demes*

Finally, although the *deme* may have been endogamous in the past, and so constituted a corporate descent group, the *fokon'olona* certainly was not, and the absence of a unilineal rule of descent means that it was not kinship alone that defined the *fokon'olona,* but also locality. This is also true of the tomb group, and since this has retained its structure the process can be easily illustrated.[27]

In other words, even for the past, Condominas' concept of the *fokon'olona* has to be modified almost out of recognition. As an explanation of what the *fokon'-olona* is at the present, Condominas' definition needs to be modified even further, and it must be remembered that it is as an explanation of the *fokon'olona* of today

41

that Condominas gives us his definition. If the *fokon'olona* was distinct from the tomb group and the *deme* in the past, now that tomb groups are smaller than they used to be while *fokon'olona* and *deme* territories are little changed, there is no reason why this should have altered. Indeed, in many ways the picture I have given above for the position of the *fokon'olona* as intermediate between the tomb groups and the *deme* still holds.

There is nonetheless one very important new factor: people do not nowadays usually live in the traditional areas of their *demes* or their tomb groups. The Merina of free descent, however, retain a tie with their ancestral villages, whether they live there or not. They retain this tie by attachment to their family tombs, and they retain their tie with their *deme* by virtue of the fact that they are associated with a tomb in the *deme* territory.[28] In this way it can be said that in spite of living away from their traditional villages, the Merina still belong to their *demes* and tomb groups. The same, however, cannot be said of the *fokon'olona*. As we shall see, one belongs by and large to the *fokon'olona* one lives in. Since recent Merina history has meant large scale population movement, it follows that there are many unrelated kinship groups in one *fokon'olona* territory, and that therefore members of the *fokon'olona* as it is today are never all kin.

Deme and tomb groups are units in the traditional system of organization, and in a way they can be said to have been unaffected in form by the changes of the last hundred years. This is because these groups are irrelevant to political and economic organization. The *fokon'olona* was part of the traditional system, but it is also part of the present day economic and political systems. Changes in the economic and political system have meant that the *fokon'olona* has had to change its form. This has meant that it has largely had to sever its structural relationship with the more immobile *deme* and tomb groups. The population movement has meant that nowadays most people living within the territory of a *deme* are not members of it, but this does not matter since the functions of the present day *demes* have little to do with matters which are dependent on locality. This means that *demes* are now dispersed groups. *Fokon'olonas* however are not now divisions of the dispersed *demes* but of the people living in a *deme* territory. This is a social unit irrelevant to the *deme* system. It follows also that for the present day the *fokon'olona* is a different kind of grouping than the *deme* and tomb groups, and is no more even an intermediate grouping between the two, but is totally separate from *deme* and tomb organization.

This having been said, the fact remains that Condominas has an important point when he stresses that this group is not just a morally neutral, administratively convenient unit, and that it is linked to feelings of kinship. Condominas' book is designed to combat a purely administrative view of the *fokon'olona,* and in his enthusiasm he, as we saw above, overstates the kinship aspect of the *fokon'olona.* Such an aspect at the level of ideology however is clearly there. That the *fokon'olona* can be at one and the same time a group which is not based on kinship and yet one which has a kinship ideology appears at first as a paradox. It can be clarified, I think, if we examine a number of typical instances in which the word *fokon'olona* is used today.

The concept of fokon'olona today

(1) When one day during field work I produced a tape recorder in the village where I was working, a very large crowd gathered to look and listen to it. Many people commented, 'the whole *fokon'olona* has come'. Here the word is used to mean 'everybody' and this is a very common usage. However, 'everybody' in a fairly small compact village made up of a limited number of kinship groups is not just 'anybody'. The word could not be used to describe a group of disparate people who did not know each other, and who had gathered at, for example, a street corner in Tananarive.

(2) In a somewhat similar sense, the word is used for describing the people who come for a ceremony, for example a marriage. Such a ceremony takes place usually in two stages. The first half (usually the first day) is described as the day of the kindred and affines *(fianakaviana)*;[29] the latter half (usually the second day) when a large number of people as well as the *fianakaviana* are present, is described as 'the day of the *fokon'olona*'. On that day all people with whom those concerned have friendly social relations are invited. In such a phrase the word *fokon'olona* is used to mean a large number of people living in the locality, indeed the whole locality as, in theory at least, everybody who lives in the village should be invited, as well as selected people from nearby villages. The interesting point here is that the notion of *fokon'olona* is here contrasted with that of *fianakaviana*. Far from using *fokon'olona* for a kinship group, the word is used here to contrast with the typical word for a kinship group. It means those neighbours with whom one has friendly relations but are *not* kinsmen.

(3) The usage of the word *fokon'olona* which we have just considered above makes another common use of the word seem at first surprising if not plainly contradictory. As in the 'sentimental' kind of literature referred to above, people often talk of the 'kinship love' which unites the *fokon'olona*: and they say the *fokon'olona* is 'one family' *fianakaviana*. How can this be reconciled with a word which in another context can be used as a contrast to *fianakaviana*? When villagers say that the *fokon'olona* is one family they are referring to a territorial group, although the exact degree of inclusiveness of this territorial group is vague. The 'kinship' unity of the *fokon'olona* is a constant topic for homilies, and with pious pride they give examples of this unity in action. The manifestations picked out by the villagers as exemplifying this sentiment are the obligations of mutual help between members of the same *fokon'olona*. This is particularly striking at funerals, when the members of the *fokon'olona* are under an extremely strong obligation to give extensive help, financial, in kind, and in labour to the bereaved family.[30] The help given at funerals is always picked out as a sign of the kind of help

expected of neighbours, and indeed it is a most striking display of solidarity. This mutual help is explained by such phrases as 'We are all one family', 'We are all parents and children', 'We are all of one womb', 'We are all kinsmen'. Clearly, however, the people referred to are not genealogical kinsmen and this is well known. Nor, as we saw above, are they 'social' kinsmen, since in other contexts the genealogical kinsmen are contrasted with the members of the *fokon'olona*. It seems to me a fair representation of the Merina view to say that these people are kinsmen by extension. Actually, Merina only make the kind of emphatic statement of kinship ties given above when they are dealing with kinsmen by extension, when it is known that the ties are not 'real'. Having made this qualification it can also be understood why the Merina feel they should call these people kinsmen.

Malagasy theory runs along the following lines: kinsmen are people who help each other on account of their reciprocal love; help motivated by love is typical of kinsmen; neighbours should help each other, therefore, good neighbours are a kind of kinsmen.[31] There is therefore no contradiction between the statements which imply that the members of the *fokon'olona* are not kinsmen and those statements which say they are. These different statements are made in different contexts and both say things which, properly understood, are not mutually exclusive. This point is important as it explains why in spite of obvious contrary evidence, so many writers like Condominas feel they must talk of the *fokon'olona* as a 'clan' or some other kind of kinship group. The *fokon'olona* is not a kinship group but a local group bound by *kinship-like* rights and obligations.[32]

(4) On the other hand the notion of *fokon'olona* corresponds in many concepts to something more than an ill-defined morally bound local community. The *fokon'-olona* can refer to a political unit whose main manifestation is its ability to gather together in a council. It is important to realise that this more formal manifestation is seen by the Merina as only one aspect of *fokon'olona*. Nonetheless, the fact that the *fokon'olona* does gather together, means that on certain occasions a fairly clear line must be drawn between those who belong and those who do not. How this line is drawn can be seen when we consider the case of one particular village and the people who belonged to its *fokon'olona*.

This case is of a village in traditional Imerina[33] where people have traditional ties symbolized by the right to be buried in a particular tomb in the village. In such a village therefore there is a moral community associated through the tombs with a particular village in spite of the fact that this community very probably never lives in the village, but simply believes that its ancestors once did.

This group of people with an ancestral association with the village would not be referred to as the *fokon'olona*. Those who live in the village are of course included in the *fokon'olona*. Others, who do not live in the village, may vaguely consider themselves to be members of the *fokon'olona*, but the villagers would not consider them as such. In fact they resent attempts on the part of these outsiders to interfere in village affairs, as several incidents during my stay showed. However, the villagers' attitude to this shadowy claim may be modified if these outsiders with tombs inside the village contribute to community expenses, such as the building of schools and roads. If they do so, the villagers might consider them sufficiently members of the *fokon'olona* to contribute to the funeral expenses of their family and to give them other forms of traditional help. Nonetheless, this category of people is not allowed to participate in village councils, nor can they affect collective decisions. Finally, of those people with ancestral ties there is a third category; the majority who neither claim nor are considered by anybody to be in any conceivable way members of the *fokon'olona.*

The *fokon'olona* therefore only includes a few of the people with ancestral ties to the village, but it also includes many people with no such ties. The fact of continued residence in the village was sufficient to establish membership of the *fokon'olona* for all except one person. This case is interesting as the man in question had in fact ancestral claims to tomb membership. He was, however, unmarried, having been a Roman Catholic priest. He had a strange and disturbing personality and was very much interested in politics, being a great supporter of the P.S.D. and considered by the villagers to be a P.S.D. spy. He regularly left the village for other villages or for Tananarive, although in this he was not exceptional. This was the only reason I heard given as an explanation of his exclusion. It seemed to me, however, that the main relevant fact was that he did not have a family and was therefore not implicated in the web of micro-exchanges which constitute daily life in such a close community. This meant that he was not concerned in most of the activities of the *fokon'olona.* He could not help at funerals nor would he require help for funerals other than his own. No member of his family belonged to the transplanting teams. He had no children to educate. Finally, and significantly, he could not be trusted to help in the current village opposition to administrative actions. He lived in the community but did not participate in it. The critical position of this man is illuminating in that it shows that even if locality is the dominant factor in *fokon'olona* membership, it is not just a matter of locality but also of community. In conclusion, therefore, it emerges that the *fokon'olona* of today is not a kinship group, nor is it associated with tombs and *deme,* but is a group of people living in one village or more whose lives interlock because of their propinquity and who express this interlocking in the idiom of kinship.

The fokon'olona as a council

If we have defined what the *fokon'olona* is as a community, we may ask what it is as a council in the sense that we have had to consider it in the historical section above. The answer is very simple, it is exactly the same thing. The reason is that there is no idea of *representation* of the *fokon'olona* in a council. The *fokon'olona* council is the *fokon'olona* doing something. When we consider different types of *fokon'olona* councils we are not considering differently constituted assemblies. Rather there are different assemblies because different things which have to be done involve different people. However, before considering this it is necessary briefly to examine various important roles in the community, so as to understand their place in the *fokon'olona* council.

The raiamandreny

There are two types of important people as far as the *fokon'olona* is concerned: The village headman and the elders. The village headman's position has already been touched upon. His main function is to read and explain the directives, whether written or not, which he has been given by the administration. He is more a servant of the administration than a leader of the village, and in terms of what goes on during meetings he has no more authority or influence than any other *raiamandreny*.

The *raiamandreny* (literally, father and mother) are the elders. They are norm-ally, but not always, men. Becoming, and therefore being, a *raiamandreny* is an ambiguous business. Some poeple, everyone would agree, are *raiamandreny*. Others, everyone (including themselves), would agree are not. There is however a third category about whom opinion is divided, but who usually consider themselves to be *raiamandreny*. Out of a population of 147 in the village considered above, six people were unchallenged *raiamandreny*, of whom only three were influential. Four others were in that difficult position of having some claim to being *raiamandreny*, but not being universally recognized as such. Some people are *raiamandreny ex officio* – chief among whom are the protestant pastor and government officials *(fonctionaires)* if any should reside in the village. Other unchallenged *raiamandreny* are the universally respected senior heads of large local families. They are main-tained in their position by their wisdom[34] and their ability to make formal speeches. However, as we shall see, this ability to make speeches and this wisdom may be as much the result as the cause of their influence. Members of the indeterm-inate category do not usually have such a clear cut right to the title because their social position is more ambiguous. They try to consolidate their position by such means as a display of their wisdom, especially in connection with astrology, and by their skill in oratory, a skill which requires personality, knowledge, and sufficient influence to ensure that one is taken seriously. To be acknowledged as a *raiaman-dreny* is rather a case of having a title than actually holding an office. It is not the fact that one is referred to as a *raiamandreny* which gives special rights and duties but rather it is a recognition of the position of such rights and duties.[35]

I now want to turn to the actual working of the *fokon'olona* as a council. We are dealing here not with a constituted council but with members of the *fokon'olona* gathering, either formally or impromptu to discuss matters of concern. If these matters are of concern to everyone then everyone would be expected to participate, but if the affairs are only of concern to a few or to only one category of people, then one would expect that only these would attend. In other words it is not the *fokon'olona* as such which is a council, but councils are made up of *fokon'olona* members, and when a significant number of people gather together to reach decisions they can be referred to as the *fokon'olona,* as this describes the kind of people they are. It is therefore in terms of the business in hand that we must consider various types of *fokon'olona* councils, rather than in terms of different types of constituted bodies. This point needs to be stressed since many of the writings discussed in the first section of this paper give the impression that the *fokon'olona* is a constituted council, and the type of cooperation typical of *fokon'- olona* members is described as though it were the result of the occasional assemblies which take place. In fact, the gatherings are themselves only one of the manifestations of the already existing community feeling.

The first type of council we must consider is the best known one, the council called as the result of the receipt of an order from the administration through an intermediary – the village headman or other government official. This type of village meeting is referred to as a *kabary* (speech) when members of the *fokon'- olona* are called to listen. This is not a meeting of the *fokon'olona* as a body but just people being called to listen to an order. Naturally there is no question of excluding anyone, and everybody, women and children included, tries to come. It is also possible for such a village-wide meeting to be called on the private initiative of any *raiamandreny* to discuss any general matter or to air a quarrel, but in fact, in the communities in which I worked, out of seventeen meetings in which the whole village was called only three were not directly and principally concerned with government business. One dealt with the clearing of irrigation ditches. (This is of importance for the *fokon'olona* but is usually discussed on the initiative of the government.) Another dealt with a quarrel relating to inheritance of land.

A *kabary* can be called in various ways. In one large village where I worked there was a town crier who, on the evening before the meeting, called everyone 'men and women of the *fokon'olona*' to attend, stating that there was government business to attend to, or, in those rarer instances when this was not the case, naming the person on whose initiative the meeting was called. In a smaller village where I also worked, the letter from the government, which the village headman had received, was pinned with a thorn to the fortifications of the village near the gate, or else the 'word was passed round'. In fact the village headman visited all *raiamandreny* in the village, but resentment occurred when certain people were not told.[36]

The actual time of the meeting was always set three or four hours too early, and as for many Merina occasions, great skill was required by those who wanted to arrive at the right time, in the right place. Nobody wanted to arrive too early, but obviously it would not do to arrive too late. The influence of a person is at stake in manoeuvres of this kind, and his effectiveness at such a meeting depends on his appearing at the right time to give the impression that the meeting is starting because of his arrival. This involves a lot of waiting about in nearby houses and sending children to spy out the land and report back. As if by magic the *raiamandreny* all appear at once at a time little related to the originally appointed hour.

This custom (infuriating for the anthropologist) is part of the prestige auction which, as we shall see, characterizes these meetings. The meeting takes place in varying places in different villages, but always in the same place in any one village. Merina villages lack any obvious meeting points like a village square, or a communal house, such as are found in other parts of Madagascar. In the community mentioned above meetings occurred near the village gate, an extremely inconvenient place as the whole meeting had to scatter every time cattle pushed through.

A typical example of this type of meeting was when the village headman called the whole community to receive their cards for the forthcoming general election in 1965. This meeting was very fluid, (only starting when sufficient people got together — and this seemed almost an accident). However, when the village headman decided there were enough people, he started a long speech about what everybody should do in order to vote, and he explained how necessary it was to vote, how good it was to vote, and, finally, who the people should vote for (the P.S.D. candidate). This speech was followed by several others who made some of the same points, and the distribution of cards began while other people of lesser importance, including many women, spoke again reiterating the same views. In such a case, as so often, there is absolutely nothing to argue about. The attendance was very fluid, although some people stayed right through. Speaking was orderly and dignified; only occasionally did more than one person speak at once and this only for a short time. Towards the end a series of other related issues was raised, discussed a little, and then dropped without any apparent conclusion being reached. The meeting ended simply with people going away. This rather desultory way of going about the whole matter is typical of those meetings which follow from a government order.

Another example of the kind of thing which may concern such a council is the discussion which took place in the village mentioned above concerning the building of a 'middle school' *(cours moyen)* in the canton. This was to offer educational opportunities beyond the primary level which had been up to then the only level available. Although presented as a spontaneous initiative of the *fokon'olona* of the canton, this idea was the result of government policy and a suggestion from the administration, a suggestion which was understood as an order. The government offered to supply a school teacher[37] if the building was built by the *fokon'olona*. In fact, although the original idea came from the government, the plan was welcomed by many of the more forward-looking villagers. Nonetheless the building of the school was an imposition. The canton head divided the responsibility between the three *fokon'olona* that were to benefit. They were each to supply a proportion of the labour for building the mud walls and wooden roof-frame, and the money for buying those materials which were not available, principally the corrugated iron required for the roofing. The *fokon'olona* was left to organize itself to supply this labour and money. In spite of this it was never proposed spontaneously either to set a day apart to work on the school or actually to contribute money. The village headman had to be prompted by the head of the canton in order to get anything done. This prompting led the village headman to make a speech proposing the matter. Only the actual date for working on the school or for paying was left to be decided on the initiative of the *fokon'olona*. This meant that these meetings took on much the same pattern as the one previously described when it was only a matter of obeying an order and this, in spite of the fact that in theory, at least, the building of the school was on *fokon'olona* initiative.

The most heated meeting I attended concerned the paying for the corrugated iron for the roof of the school. The original speech by the headman was again followed by two other speeches by the *raiamandreny*, the main point of both being the advantage of education in general. It was only in the discussion by the lesser people who followed the elders that it emerged that each household would have to supply either 3m^2 of corrugated iron or 600 F.M.G. (17s.2d.).This was a bitter pill to swallow and many, largely impracticable, alternative modes of roofing were considered, as well as a close discussion of exactly how much roofing was necessary. The discussion was fairly heated between the junior members of the council. The elders steered clear so as not to lose dignity. It was clear that the decision was really already taken and the resistance was only a show. The counter-proposals were left unanswered. It was left at that, but the actual collection of the money was a very long and difficult business. Matters connected with this and with the building of the school were continually brought up by the *fokon'olona* subsequently.

These two examples of the kind of thing discussed by the large *fokon'olona* meetings, called by the village headmen as the mouthpiece of the administration, give an idea of how such matters are handled, and we may now turn to a more general account of the procedure at this type of meeting.

Procedure

The meeting always opens with a speech by whoever has convened it. This, of course, is usually the village headman, who is introducing an order he has received from the administration. The speech he makes however is a formal Merina speech, on a pattern which is typical of all important occasions. However, speeches given in the *fokon'olona* are, by Merina standards, relatively simple affairs, although by European standards they would be considered very elaborate.

All speeches begin with an introduction called *miala tsiny*, which literally translated, means the removing of faults. It is in fact a long and elaborate apology for speaking, considering how unworthy and junior the speaker is. The phrase which nearly always begins this part of the speech expresses well the general gist of it: *Tsy zoky fa zandry, tsy ray fa zaza,* which means, 'I am not an elder brother but a younger: I am not a father but a child'.

These introductory sentences are greatly appreciated by amateurs of speech-making and the more elaborate the conceit the better it is liked. Formal though it is, the idea of *tsiny* is not just an empty show of humility. It corresponds to the idea of removing impiety. The rationale behind this is that since any act is bound not to match up to somebody's expectations, to disappoint somebody, to slight somebody, it must be excused. This is a key concept, as is demonstrated by R. Andriamanzato in his short book: *Le Tsiny et le Tody dans la Pensée Malgache,* and the expression of this sentiment is regarded by the Merina themselves as a typical feature of their way of seeing the world.

After the *miala tsiny* there follows a section expressing general moral sentiments. These usually deal with such things as the unity of the family, the need for love amongst kinsmen, the goodness and justice of the government, and the good fortune of the people in having such a president of the republic and so on. This section, which again is fairly standardized, is judged by the wealth of illustrations it includes. The illustrations are of two kinds, first the *teny drazana* or proverbs, and secondly biblical illustrations, especially from the Old Testament. This second part, which again has usually little, if anything, to do with the matter in hand, merges into the third and final which contains the actual proposal, still ornamented with elaborate decorations. Not only is the form of the speeches characteristic and traditional, but also the mode of delivery. The *miala tsiny* part is delivered very quietly, head down, and very slowly. Only imperceptibly does the speaker get more confident so that the rhythms of the proverbs can be stressed and the significant parts emphasized. After a speech by an important man there is usually a short period of silence.

The introductory speech of the village headman is followed by others of the same pattern delivered by other well accepted *raiamandreny.* These say very little that is new and are definitely not controversial. They state how good and how moral the proposals are, how good the government and administration are, and so on. The formal speeches usually take about half the time given to the proceedings. Up to this stage there is no trace of disagreement; indeed opposition is usually not possible as the meeting is dealing with a government proposal. Then the first person to introduce the discussion, or someone closely linked to him, will bring up concrete proposals for action. For example, at what time will they go out and dig the drainage channels; on which day and what tools will they bring with them. Then it seems as if something is really being discussed in the way we understand the word, but the method of reaching a decision is still unfamiliar to us. It is generally at this stage that the junior members of the *fokon'olona* take part in the discussion. Even now the argument never appears on the surface as a conflict of views. The discussion happens as a series of mutually exclusive statements. One person makes a speech the gist of which is a proposal to come on a particular day. This may well be followed by another speech which seems to be in support of the proposal and full of praise for it, but in fact contains, hidden within the mass of polite sentences, a counter-proposal for another day. There is no argument and it is very difficult to realize that the statements are contradictory. What is more, no decision seems to be reached at the time. However, if a large number of people mention one time rather than the other, everyone knows that this is the right time. Often, however, the matter is left in the air and the chosen day is understood to be that proposed by the more influential man. In this way these contradictions may be tests in a power struggle between different individuals. Very often it is not clear to the participants at what time they should turn up. If this is so on the first day mentioned the supporters of one side will start to gather. If they are few, they will soon disperse. If, on the contrary, they are many, they will be joined by waverers and then the whole thing snowballs, until ultimately perhaps even the proposer of the alternative day will be drawn in. It must be remembered that such instances when the *fokon'-olona* is called to work together are usually at the request of the government, for such purposes as reafforestation, road mending or irrigation channel clearance. Even though this last task is to the benefit of the village as a whole, and until recently was done spontaneously, it is now regarded as a government imposition, although it is done more cheerfully than the much resented compulsory reafforestation.[38] Much of this work is done with particularly bad grace and nobody is willing to push anybody very much into doing it. Thus the communal work aspect of *fokon'olona* activity, much praised by the government and by many writers on the area, is in fact resented and is often the occasion for a dismal display of lack of cooperation and goodwill. The difficulty in reaching a date for doing this type of work is connected with this general unwillingness. Nonetheless, this does not mean that the peculiar imprecision of this type of decision-making is to be explained as a function of the particular circumstance of this type of work. Rather the circumstance gives particularly full play to a typical mechanism of Merina decision-making.

There is another way, perhaps more straightforward, in which a proposal may be rejected; that is by irony. If a person makes a proposal his opponent may interrupt with a joke, making fun of it. This may have one of two results. In the first case lots of people join in and the speaker is laughed down. (If this happens the speaker himself may well turn the proposal into a joke and in this way abandon it.) The other possibility is that the joke will not be taken up, and the speaker will just carry on, ignoring the joker, and in such a way he carries his proposal forward. In fact this mechanism is, in my experience, the most important factor in the process of rejection or acceptance of a proposal. Clearly in the open outbursts mentioned above, the subtle effect of potential irony is a continuing ground base to the speeches of lesser men, but as such it is difficult to describe and even to record. The possibility of being laughed at is always present and the speaker is on the watch for the slightest hint of irony in the facial expression of those around him.

These two mechanisms, the non-recognition of opposing views and the expression of irony, avoid open confrontation of conflicting points of view. In this sense the mechanisms can be said to stress consensus as a system of decision-making. It is not however consensus reached as a result of compromise, but consensus which appears to follow from the assumption that there can be no disagreement among people linked by such strong moral ties. Finally, if only for the sake of accuracy, it should be mentioned that there were, on a few minor occasions, actual open clashes of opinion. These were very rare and they made everybody uncomfortable. The onlookers changed the subject and in one case just went away. This avoidance of open verbal conflict is typical of Merina interpersonal relations at all times, and not simply during meetings. Open clashes are extremely rare and during my eighteen-month stay in Merina villages there were only three quarrels involving people shouting at each other. This is a general rule controlling behaviour. Conflicting interests are not received orally and the formality of oral communications between adults does not allow for the expression of hostility. This presents only a limited problem for the type of meeting which we have considered above, since, as we have seen, little of substance is left to be decided in the council. We noted some of the mechanisms for dealing with conflict, but the picture must be completed with an account of what happens in those other meetings of *fokon'olona* members where it is more important that decisions be reached.

Village meetings concerned with the settlement of disputes

This type of gathering differs from those I have considered above in that it does not deal with an administrative order but with a matter which arises from within the *fokon'olona,* usually a quarrel. It should however be remembered that quarrels are not normally dealt with by an assembly of the *fokon'olona* any more, but tend to be taken directly to the mayor or the *chef de canton* who are sometimes joined by such government employees as the local school teacher and the agricultural adviser. Only minor quarrels are dealt with by the *fokon'olona,* mainly cases dealing with the depredations of straying animals, cattle, sheep, geese and ducks (a continual cause of tension); some disputes concerning irrigation (since the complicated network of channels is dependent on intimate cooperation and considerate behaviour);[39] and finally petty thieving. Even then, not all these types of case are dealt with by a grouping of *fokon'olona* members. Nonetheless, some cases do still occur which are not, at least at first, taken to the officials. The reasons for this vary. It might be that the group within which the quarrel occurs does not want the news of the dispute to be widely known; it might be that the parties do not want to pay the small fee which the administration charges for arbitration; or it might be that for one reason or another the parties concerned do not trust the administrator. Finally, although it is normal to by-pass the *fokon'olona,* this is an action which carries with it a certain amount of blame. In one case which I recorded, public opinion in the village which had previously been supporting one side in a dispute in a *fokon'olona* discussion swung round to the other side when the opponents took the matter to a government court.

The *fokon'olona* assembly deals with disputes relatively rarely, and I was able to attend only two such meetings. I suspect, however, that they are not as rare as this figure suggests since a desire for secrecy is often one of the reasons for using these meetings for dealing with disputes rather than going to the officials; and for this reason it may well be that the number of people attending such meetings is kept to a minimum. This may have meant that I was not aware of such assemblies even though they were going on.

By way of example we can consider one of the cases I listened to. This was concerned with persistent chicken thefts. Several of the *raiamandreny,* having heard of the repeated thefts, decided to get together to discuss the whole matter. One prearranged evening they all gathered inside the village headman's house – not the usual place for such meetings – until about twenty-five people had assembled, a fair proportion of the men concerned.[40] The procedure was much the same as at any gathering of *fokon'olona* members. The speeches were long and formal and their main points were that, (1) the thefts had been taking place, (2) that they were very wrong. The longer speeches were followed again by shorter ones which were more factual, stating more clearly where and when the chickens had been stolen, and the suggestion was made that the chickens must have been stolen by someone within the village. This is as far as the meeting went. No specific accusations were made and the whole thing was left in the air. When I discussed what seemed to me this rather inconclusive end to the whole matter with one of the main participants in the meeting, I was assured that everyone knew who the culprit was, and that the whole proceeding was to make him feel bad and give him a warning. In fact the meeting was successful in that the chicken thefts stopped. A similar type of meeting can occur when two people are said to be quarrelling regularly.

Finally, in order to show how unstructured is the concept of the *fokon'olona* as a court and how close it is to a simple gathering of the people concerned, we may consider the following example. This case concerned a sheep which, as continually happens, had wandered into a rice field and eaten some of the seedlings. The owner of the rice field, after having tried to break the sheep's leg, the usual retaliation for this type of offence, caught it and told its owner that he would not give it back. A group of ten or twelve people gathered as both sides argued, each side making relatively formal speeches. Nearly everybody present chimed in with their opinions until a *raiamandreny* proposed a sum for compensation which, after a little haggling, was accepted by both sides. As far as I could understand, this sort of procedure was not seen as being in any way different from the rather more formal proceedings described above. This episode, slight in itself, is interesting in that it shows just how imprecise a group (including only one *raiamandreny*) can be referred to as the *fokon'olona.* It is also interesting in that this is the most direct piece of decision-making 'in council' I came across. It shows clearly that even here it is only in a mediating capacity that the *fokon'olona* acts.

Decision-making in village meetings

We now turn to the more general question of the type of decision-making processes which are at work in the kind of meeting we have been considering up to now: that is to say the large meetings. The first point to notice is that very little is left to the *fokon'olona* members to decide. Usually the important issues are already decided by the administration and it is only the way they are to be implemented which is left to the villagers. Even such matters as when to clear the irrigation channels for the rice fields, a traditional concern of the *fokon'olona*, are taken out of their hands and the village headman receives orders about what is to be done. Even when there is something to decide, the decision-making process with its clear implications of considering differing opinions and choosing one of them is avoided. Whether this is the result of the habit of having nothing substantial to decide it is difficult to say and the point can be considered again when we have seen how women reach decisions. One thing, however, is certain: apart from the substantive matter in hand, the meetings we have described are part of the continuing process of assessing who is, or is not, a *raiamandreny*. This accounts for the, at first baffling, fact that even on the occasions when there is nothing to settle when; in fact, the council is dealing with a decision from above which it is powerless to affect; there is often prolonged and even emphatic discussion.

As we have seen, nothing marks out a *raiamandreny* so much as the type of speech he makes. A *raiamandreny* makes long ornate speeches with a fixed structure which are listened to from beginning to end without interruption and in silence. By contrast, a person of no importance only makes short speeches which can be interrupted by counter-proposals or by ironic jokes. A man without importance would never attempt a fully developed traditional speech for the simple reason that nobody would listen. Also, it is assumed that such a person would not know how to make this type of speech and does not possess the much appreciated skill of entertaining an audience in that way.

Obviously it is in the field of speech-making by those people whose status is uncertain that the ambiguities occur. An aspirant *raiamandreny* tries to make traditional *raiamandreny* speeches but is not listened to. The reasons given by the actors are in terms of his lack of knowledge of traditional forms of 'custom', of proverbs or anecdotes. Clearly, someone without this knowledge cannot hope to be considered in the running at all. However, in my experience, the final selection is not done purely in terms of oratorical ability. The power to command an attentive audience does not only depend on the ability to make a speech but on the willingness of the people to listen. The rejection of a speech by a person trying to be recognized as a *raiamandreny* is characteristic. When such an orator launches into the long solemn form of a traditional speech other people present interrupt him, adding comments, which he can either answer and risk losing the dignity associated with this type of speech-making; or ignore, and run the risk that the interruptions will become more and more frequent, and that the same effect will be produced. More significant are jokes making fun of the speaker and of what he says. These are weapons in the hands of the audience which they might choose to use to expose the pretensions of the speaker. When such a joke is made one of three things can happen. First, the joke may be ignored by both speaker and audience, in which case the speaker gains in status. The second possibility is that the joke is taken up. A speaker can only weather a few such jokes and maintain his dignity. The third alternative is for the joke to be taken up by the audience in general and when the speaker realizes this, seeing himself beaten, he laughs with the others against himself, as if to say that his claim to be a *raiamandreny* was not really to be taken seriously. Clearly therefore the acceptance of the claim to be a *raiamandreny* depends on the audience. The audience reacts, in part, in terms of the power and influence wielded by the speaker in the everyday life of the community, and in this way the acceptance of a speech by a certain person can be seen as the public demonstration of the evaluation in which he is held. Nonetheless, I feel that we should not underestimate the very real value attached to traditional speech-making as such by those concerned. It is quite clear that someone with the great ability and knowledge necessary for this type of speech-making is likely to be recognized as a *raiamandreny* in spite of the fact that his control of wealth and of power in everyday affairs might be considerably less than would otherwise warrant the rank. I know of one clear case when this had in fact happened.

The meetings of members of the *fokon'olona* therefore can be seen, less as occasions for making decisions about the matters in hand, than for making decisions about ranking in the community. Those few clashes of opinion which do occur are insignificant and are often little more than the side effects of competition between individual members.

Meetings of women members of the fokon'olona

I now want to continue this examination of decision-making in councils by considering this process in a totally different type of assembly, those consisting entirely of women. It is obvious that there is nothing different in a meeting of women of the *fokon'olona* from that of any other meeting of a group of members of the *fokon'olona* for any other purpose, since in no case are we dealing with the *fokon'olona* as a complete body but only with certain members of it. There are two important occasions on which the women of the *fokon'olona* meet. The first concerns meetings of the Malagasy Red Cross; the second those dealing with the organization of the transplanting of rice seedlings.

Red Cross meetings

The rank and file organization of the Malagasy Red Cross is at first surprisingly wide. In fact in the villages the Red Cross is seen as an arm of the government and it is felt that *all* women should belong, and nearly all do, the membership fee being minimal. The actual functions of the Red Cross are less clearly defined. In the village its main job is concerned with the weekly distribution of anti-malarial drugs, organized on a local level, and the distribution, when available, of such things as powdered milk or in some cases sweets and biscuits.

The meetings of the Red Cross are attended by women alone and the decisions to be made are few. The most significant of these consist in the choice of the officers of the Red Cross. This occasion contrasts to a certain extent with the way the men who are elected to government offices in the village are chosen, in that, as far as I was aware, the higher echelons of the Red Cross does not try to influence the choices which are to be made. On the other hand, these Red Cross officers did not emerge by the same type of mechanism by which the *raiamandreny* emerged. The main contrast is that the formal speech is not used by women, at least at these meetings. Much shorter, to-the-point, speeches are made. In addition, in contrast to what we have seen in the case of the wider *fokon'olona* meeting, there is no avoidance of open conflict and indeed it is a characteristic of the meetings of women that they are loud, bad-tempered and back-biting. This at any rate is the accepted stereotype; and in my experience it does seem to correspond to reality. This is not really surprising since the extremely polite, reserved, controlled behaviour expected of the *raiamandreny,* and characteristic of many village meetings, is not expected of younger men, and even less of women. The difference of behaviour between meetings of women and meetings dominated by men corresponds to the more generally expected behaviour of these two categories of people. An interesting aspect of this type of behaviour of women is that it is accompanied by actual voting by a show of hands. This procedure is said to be a European introduction, but fits very well with the way women conduct their deliberations. By contrast voting would be unthinkable at a village meeting.

Meetings for organizing transplanting

The second type of meeting of the women of the *fokon'olona* is an even more important, although rare, occurence. It is the meeting which occurs once a year when the women arrange when their village team will transplant in the respective fields of its members.[41] The decisions to be reached are vital, as the labour of women is very scarce during the period of transplanting, and since the livelihood of everyone involved depends on the arrangement. The general principles are clear but they do not specify the day on which fields will be done. I have unfortunately not attended such a meeting but I understand from informants that there is a lot of haggling and quarrelling and that certain decisions have to be voted on. In other words the process of decision-making seems to correspond with the general pattern for women's assemblies.

Conclusion

It is interesting to examine, by way of conclusion, to what extent the material presented here fits in with the conclusion that Bailey reached in his article on decision-making in councils.[42] First of all Bailey distinguished between two kinds of activity, '(a) There is a range of behaviour from clamping down a *dispute* to allowing it free expression. (b) There is a range of behaviour from readiness to compromise to intransigence'. For Bailey (a) and (b) are not the same thing and (a) need not be taken into consideration when we are dealing with (b). A few lines later he adds that (a) is symbolic action, or ritual, while (b) is substantive action. By this Bailey means that the form of the process by which disputes are dealt with is traditional. While some societies have mechanisms for expressing division, others have not, but this does not mean that there are necessarily more divisions in the first type of society than the second. This is no doubt true, but the question Bailey is dealing with is not which societies have more conflict than others, but how different societies reach decisions. Bailey wants to carry over his basic distinction into the actual processes which go on in councils. However, in this case it surely is invalid, since he is not talking of the state of being in conflict, but of what happens when the conflict is recognized and when the situations have to be transformed so that unified action can be taken. This transformation takes place as a result of what people say to each other, or possibly do to each other, in other words, as a result of what happens in council. This is both symbolic and substantive action, indeed I find this distinction difficult to use if only for the reason that it is difficult to accept that the behaviour that I observed during councils was in any way 'unsubstantive', and equally difficult to conceive of a human activity without a symbolic element. Clearly when we consider an assembly of women deciding on the order of trans-planting fields in a Merina village the particular way or procedure whereby a decision is reached is what we are studying. This is not an elaborate front for some sort of *realpolitik* going on in the background. We do not need to accept statements by participants at their face value, but it is within the framework of these state-ments and indeed within the whole institutional framework that decisions are reached. This framework determines the range of possibilities of ways by which decisions can be achieved and no doubt the kind of decisions reached. Perhaps what Bailey is implying is that when we want to understand the decision-making process in a council, we should not limit ourselves to the symbolic exchanges going on in the actual assembly, but should also take into account those other instances of less formal social intercourse (equally symbolic) which take place before the council meets. These may not occur at the meeting place but in the fields, or around the hearth, or at street corners or anywhere else. If this is what Bailey means I would agree with him, but his actual statement suggests that anything we observe people doing and saying is a shadow play for the real, naked, wordless and actionless struggle of wills which goes on in a place and in a way which cannot be observed. Unfortunately, we are stuck with reality, however naive this might seem to the conflict theorist. As anthropologists we cannot afford to say that what we can observe is unreal but what we can only guess at is real.

If we ignore this theoretical point, Bailey's conclusions become well worth test-ing against the material in hand. At first sight all the councils we have considered are in Bailey's term 'arena councils' in that everyone in the village attends and therefore all tendencies are represented. However, on closer examination members of the *fokon'olona* have some of the characteristics of 'elite' councils in that, although everyone is present, it is really an occasion almost entirely dominated by the *raiamandreny* and the aspirant *raiamandreny* and these are, in a very important way, in opposition to the rest of the people. In these circumstances this type of assembly is really an elite council with the 'audience' present. It contrasts with the women's meetings for organizing transplanting, which have more of the character of arena councils, in that in those meetings there is no clear elite as there is in the wider village councils. This may explain, as Bailey's theory leads us to believe, such differences between these councils as the emphasis on consensus in the one and the use of such contrasting and contradicting procedures as voting in the other. In the councils of the whole village the opposition of the elite to the mass and the resulting need on the part of the elite to present a united front can be sensed. Nevertheless, other facts make us more wary of such a conclusion. By contrast with the meetings of women called to organize transplanting, the meetings of women for administering the Red Cross council are more like the village meeting. Here the same division between the elite and the mass can be seen and the important women in these meetings are in fact usually the wives of the *raiamandreny*. In structure at least the Red Cross meetings are very similar to the village meetings, yet their decision-making procedures contrast most sharply. In other words, although Bailey's hypothesis does seem to explain the difference in decision-making procedures between the village meetings and the meetings of women for transplanting, it fails to account for the difference between village meetings and Red Cross women's meetings.

Bailey establishes another criterion which he sees as linked with decision-making procedures. He distinguishes between those councils concerned primarily with policy-making and those councils dominated by administrative tasks. The former would tend towards consensus decisions, the latter to majority decisions. It is clear that the large assembly of the village, called by the village headman, is normally only administrative and its lack of policy-making functions is striking. This is also largely true of the Red Cross women's meetings. By contrast the village meetings not dealing with government orders also have a policy-making function, and the meeting of women to organize transplanting certainly do. According to Bailey therefore we would expect the purely administrative councils to tend more towards consensus procedures than those which also have a policy-making function. Here the evidence is less clear; though again it seems to me that within the village assemblies those more concerned with policy-making reach consensus less easily. This again may be true within the category of women's meetings. However if we begin to take all councils discussed here as one set, then again the generalizations of Bailey do not fit easily, in terms of this second criterion. The council dealing with the stealing of chickens described above had a more pronounced policy-making function than the council of women dealing with the Red Cross, yet it was the latter which resorted to voting procedures. In other words, although such generalizations may well work within one category they do not work across such institutional differences as the accepted norms of behaviour for men and women.

We are faced with two radically different ways of reaching decisions. On the one hand those characteristic of the assemblies attended by both men and women, but dominated by the almost exclusively male *raiamandreny*; and on the other the methods of decisions practised by the assemblies of women.

What other factors than those already considered can explain these differences? First of all there is the historical factor. Clearly, we can only understand the meetings of the *fokon'olona* called by the administration in the light of what we know of the traditional behaviour in the *fokon'olona* in the past. Only in these terms can we understand why there is any need for the forms of a decision-making council when normally the only thing to be done is to listen to orders from above. It is in this perspective that we can understand the total absence of conflict manifested in these councils and the apparently unchecked development of ceremonial forms of speech-making. The whole procedure of these councils only becomes understandable when it is realized that these councils were in the past the organ whereby most of the significant decisions for the organization of the community were taken, and that subsequently the power of reaching these important decisions has been lost. Hence the presence of a mechanism and a procedure for dealing with matters of greater weight than those which the *fokon'olona* is usually confronted with today. Hence also the surprisingly important place of the *fokon'olona* in the system of belief and values of the Merina. An explanation of why Merina *fokon'-olona* behave as they do cannot be given just in terms of the function that they fulfil now. The institutionalized form of these meetings is only explicable in terms of the history of the Merina kingdom and subsequently of the colonial and post-colonial period. Given an institution which does not really 'fit', we can then understand how the villagers make use of it and change it to a certain extent to achieve ends which are relevant to present-day organization. An example is the use made of the meetings of the *fokon'olona* for demonstrating and defining who are the *raiamandreny*. However, if the *fokon'olona* meetings did not exist, it seems incredible that such an institution and its particular form would grow up to perform what is really such a peripheral function. I am not claiming that these assemblies have lost all function and are in this sense 'survivals', but their form cannot be explained as an epiphenomenon of those functions.

There is another factor besides the historical, or perhaps it is the historical factor in another guise, which must be taken into account; that is the cultural. When we contrast the assemblies dominated by men and those composed exclusively of women, an explanation of why the latter turn more willingly to procedures such as voting seems at first obvious. While the village meetings have nothing to decide, the decisions having already been taken for them, such women's meetings as those dealing with transplanting have very vital matters to agree upon. We would expect those meetings which have important matters in hand to adopt procedures such as conflicting arguments and voting. This sort of explanation however is not sufficient.

When the larger village council does consider vital issues, the same sort of decision-making procedure occurs, insofar as the way speeches are made and how they follow from each other, as in the meetings in which they have nothing to decide. This is not to say that there is no difference in such elusive phenomena as the degree of tension in the meeting, or allusions intended to influence such and such a person. There is more pressure behind the proceedings but the behaviour follows the same pattern and the same apparently inconclusive way of reaching a decision is used. Furthermore, in those meetings of women when there is little to decide, as is the case for the Red Cross meetings, we get similar procedures and a similar type of meeting as when transplanting is discussed. In other words, it seems to me clear that such factors as the type of issues considered, or the type of the council, are not sufficient to explain why a particular process of decision-making is used. More significant is the accepted way for men and women to behave and argue. This is not limited to behaviour in councils, and is ultimately linked up with the way the sexes are educated and the beliefs held about their respective natures. This is linked to the significant sociological fact that men are permanently locked in a struggle for rank. This manifests itself in an unwillingness either to challenge anyone's rank for fear of his hostility or of placing oneself in a situation where one might lose rank. These fears paralyse men with respect to what they may say and do. Women on the other hand are much less inhibited since rank is of much less significance for them. Only in this way can we explain the most significant cleavage in decision-making procedures; that is to say the cleavage between the councils dominated by men and those dominated by women, a cleavage which over-rides all other differences in spite of similarities or differences in the functions and structure of councils. The functional sociological pressures can only be seen to operate within the historical—cultural framework.

I wish to acknowledge the generosity of the Nuffield Foundation of Great Britain which financed my research. I also take this opportunity to thank Dr J. Loudon, Dr A.I. Richards, Dr A. Sharman, and Mrs J.H. Bloch for many useful suggestions on an earlier draft.

Notes

[1] M. Bloch, 1971.

[2] M. Bloch, 1967b..

[3] This is a history of the Merina based on extensive records of oral traditions collected at the beginning of the century. Its value cannot be overestimated, but clearly, like any oral history, it must be treated with great caution (see M. Bloch, 1967b).

[4] G. Condominas, 1960: 37. The translation of the terms *hova* and *andriana* poses an acute problem. Since the meaning of these words is of little significance here I shall retain the words 'commoners' and 'aristocrats' for the sake of simplicity and comparability with other words. However, I am clear that this could be misleading.
(For a fuller discussion of this question see M. Bloch, 1967b).

[5] I recorded an almost identical origin story for a (presumably) different *fokon'olona*.

[6] G. Julien, 1908: 1, 367.

[7] H. Isnard, 1953: Chapus and Ratsimba, 1953: 421.

[8] Chapus and Ratsimba, 1953: 753.

[9] See L. P. Mair, 1962: M. Fortes, 1953.

[10] Various European coins had been introduced in Imerina. They were cut up to obtain smaller denominations.

[11] Julien, 1908: 363.

[12] Chapus and Ratsimba, 1953: 421.

[13] Condominas, 1960: 103.

[14] Condominas, ibid.

[15] 'Administrative villages, may be made up of one or more localities. They are in fact a compromise between traditional groupings and (more important) administrative convenience.

[16] In some cases the *fokon'olona* has a separate 'chairman'. In the only case of this I know, the official seemed to have no functions whatsoever.

[17] The hierarchy of mayors and councillors runs parallel to the one of village headman, head of canton etc. During my fieldwork the respective competence of these two hierarchies was not clear. This was perhaps due to the fact that the mayors etc. were a recent innovation.

[18] Legamble, 1963. I am indebted to P. Verin for drawing my attention to this publication.

[19] Ibid. p.64.

[20] Ibid. p.65.

[21] Condominas, 1960: 24.

[22] Ibid. p.112.

[23] M. Bloch, 1971: A. and G. Grandidier, 1908: 1, 236-7

[24] M. Bloch, 1971.

[25] W. Ellis, 1938: Grandidier, 1892.

[26] The relationship of tombs to people is extremely complex and cannot be discussed here. It is explained in part in Bloch, 1968a, and more fully in Bloch, 1971.

[27] M. Bloch, 1971.

[28] Ibid. and Bloch, 1968a.

[29] Bloch, 1971.

[30] Ibid.

[31] Bloch, 1967a.

[32] This point is made more extensively in Bloch, 1967a, where the group of *havana* or *mpifankatia* together can be considered as forming the *fokon'olona*.

[33] Ibid.

[34] M. Bloch, 1968b.

[35] The government, whether French or Malagasy, has always considered being a *raiamandreny* as being the holder of an office. This means that in administrative contexts it may actually be so.

[36] The cases I have in mind are of people who considered themselves *raiamandreny* but who were not so considered by the village headman.

[37] It actually failed to do this.

[38] On the occasions when the *fokon'olona* is expected to carry out this type of work, the meeting is, so to speak, carried on during the work itself. Every adult man is expected to participate but only informal pressures are brought to bear on those who do not. In my experience people did in fact all turn out except for those with a valid and accepted excuse such as illness. A few sufficiently important men, who knew that nobody would dare blame them for not coming, did not do so. Most important men in fact come but try to direct the operation. Here too there is much scope for trying to establish and demonstrate status as a

raiamandreny. A *raiamandreny* can give orders and these are accepted but a claimant to the status takes a risk with every order he gives. He may be obeyed, in which case he gains status, or he may be laughed at and asked to join in, in which case he loses status. As a result of this competition and also of the general unwillingness, organizing into teams under various leaders can take a very long time. In one case I witnessed, the time they spent was much longer than the time spent on the actual job. Here the decision is reached by means of compromise and irony, but again opposing views are hardly ever expressed.

[39] This contrasts with the situation in Ceylon described by E.R.Leach (1961). In Pul Eliya water is not normally a scarce resource except at the very beginning of the wet season, and as such is not a cause of conflict.

[40] No women were present as the meeting took place at the time when the evening meal was normally prepared.

[41] Sometimes there are several rival teams, sometimes more than one village may join to form such a team. Obviously only in the villages practising transplanting did these meetings take place.

[42] Bailey, 1965.

COUNCILS AMONG THE CENTRAL IBO

By G. I. Jones

I. Introduction

This paper is concerned with village and town councils among the central Ibo, the groups previously referred to as the Nri-Awka and Isuama Ibo.[1] Data was collected during the years 1927-46 supplemented by later visits in 1955, 1964-5 and 1966-7. The system described in part II of this essay is the one that prevailed in the nineteenth and early twentieth century and I have used the past tense to make this clear. Subsequent changes are described in part III.

The central Ibo consist of a large number of autonomous communities averaging about 5,000 people and usually referred to as towns (Obodo). Along the Niger, and in the mid-western region beyond it, these towns are compact residential units and their primary segments (Ebo) can more properly be referred to as quarters, or wards, but in most of the central Ibo area the residential pattern is more dispersed and towns are scattered in a maze of palm trees, shade gardens and secondary forest growth. The primary segments are here usually referred to as villages and the towns as village groups.[2] The local English term for them is however 'towns' and I have therefore retained this word. As one moves away from the central area, villages become more dispersed and independent and they combine together into larger structures referred to in official documents as 'clans', though they are more properly termed 'tribes'.

In considering the traditional social structure of the people of the former Eastern region of Nigeria, it is well to distinguish two varieties of political systems, namely, a wider extensive system which brings together most of the communities in the region and beyond, and a narrower small-scale type which characterises the very large number of towns (or village groups) and small tribes of which the region is composed.

The wider system was essentially segmentary in character and was held together by a network of trade routes and markets. The order which prevailed in this system depended on a relative balance of power between its component segments (the towns and tribes) which tended to be of the same size and strength in any given area, although they increased in size in the region of more recent expansion towards the Cross River. Central Ibo towns had an average population of about 5,000 people (1953 census). The kind of law which governed the relations between these towns was 'international' rather than national and its most effective sanctions were economic e.g. boycott or avoidance of markets.[3]

In the narrower political systems the government was more coherent and centralized. There were no chiefs in the accepted sense, that is to say 'strong chiefs', to serve as a focus of town or tribal unity and as the ultimate source of political authority. Power remained with the primary segments of the town but authority was vested in, and decisions made by, a council of representatives from these villages. Such councils were multi-purpose. They made and they upheld the law; they acted as the supreme court as well as the legislative assembly; they were the supreme political authority deciding when to make war or peace; they were the financial authority, imposing and organising the collection of taxation whenever there was need for it, for example to buy the powder and guns needed to fight a war.

The structure of these towns and small tribes was that of a hierarchically integrated segmentary system which in most Ibo towns was represented as the ramifications of a patrilinea derived from a mythical founding ancestor. There was a council for each of these segments at every structural level, but the important ones for the purposes of this study are those of the villages which were the feuding units, and of the towns which were the warring units. A town in the central Ibo area considered itself an independent state in a position of armed neutrality with its neighbours. But this autonomy was limited by the position of the town in the wider political system on which it depended for its survival. Though a town might go to war with another town, these territorial units were mostly too evenly matched to be able to annihilate each other, and any prolongation of active hostility would involve each side in a loss of trade. This would force both towns to submit their dispute to the arbitration of neighbouring towns or else to lapse into a state of inactive hostility. At a lower level of segmentation each village had the right to engage in a feud, with other villages, but it was not allowed to feud against fellow townsmen. Thus if it wished to remain an integral part of the town it had to substitute for a true feud an innocuous raid followed by a settlement involving compensation for the original homicide.

The political elite which ran these political systems, and which is referred to in government reports as 'the elders', can be polarised into two types, referred to by the regional government as 'traditional heads' and 'natural rulers'. The former embodied the ancestral authority derived from the founders of the community and held the *ofo*, the symbol of this authority. Succession to their offices was on a basis of age, and in most Ibo communities the eldest male *(okpara)* in a lineage whether minimal, minor, major or maximal, held the office. In the case of a maximal lineage this office was that of village head. In many central Ibo towns, however, these lineage heads *(ndiokpara)* were the eldest sons of the previous holders.

'Natural rulers' were normally mature men still in full possession of their faculties and physical vigour. They were men with a natural aptitude and liking for politics and administration and could more accurately be described as leaders than rulers. The two types merged into each other and it was normal for a 'natural ruler' to become a traditional head when his age and lineage position made him eligible for the office. The roles however, were and are distinct; the 'natural rulers' were the men who actually ran the meetings and who were responsible for the routine day to day work of village government, but they represented their actions as sanctioned by the 'traditional heads'. They described themselves as 'carrying out' the latters 'orders'. The 'traditional heads' were expected to preside at meetings but took no active part in them except in cases where a 'natural ruler' was also a traditional head.

In the central Ibo area these 'natural rulers' or leaders tended to be specialists who made their living from this occupation. They remained at home to run their villages and the town while their brothers were working abroad. Their income derived mainly from what can be called the 'spoils of office', that is, from the rewards they got from making the system work for those who sought their aid (particularly in the field of litigation, in settling disputes out of court). There was some measure of competition for such positions of political leadership. They were not inherited, though an able son might well acquire the position held by his father particularly if there was no one else of equal capacity in the lineage. Some of them succeeded in reaching the position of being the accepted leader of their village, and exceptional men became the de facto ruler of a town or group of towns. In all cases their influence and authority depended ultimately on public support which could be withdrawn should they lose their public's confidence. Their value to their people and hence their authority over them, lay in the degree to which they could influence natural rulers in other villages and towns. Conversely the more they could influence people in their own village and town, the more they were valued by and the more influence they therefore had over 'natural rulers' in other towns and villages. This 'horse trading' network of natural rulers was one of the more important factors making for peace and a rule of law in this part of Nigeria in the pre-colonial past. War was the last thing that a natural ruler wanted in the central Ibo area. It interrupted or destroyed the lucrative connections with neighbouring big men.

There were and are two cardinal principles which regulate the social organisation of these communities; the segmentary principle which stressed the equality and the equivalence of individuals and of the groups to which they belonged, and the age principle which stressed the opposite. There were a number of conventions which governed their application, and the political elite was expected to apply them both in individual cases, for example in the enforcement of laws and the settlement of disputes, and collectively, for instance at council meetings and in the allocation of public works and rewards.

In the case of the segmentary principle the two most important conventions were those of 'blood', that is patrilineal descent and 'soil', that is, local residence. Members of an Ibo town or of its sub-divisions referred to themselves as 'sons of the soil' and, as in the case of the Tiv, descent and local residence were regarded as synonymous. A territorial residential unit of whatever size was a lineage (putative or actual) and its members lived and farmed on land which belonged to the lineage.

A central Ibo town consisted of a central residential area of palm groves interspersed with compounds and shade gardens surrounded by a larger area of bush and farmland. Each village occupied its own section of this residential area and its members farmed the land extending outward in a particular direction from this centre.

But not all the members of a lineage were living in the lineage residential area, or farming on the lineage land. Some were living and farming on other lineage land. A lineage of larger size (major and maximal) contained people who were of cognative, stranger and of slave descent, who if at all numerous formed minor lineages within the larger lineage structure. The central Ibo, unlike the inhabitants of some of the riverain towns (e.g. Onitsha, Osomari) intermarried with slaves and those of slave descent *(ohu)*. There was however the *osu*, a group of people who were bought and given to a tutelary village deity, along with their descendants. These formed a caste with whom marriage was forbidden on pain of becoming an *osu*. The *osu* of each town were grouped into a quasi-lineage (minor or major) which observed the regulations of ordinary lineages, for example in the matter of exogamy. Thus the convention of descent might conflict with that of local residence. When it did, local residence prevailed in matters of the group's external relationships, for example in defining group membership and with it political affiliation. A man belonged to the group with whom he was living and as a proof of this he could show he had been given land to live and farm on. In matters of internal relationship descent prevailed. An agnate ranked above a cognate, and the latter above an incorporated but unrelated member of the group. Local residence determined and defined the segmentary structure but descent co-ordinated it on the basis of a genealogical charter which distinguished and ranked the various segments as the descendants of the mythical, senior and junior sons, sisters' sons and other offspring of the village or town founder.

The age principle provided the legitimation of authority within the group. It distinguished those who had the right and the duty to govern, those who should enforce their orders, and those who must accept and obey them. It graded people as superordinate and subordinate, but never as equal unless they happened to be in the same age set. It used two conventions. One was divisive and genealogical, the charter referred to above, which ranked people and the groups to which they belonged in terms of descent from an apical ancestor. The other was collective and stratifying. It cut across the segmentary system and the charter which validated it, and grouped all the members of the community into a single organisation of age grades and age sets in which authority was concentrated at the top in the sets in the senior grade and diminished as one descended from top to bottom. The genealogical convention found expression and support in the institution of the *ofo,* the symbol of the authority of the father and by extension of the founders of the community and of its subdivisions. When a man died his eldest son *(okpara)* made an *ofo* (from a faggot of a particular tree) which he used in rituals of communication with his dead father. He did this unless his father already had an *ofo* in which case he took over his father's one. There are thus *ofo* and *ofo* holders *(ndiokpara)* for every lineage in the community, and, in the case of the larger units, the *ofo* and the office passed, either to the eldest son of the previous holder (e.g. amongst the Isuama and many Nri-Awka communities) or to the next oldest man in the lineage.

This collective and stratifying convention found support in the cult of the ancestors (the collectivity of former elders of the group), but this cult also co-ordinated the age organisation and territorial segmentation; for each segment which considered itself a lineage, [4] had a shrine for its own ancestors as well as an ancestral *ofo.*

When the genealogical convention conflicted with the stratifying one the latter won, e.g. an *okpara Uku* who succeeded to the office as a boy or younger man would perform the rituals of his office and would sit with the elders of his group, but would not be accorded the authority given to an elder. When, for example 'the elders' retired to consult, he went with them but did not take any part in the discussion. Similarly it was the stratifying convention that dominated the genealogical ranking order of segmentation, for example, in council meetings where although people sat and debated as members of their respective territorial segments, the decisions were made by 'the elders', the senior age grade, who retired as a body to consult and returned to announce their decision.

The segmentary and age principles were neatly combined in the institution of 'sharing'. All public work and collective contributions of labour and wealth were divided out equally between the component segments, each having to contribute an equal amount. The same applied to the distribution of food and of other rewards and spoils. The organisation of this distribution was one of the functions of the councils and every council had an official, the 'sharer', whose duty it was to divide spoils into as many approximately equal shares as there were primary segments. These segments then chose a share according to their ranking order, the senior ranking segment choosing first, the most junior taking the share that remained after the other segments had successively made their choice.

In the ranking of individuals the principle of age was again modified, particularly in the central Ibo area by the recognition and rewarding of superior organisational and entrepreneurial ability. Such men, if successful in political and economic affairs, were accorded superior social status and authority provided that they used their talents and wealth in the public service and for the public benefit, e.g. in making the system of government operate for the community by organising community work, by organising council meetings and by maintaining law and order; and provided they shared their wealth by providing feasts for the community and gifts (or fees) for its important people. Such expenditure either validated a position of power or influence built up by a local political leader or bought such a position for a person who had accumulated the wealth working abroad and who wished on his retirement to occupy a superior political and social status. South and east of the central area this distribution of wealth brought its maker the title of *ogaranya* (big man). Amongst the riverine and some of the central Ibo communities, a man who could feast the whole community and buy the support of its leading men could acquire the title *eze* (king) and the status of political head of the town. Amongst the central Ibo, such expenditure became institutionalised in the *ozo* title society which contained all the men that mattered in the community. Although in many towns the *ozo* society, like the *ogboni* society in some Yoruba areas, was the de facto government it had no official position or separate representation in town or village government, for example, in town council meetings its members sat with their respective villages as elders of their village. But the private meetings of the *ozo* society brought together all the men of wealth and influence in the town and provided them with a forum for the informal discussion of political business. The *ozo* society also functioned as a very effective court for the settlement of civil cases. Criminal cases were tried at town council meetings. The financial rewards of membership (mainly from the fees paid by initiates) made the *ozo* title a very profitable investment for anyone who could afford to join it, and not everyone of these was interested in politics. But any man who wished to become a 'natural ruler' had first to achieve an *ozo* title.

II. The central Ibo town council

An Ibo village was, and still is, a closely integrated residential land-owning unit which represents itself as a maximal patrilineage solely responsible for ordering and determining its internal affairs. The day-to-day routine business of its government was carried out by persons referred to in official reports as 'the elders'.

More important business was dealt with at village council meetings, for example matters involving decisions affecting the whole community, or where 'the elders' felt that public support was needed for their actions. Similarly matters which affected all the villages in a town were determined at a town council meeting convened by 'the elders' of its component villages.

Such council meetings were not held on any particular day of the week or month. They were only convened when the occasion demanded. Village council meetings which had more regular business to deal with were convened more frequently and, because the status of their members was well known, were more informal. There were no executive or other committees for either village or town councils but 'the elders' of a village were in regular association with each other, and the leading elders maintained informal contacts with their counterparts in other villages of the neighbourhood, particularly with those belonging to the same town. [s]

People were notified of the time and place of a council meeting by an official 'crier' who went round the village or villages sounding a bell or gong and shouting out the details. Each village had such an official and one of them ranked as the town crier. The office was an acquired one in most villages; in others it was vested in a particular lineage. A council always had a specific meeting place, usually a clearing in the residential area of the group concerned, which also served as a centre for most other gatherings, ritual, recreational and economic (e.g. markets).

The personnel of a council meeting was exclusively masculine, 'government' being a male function.[6] Conversely men had no jurisdiction over matters which were considered the concern of women and which were ordered and governed by a council composed exclusively of women.[7] Women and children could be present in the meeting place and listen to the council's proceedings but they could not sit with any part of the council. The exceptions were a few small boys who accompanied some of the elders to carry their bags and stools and who then sat at their feet.

The members of the council meeting were graded on a basis of age into elders, (ndichie, ndioke, ndikenyi, lit. 'old men', a term also used for the ancestors), men (nwoke) and young men (ndi-ikoro, or ndokoro). Age however was considerably modified by achievement. An onye nze (ozo titled man) whatever his age sat with the elders, but was always a man of mature years. The men were normally married men of varying age (20 to 60 years) the young men were those who were unmarried and included adolescents. An unmarried man of middle age, if he attended a meeting, would sit or stand with the men. Okoro or okorobia when used as a term of address to a young man was, on most social occasions, a praise name carrying connotations of strength and physical prowess. When used by an elder to anyone younger than himself it was a derogatory indication of inferiority and subordination. The polite form of address was nwam ('my son'). When talking about councils informants maintain that it was the elders who ruled, and the men who worked together with the young men who had yet to prove they were capable of being men. In the Isuama towns the word oha designated a council or meeting and 'the elders' were divided into senior and junior elders. The former were called the ndi-oha (the councillors) and they corresponded to the people previously termed 'traditional heads'; the latter were the ikoro oha (the young men of the council) who corresponded to the 'natural rulers' and who were represented as the men who carried out the orders of the ndi-oha.

Despite this emphasis on age and on an elite category of councillors (the ndi-oha) a town council meeting was in fact a federal assembly at which each village was represented as a separate unit.[8]

The decisions of the meeting were by consensus and no village was bound by it unless it had been represented at the meeting and had accepted the decision. The delegates from each village occupied the particular area of the meeting place reserved for their village and they were expected to express the views of their village, and to be unanimous – 'to speak with one mouth'. Before attending a town council meeting a village should have held a village council meeting at which all its primary segments were represented and should have decided upon what it was going to do and say at the town council meeting.

Town council meetings were held in the morning, the elders representing each village and their supporters arriving between 9 and 10 a.m. and taking up their customary location in the meeting place. When all the villages had assembled they formed a rough circle around a central area which each speaker entered when addressing the assembly, retiring to his own group after speaking. Any man was free to attend the meeting and to speak if he so wished. The number who attended depended on the amount of popular interest in the matters under discussion. Normally only those involved in local politics and administration and their supporters attended together with any young men who had nothing better to do. The number of persons representing a village could range from under ten to over a hundred people. The actual number was irrelevant, what mattered was that the village should be represented at the meeting and that its representatives should be persons known to the other villages as its heads *(ndi-okpara-uku)* and leaders.

The meeting was opened by one of these leaders who introduced and explained the subject to be discussed. Any person who wished was then free to address the meeting, but other people had the right to shout him down and tell him to stop if they felt he was 'wasting their time', i.e. was raising personal, irrelevant, or controversial matters which they did not want ventilated at the meeting. The people who shouted him down were his peers, that is men of the same age grade and and village. Men who aspired to political leadership began by trying out their capacity at these meetings. The less they were shouted down the more they were likely to develop into political leaders. Veteran leaders took care to speak towards the end of the discussion when they could judge the general feeling of the meeting and put forward arguments which would win general support. In any really controversial issue each village would be expected to have one opinion (mouth) which would be expressed by one of its leaders.

Should an uproar develop with a number of people trying to talk all at once and others shouting at them to sit down and be silent, the leaders would rouse the *ndi-okpara-uku* into action. When they all stepped forward together holding up their *ofo* the meeting became hastily silent while they struck their *ofo* on the ground at the same time calling upon the ancestors to punish anyone who should speak out of turn or create a disturbance.

When the leaders felt that the matter had been fully discussed and some degree of unanimity had been reached they aroused the senior elders *(ndi-okpara-uku)* once again and retired with them, 'to consult'. They stood out of earshot of the meeting literally putting their heads together. All appeared to be talking at once, but gradually the babel subsided as a decision was arrived at. They then returned to the meeting and one of them, 'the spokesman', usually a leader accepted by his fellows as their best public speaker, announced the decision, pausing after each important point for the assembly to indicate its assent by acclamation. When he had finished, the tension was relaxed and everybody began talking at once while they hurried off to their homes leaving the leaders to discuss amongst themselves how best to implement the decision.

The assembly always accepted the elders' decision for the simple reason that it was in fact their own decision. The elders, when they retired, were not making a new decision but consulting how to give precise definition and expression to the general feeling expressed by the meeting. Should the general discussion fail to reconcile the conflicting views of particular villages and their leaders and achieve some degree of unanimity, the elders never retired to consult. Arguments became more heated, tempers more frayed, the speakers and their opponents and their respective supporters became more and more abusive. The uproar eventually became so great that either the invocation of the ancestors failed to quieten it or the *ndi-opara-uku* were too frightened or angry to invoke them, and the meeting broke up in confusion, each village going off home and hurling abuse over their shoulders at those who had disagreed with them, but getting further and further away all the time; for the town layout ensured that the paths leading from the meeting place to the various villages led in different directions and never crossed. If it was necessary to reach a decision the town leaders would come together and, having arrived at a modified policy, work upon people in their respective villages until they were prepared to accept a decision along these lines. Then when they felt that tempers had cooled sufficiently they called another meeting and tried again.

It will be seen that these council meetings were both 'arena councils' in that decisions were by the consensus of all the segments and 'elite councils'[9] in that these decisions were framed by an elite – the 'elders' who were represented as the authoritative body.

There were four constitutional principles affecting these meetings which should be noted, namely (1) that only one level of segmentation was represented at a council meeting, e.g. villages at a town council meeting, primary village segments at a village council meeting and so on, (2) that a segment must express a unanimous opinion, the principle of 'one segment, one voice', (3) that a segment not present at a meeting was not bound by that meeting's decisions –,but, as a corollary of this, (4) that a segment that did not accept the collective decision of the other segments of a council meeting could refuse to attend the council meeting. The position resolved itself if this continued and was not satisfactorily explained away by the segment being regarded as in a higher position and outside the political system at that structural level. For example, a village that would not accept the decision of the other villages of the town defined itself as a separate town, and had to be prepared to accept the consequences of this, that is to say that instead of being able to count upon the support of the other villages, it had to reckon with their collective hostility. In the same way a village segment that did not attend the meetings of its village council defined itself as a separate village. This was one of the principal ways in which villages or village sections which had expanded at a greater rate than their fellows, established themselves as new towns or villages. It was also, should they fail to maintain their position, the cause of their disintegration and disappearance, their members becoming absorbed into the lineages of their cognates and affines in the surrounding communities.

III. Councils during and after colonial rule

With the introduction of colonial rule the country was divided up into administrative provinces and divisions, the latter in charge of District Commissioners (later called District Officers). The D.C. was responsible for the maintenance of law and order and for the development of the system of local government which, it was hoped, would ultimately make his presence unnecessary. Towns and villages were considered too small and too numerous to serve as units of local government and the aim of the colonial administration and of the regional government which succeeded it, was to integrate them into larger units intermediate in size between the town and the division. There were four successive systems of local government, two introduced by the colonial government and two by the regional government during and after the transition to independence.

Each was radically different from the one which preceded it, and each was introduced with a minimum of consultation with the people affected by it. The first, later condemned as the warrant chief or direct rule system, developed out of the earlier consular jurisdiction in the Oil Rivers. Its primary objective was to provide effective machinery for settling disputes between the small independent communities characteristic of this region. Such disputes could not be determined peacefully under the traditional system and were a constant threat to law and order. The institution which was evolved for this purpose was the Native Court, four or five to each administrative division, in which the District Commissioner sat with a panel of assessors who were local 'chiefs' drawn from the area under the Native Courts jurisdiction. Pressure of more important work soon led to the withdrawal of the D.C. leaving the chiefs to adjudicate on their own and giving the D.C. powers to review their judgments. Experience in the Delta and on the Lower Niger had convinced the colonial government that the communities in this region were headed by chiefs who could be recognised by government for this purpose. The system as it developed was analogous to the English system of rural justices of the peace. It recognised a number of such justices (warrant chiefs), as responsible for the maintenance of order and for the enforcement of various government regulations (mainly relating to corvee labour) within their respective towns and it empowered them to do this by giving each a judicial warrant to sit on the bench of a Native Court which in addition to trying civil cases could punish law breakers and those who disobeyed their legitimate orders. The Native Court thus became an executive and administrative as well as a judicial instrument of local government. It had its own bailiffs or police force (court messengers) and a panel of warrant chiefs, ideally one for each town in the Native Court area, who took turns to sit on the Native Court bench. There was no council of chiefs or similar body and co-ordination between them and communication with the D.C. was effected through the clerk of the Native Court.

The acceptance of and adjustment to this system of local government and to its successors varied considerably in different parts of the Eastern region. The central Ibo towns had no difficulty in adjusting to colonial rule and never lost their cohesion. The establishment of the Colony and Protectorate of Nigeria provided ever expanding opportunities for employment outside the area, particularly for those towns already specialising in trade and employment away from home. At the same time improvements in communication (roads, railways, postal services) enabled those working abroad to keep in contact with their homes, though removed from any direct contact with home politics. Indeed what these 'breadwinners' as they came to be called, wanted and eventually were able to insist upon, was for their lineages, villages and towns to be peacefully and efficiently administered in their absence so that they could be free to continue in their employment abroad unhampered by appeals from their relatives to return home to protect and defend their family and lineage interests. The governing elite of these Ibo towns, particularly the wealthier ones (e.g. Awka, Nkwerri, Awguku) retained and if anything increased their efficiency, each village being headed by a relatively able and responsible natural ruler who in many cases (e.g. in villages where primogeniture prevailed) was also a traditional head *(okparauku)*, and who was supported by village section and other lineage heads of similar calibre.

They had no difficulty in adjusting to the warrant chief system. If a town had a 'natural ruler' who had established himself as its de facto head, he became the warrant chief. In default of such a big man, the 'natural ruler' of the senior ranking village was put forward for a warrant and the town was run by a committee consisting of the warrant chief and the leaders of the other villages (referred to by government as his 'headmen') together with any other supporting elders who might wish to accompany them. They met informally in the warrant chief's compound or, when they needed public approval for their actions, they came together more formally at a town council meeting accompanied by more people from their respective villages.

In the Ibibio divisions and in the Ibo divisions in the Southern and Eastern parts of the Owerri provinces there were few towns, villages were more dispersed and independent and were grouped into the far less coherent tribal units which government reports referred to as clans. The people found it very difficult to adjust to any system of local government and just when they were beginning to, the system was replaced by a radically different one. It was precisely these areas which also reacted most strongly to the outlawing of war and other forms of aggressive self-help, by the colonial government. It was largely the fear of attacks from their neighbours that had previously held them together, and now these sanctions were removed, villages and village segments were free to disassociate themselves and go their own way if they so wished. At the same time the title and secret societies, which had united the important members of a community, lost their influence and failed to attract any more members now that men were finding other more profitable and socially rewarding investments for their wealth. At the same time wealth was getting into the hands of a limited number of younger and 'part educated' men and out of the hands of the older men who had formerly had a greater share of it.

No real attempt was ever made to adapt the warrant chief system to meet the different types of social organisation of these areas. The tribal units were too large and too incoherent to be represented by a single warrant chief even if the people could have managed to select one, while the colonial administration was not prepared to meet the demand for a warrant chief for each village. Only a limited number of warrant chiefs were appointed and the villages which had been unsuccessful in getting one, and these were naturally the majority, were left with a permanent grievance against the administration and hatred of the warrant chief under whom they had been placed.

The colonial government did not interfere, except indirectly, with the deliberative and administrative functions of town and village councils. It deprived them of the right to use force to implement their decisions, and it altered the balance of power within the council in favour of those 'natural rulers' who had secured a government warrant. What it did do was to deprive these councils of their judicial functions. It was now a criminal offence for a criminal case to be settled out of court, to be heard, that is, anywhere except in a Native or Protectorate court. They were not debarred from hearing civil cases, but town council meetings had never been a popular method of settling civil disputes. The fees which had to be paid to its members were considerable, and their judgments as was only to be expected from such a large assembly, unpredictable and unsatisfactory. The reasonable central Ibo man preferred to settle his disputes 'out of court' or, if this failed, to submit it to the private adjudication of a 'natural leader'. The difficulty with such private cases however was to enforce their judgments should the parties be from different towns or villages and the loser refuse to comply. The creation of the Native Court rectified this position and provided 'natural leaders', particularly those who were warrant chiefs, and their headmen, with a tribunal to which they could refer their client in such cases. To judge, for example, by the volume of civil cases which they heard, the Native Court very soon became and remained a popular institution and for good reason, it met a local need and its justice was cheap, speedy and efficient (being under the close supervision of the D.C.) and town councils ceased to exercise any judicial functions. Village councils, however, in the interests of village unity still continued to settle disputes between their members.[10]

Indirect rule

Complaints against, and criticisms of, the warrant chief system came to a head after the first world war, and it was replaced by a system which had previously been introduced into Southern Nigeria in 1914, but had not as yet been extended to the Eastern Provinces. This was the system usually known as indirect rule or native administration. The change came in 1928/9 just when the process of disintegration and anomie mentioned in the previous section had reached its climax and just when the full effects of the world economic depression had reached Nigeria with a catastrophic fall in the world prices of palm oil, the principle export of Eastern Nigeria. The principles which governed the new system were that it should be based as far as possible upon the local traditional systems of government; that it should have the responsibility for collecting and spending its own funds, and that a separation should be made between executive and judicial institutions. The former was to be the Native Authority and the latter the Native Court. The recognition of warrant chiefs was withdrawn, corvee labour was abolished and replaced by a tax on all adult able bodied males to be collected by the heads of the 'highest functioning units' of the local traditional political systems. These according to the reorganisation reports were 'heads of families'.

A family was a lineage and in the central Ibo area it was, for tax collecting purposes, either a village (maximal lineage) or a village section (major lineage). Elsewhere it was usually a smaller unit, a minor or even a minimal lineage. Taxation however was introduced at once (in 1928) before these reports had been made and before these family heads had been identified it was collected through the native court organisation in default of other local agencies and by the warrant chiefs. The tax was paid into a Native Administration Treasury[11] and apart from a small percentage paid over to the Nigerian government was used for local government purposes. The Native Authority was defined as a council to which all the communities in the area would send representatives. It was presumed that these representatives would be some or all of the 'heads of families', but the decision as to how they were going to select these council members, and how they were going to combine to form Native Courts was left to the communities themselves. This meant, amongst other things that in the initial period there were a great many N.A.s and Native Courts. But by 1945 most of the smaller N.A.s had combined into units whose boundaries corresponded very closely to those of the original Native Court areas of the warrant chief period. The popularity of the Native Courts and therefore the number of newly established courts remained unaltered. In the central Ibo area the change to this system was accompanied by a very brief period during which the Native Courts and Native Authority councils were flooded by anybody who could lay any claim to being an elder of any sort, these being under the mistaken idea that they were being paid for their services. When they discovered that there were no council fees, and that the court sitting fees were negligible when divided between so many judges, most of them found they could not afford to waste their time so unprofitably, and left the field to the former warrant chiefs and other semi-professional specialists who were prepared to make their living as local government experts.

The local government system

The transition to independence was accompanied by radical changes in local government. 'Native' was now a perjorative epithet in the Eastern region and 'indirect' synonymous for phoney. The N.A. system was replaced by a truly 'democratic' one modelled once again on an English prototype. This time there was to be a hierarchy of 'democratically' elected County, District and Local councils. County council areas corresponded to the Native Authority areas which they replaced; District council areas were more various; Local councils were to replace town councils, which for the first time were recognised as local government units. The Native courts remained unchanged except in name; they were now 'Customary Courts'. At the same time the supervisory powers of the District Officers over the new 'local government' system, as it was now called, were removed. Their main function was henceforth to be that of preparing electoral rolls and organising elections for all these councils. The central Ibo communities again adjusted to these changes without any difficulty. While the Ibibio electors returned as their County and District Councillors educated young men with no political experience and with no authority over the illiterate village and family heads and the leaders whom they had displaced, the people who were returned unopposed as central Ibo County Councillors were the men who had filled the same positions on the Native Authority councils. When a few years later, the Ibibio councils were in trouble with the regional government through failing to collect their taxes, the central Ibo councils had collected theirs without difficulty and the Orlu County council had revised its nominal rolls and collected considerably more tax than before, as it wished to use the money to provide free primary education in its schools.

In the case of the Local councils which should, at least in theory, have replaced the town councils I could not trace any record of a central Ibo elected County council replacing a 'traditional' town council, or of any government officers having had the time to organise any Local council elections after the initial year in which they were introduced. My informants all said that there was no change. The electoral wards of these Local councils were the same as the villages or village primary segments of the town concerned and the political leaders of these segments or villages were returned unopposed.

Local government – the second phase

By 1955 the financial shortcomings of the new County and District councils, mainly in areas other than the central Ibo, had become so manifest that the system was drastically changed. The supervisory powers of the D.O. over the councils was restored, the collection of tax was now made a regional government responsibility and the District councils were abolished.[12] The most ominous change however was in the personnel of the Customary Courts whose judges once more became 'chiefs' recognised by the regional government under a special ordinance which defined and graded them as 1st, 2nd, 3rd and 4th class chiefs and which brought the courts under the direct control of a minister of Customary Courts and Chief-taincy Affairs. He was not concerned with the justice administered in the courts but with the distribution of party political patronage in the appointment of the chiefs who sat on the court bench.

In January 1966 following the first military coup, the entire system of local government and customary courts was suspended pending enquiries into alleged corruption, particularly in the courts. The suspension was still operating when the Nigerian–Biafran war broke out in 1967.

By this time however, that is after 1956, it was becoming less needful for the leaders of central Ibo towns to take any active interest in the higher local government councils. In the colonial period, particularly under the N.A. system, there had been a considerable measure of decentralisation. The District Officers were charged with implementing the central government policy of developing in local leaders an active and constructive interest in local government affairs and of making the Native Administrative councils, of which they were members, responsible for raising and spending the funds needed for all local services and developments. After 1955 there was a complete reversal of this policy, particularly financially. Tax collection became a regional government responsibility and although there were now, for the first time, considerable government funds available for development these were tightly controlled by various government departments in Enugu, the regional capital. The regional government found it convenient to use the machinery of the county councils for the maintenance of local services, giving them grants in aid for this purpose. Town leaders however found they could advance the interests of their towns more successfuly by by-passing the County council and negotiating direct with the particular government department through the agency of any members of the political (N.C.N.C. party) or of the bureaucratic heirarchy at Enugu, who belonged to their neighbourhood.

Relations with the progressive unions

By now power and authority in these towns had shifted from the 'elders' at home to the 'young men' abroad, who were now organised into the associations variously called Progressive, Improvement, Patriotic and Family Unions. Each town had one of these unions which included all their members working abroad as well as many who might be living at home or in the neighbourhood. It was the officers of the union who planned the development of their town or 'clan' (a group of towns) who negotiated directly with the appropriate regional department and which organised the collection of the necessary funds and paid them over to the government.[13] When it suited their purposes the unions made use of the County Council organisation (for example in getting Isu County council to levy a water rate) but in most cases the union organised, levied and controlled its own system of taxation for local development.

This community development in the central Ibo area was spectacular particularly in the field of education (secondary schools and university grants), health (hospitals and dispensaries) and in water supplies (artesian pipes borne to storage tanks and stand pipes). Like the organisation of these unions it cannot however be discussed here. The success of the unions was very largely due to the fact that they avoided any involvement in politics either at the national, regional or local levels. They included all members of the town regardless of their political, religious or other divergent views, who by combining to advance the interests of their town or 'clan' could also advance their own.

There were now two organisations governing a central Ibo town, the town council with its local political leaders and traditional heads which has been described in this paper and the town union of 'progressives' and 'breadwinners' and other members of the town, most of whom were residing abroad. The unions' organisation followed British patterns. Its officers had the same names and functions as those of Friendly and similar societies in Great Britain; it had branches in most of the important centres of employment in Nigeria as well as a home branch. It had its steering and other committees and its annual general meeting held in December in the home town, to which all the branches sent delegates. There was no clash of interests or of personalities between the two organisations. Most of 'the elders' were members of the union: many were in any case retired 'breadwinners' while others were persons whom their lineages wanted to remain at home to manage their affairs, and who were supported and, if need be, subsidised by their wealthy brothers working abroad.

There was also a clear division of functions between the two organisations. The union with its expert knowledge of regional and national policies was responsible for the external relations of the town. 'The elders' with their expert local knowledge were the people responsible for government at home and in the neighbourhood; and their organisation was separate from that of the union. For instance the officers of the home branch of the union were not village political leaders, but school teachers and other men in local employment. Most unions took great care to avoid being involved in town or neighbourhood politics and because of this they constituted a tribunal which could intervene decisively to settle disputes between 'the elders' when it was felt they were 'spoiling the town'.

By the 1960s many of the more energetic unions were taking steps to involve all sections of the town in their development plans by convening a mass meeting of the whole community, both men and women, to accept and ratify them. This assembly was far too large for deliberative action; it was there primarily to listen to the union's plans and to approve the amounts to be contributed by the different sections of the community, namely, by the respective branches of the union, by the component villages of the town and by the women's organisation. In addition to these practical functions, these assemblies were developed as a ritual occasion, the supreme ritual ceremony of the year when all people assembled irrespective of their different creeds and political interests, to demonstrate the unity and solidarity of their community, their belief in its destiny, their pride in its achievements and their trust in its leaders.

Notes

[1] Daryll Forde and G. I. Jones, 1950.

[2] C. Meek, 1937: Margaret Green, 1947.

[3] The system did not correspond in any way to the tribal political units of today; its frontiers were economic not linguistic.

[4] Dual and triple divisions of a town did not.

[5] For example, each town had a market held every eighth day and on market day leading elders were normally to be found sitting together and talking and drinking in the vicinity of the market.

[6] There were occasional exceptions to this generalisation but only where a woman had for various reasons been accorded male status.

[7] See Green, 1947.

[8] In the same way a village council meeting consisted of a federation of village primary sections.

[9] In the sense used by Bailey, 1965.

[10] There is a parallel here to the Southern Tiv as described by Bohannan (1957). The Tiv *mbatareg* are 'natural rulers'. Some of them are also members of the Native Court. Bohannan's Moots(*jir* at home) correspond to the Ibo village and village section councils whose primary objective is the maintenance of village solidarity, epitomised in the Ibo expression 'keeping the ground cool', and the Tiv 'restoring the tar'.

[11] Which until the N.A.s had been approved, defined and gazetted was at the Divisional Headquarters in the charge of the D.O. Even when N.A.s had their own treasuries, the key of the safe or strong room remained with the D.O. who was financially responsible for its contents.

[12] Except in the Orlu division where the county which was coterminous with the division was abolished and its five District councils became County councils.

[13] For government grants for development were not normally provided gratis, they had to be matched by corresponding contributions from the local people.

THE KGALAGARI LEKGOTA

By Adam Kuper

I

The Sotho-speaking societies of Southern Africa are remarkable among Bantu tribal states for their higher level of citizen participation in the regulation of public affairs. This participation is channelled mainly through the popular assembly, termed *lekgota* by the Kgalagari and *lekgotla* by most of the other tribes. Schapera has suggested that this characteristic is related to the comparatively dense settlement pattern of the Sotho, which in turn is necessitated by the concentration of water in only a few places in the areas where they live (Schapera, 1956:65); and ready communications are certainly fundamental to direct democracy. In any case, as Casalis remarked over a century ago, 'there are among these people all the elements of a regular government, nearly allied to the representative form' (Casalis, 1861: 236).

Casalis went on to warn, however, that the involvement of colonial power had the effect of bolstering the power of the chief and reducing his dependence on popular support for his government. His prediction has been borne out by events, at least in Lesotho where he spent the bulk of his time. Ashton reported in 1952 that governmental protection of the chiefs had been the direct cause of the neglect of the *pitso* (meetings of the popular assembly) (Ashton, 1952: 217). (Today, the independent governments of Botswana and Lesotho have moved to check the powers of the chiefs, and it will be interesting to see whether the popular councils will become more important.)

In other areas, however, the influence of the popular assembly did not decline so radically and the effect of colonial overrule on the fate of the popular councils should not be exaggerated. The size and density of the political community are important independent variables. In general, the larger the political community the more powerful the chiefs and the weaker the councils, although this effect was counteracted, to some extent, among the Tswana by the concentration in the capital. It is true that the larger communities with their more powerful chiefs also, as a rule, attracted greater attention from the colonial powers. On the other hand, the small Sotho-speaking communities of the Northern Transvaal, for example, have been closely administered over a long period, and yet the popular assemblies seem still to be significant.

If one were to place the various Sotho-speaking peoples along a continuum, according to the extent of citizen participation in tribal government, the Basuto, a large nation with, until very recently, a powerful king and privy councils and neglected popular councils, would probably figure at the extreme authoritarian end. Somewhere near the centre, but inclining to the authoritarian end, would come the large Tswana tribes of eastern Botswana. Then, perhaps, would come the Transvaal Sotho, and, at the extreme democratic and republican end of the scale, the Kgalagari of western Botswana.

But I should like to go further than this. All the Sotho share the same constitutional forms, *mutatis mutandis,* and, in the larger tribes, these forms are repeated – on a smaller scale – through the various levels of government, typically the tribe or nation, the district, and the village or parish.[1] The authoritarian/popular scale could be applied equally *within* the larger tribes, where one moves from the authoritarian to the democratic extremes as one descends from the central authority through the levels of tribal local government.

The western Kgalagari, whom I discuss in this paper, are organized in small self-governing village communities, and the citizen body exercises considerable power. The Kgalagari may be taken to represent both the extreme democratic twist of the Sotho form of government, and the general type of Sotho government at the village level.

II

The Kgalagari-speaking peoples pioneered Sotho immigration to Southern Africa. Culturally and linguistically they belong to the Sotho complex, with special affinities to the Tswana. They established themselves first in the western Transvaal and the northern Cape, were later pushed into what is now south-eastern Botswana, and are today scattered throughout Botswana. The Kgalagari engage in various forms of economic activity, pastoralism, agriculture (plagued by unreliable rainfall), hunting and migrant labour to the urban areas of South Africa. It was these activities, as much as the development of the colonial government, which drew them into wider social and economic worlds, particularly after World War II. The recently booming demand for beef in South Africa greatly enhanced the money value of their cattle during the 1960s.

The Kgalagari in eastern Botswana are subject tribes in Tswana reserves, but in the central and western State Lands (Kgalagadi and Ghanzi Districts) they have lived for six or seven generations in independent village communities, varying in size from about 400 to 2,000. Here they have conducted their own affairs subject only to the overriding authority of the District Commissioners, who represented first the (British) Bechuanaland Protectorate Administration, and, since October 1966, the government of an independent Botswana. The village was, until recently, the only unit of African administration in western Botswana. In the northern Kgalagadi District, the British in the mid 1950s united the administration of five villages under one of the headmen, who became a 'sub-chief'. The result of his enhanced authority – and increased police support – has been to reduce the power of the *lekgota*. I shall concentrate here on the villages in Ghanzi District, where there have not been administrative changes of this kind. There are four Kgalagari villages in Ghanzi District (which contains five villages altogether, plus the District capital, a police post, and European and Coloured ranching areas). The distance by road from the first village to the fourth village is about 120 miles, and the most distant village is nearly 200 miles from the District capital. There is little traffic, and few visitors stop in the villages. Government personnel may visit a village once or twice a month, but seldom spend more than a couple of hours on each visit, exerting an intermittent, often somewhat baffled, control.

The Kgalagari constitution – the ideal structure – envisages a partnership between headman and citizens. The well-known Sotho proverb says, 'A chief (or headman) is chief by the tribe'. Or as one man put it, discussing a law proposed by the headman at a *lekgota* meeting, 'It is a law, not one hand' (i.e. the citizen body must concur if it is to be a true law). The Kgalagari headman enjoys less personal power than any other Sotho tribal leader, but he does have various traditional executive rights and duties, not least among which is the chairmanship of the *lekgota* itself – a right sometimes usurped today by the elected District Councillor. The counsellors and the court-scribe, the other officers of the government, also have some executive and supervisory functions which allow them a degree of free action, though the counsellors at least are strictly accountable both to the headman and to the *lekgota*.

When I speak of the citizens I refer to the adult male Kgalagari and, in some villages, to minorities of other pastoralist tribes. I exclude women, children and Bushmen,[2] the legal and political minors of Kgalagari society. Within the citizen body there are always a few men who rise above the mass by virtue of close kinship with the headman, leadership of sub-clans within the village, or sheer ability. They share effective power with the headman and the officers of government, and together with them dominate the activities of the factions within the *lekgota*.

The extent to which this group dominates the *lekgota* may be illustrated by evidence from Kuli village in Ghanzi District. Kuli has a Kgalagari population of about 350, plus perhaps 100 Bushmen. In 1964 I attended thirty-one *lekgota* meetings in the village. Attendance at these sessions ranged from about a dozen to just over forty (and taking into account those absent on migrant labour or visiting abroad, there seldom were more than about forty citizens in the village during most of the year). However, eleven citizens accounted between them for 84% of the contributions to debates. They made 361 of the 433 contributions to debates which I recorded. When it is added that many of the remaining contributions were made by witnesses or parties in law-suits, or by visitors, including government personnel, it will be appreciated to what extent the dominant group – about a quarter of the membership of the *lekgota* – monopolized the proceedings. This group constitutes the effective decision-making unit within the *lekgota*. Its members not only do most of the speaking in debates, but also largely determine the final outcome of the debate.

Five of these dominant men in Kuli village were the office-holders – the headman, the court-scribe, and the counsellors. Three others were close agnates of the headman; his eldest son, and two leaders of the main opposition faction, including a half-brother of the headman. The remaining three members of this group included the leader of the minority sub-clan in the village, and two political independents with no kinship claims to influence. On returning to the village in 1966-7 I found a few minor changes in the composition of this group: two close agnates of the headman had returned to the village after absences and joined the leadership of the opposition faction (displacing one of the interim leaders), and one of the political independents had left. But one development which had marked a real break with earlier years was the emergence of the District Councillor, in this case an import from a neighbouring village, as perhaps the leading member of the *lekgota*. The power structure in the councils of all the western Kgalagari villages follows a similar pattern to that which I have outlined for Kuli, and I found the sudden prominence of the democratically-elected District Councillor repeated throughout the villages in this area.

The dominant group of citizens is not a unified elite. The citizen body is split into factions, and these are led by some members of the dominant group. This factionalism is not peculiar to Kgalagari politics, but is endemic among the Sotho-speaking peoples. Indeed, as Casalis noted in Lesotho in the mid-nineteenth century, 'Here, as everywhere, there is always a party for and a party against the government'. (Casalis, 1861 234)

These factions are the political aspect of the residential/kinship groups into which the village is divided. Each group has a core of two or three family-groups whose heads are close agnates, but often includes matrilateral or affinal kin as well, some of whom may have great influence. The agnatic cores are not equivalent to lineages, and a single lineage is often split in not altogether predictable fashion between two factions.

Every Kgalagari village, then, contains at least two factions, whose existence has an important effect on the operation of the *lekgota*. Typically, one faction is led by the headman, who is supported by some of his close agnates, while an opposition faction is led by a half-brother or paternal uncle of the headman, supported by other close agnates. Subordinate sub-clans (the local members of clans other than the headman's) may also function as factions. In addition there are usually a few influential men who do not belong to the major constellations of political interest, and who have an important role as 'neutrals'.[3]

Factions do not emerge in all political contexts. As a rule, factional activity is significant only when an issue touches on the internal power structure of the village, or on the distribution of jobs, but does not involve confrontation with outside authorities. Moreover, the opposition of these factions to the headman is inhibited by cross-cutting ties with him, and by a shared interest in the achievement of many political and administrative ends.

The emergence of factions and pressure-groups based on political party member-ship or shared 'progressive' interests is a recent development stimulated by the activity of the Botswana Democratic Party before Independence, and now by the participation of Africans in national and District policy-making. This development is not uniform, and still depends largely on the calibre of individual District Coun-cillors, who provide the leadership.

III

The council-place, the venue of the meetings of the *lekgota*, is termed the *kgota*. [4]
The *kgota*, always sited near the headman's compound, was traditionally a fenced oval area, perhaps twenty yards long, usually including a shady tree. Today, how-ever, most council-places are fenced only on two or three sides, and in some villages there is no trace of the traditional structure, the *lekgota* meeting under a large tree or, in one village, in the compound of the tribal offices. In some villages a shelter has been put up beside the *kgota* to store the court-records and a table and chairs, but this development is unusual.

Traditionally the *kgota* served as the men's club-house. Youths and unmarried men camped and ate in the *kgota*, and visitors gathered there. The citizens came to the *kgota* regularly, even if there was no meeting on. They would exchange news, question the visitors and discuss the topics of the day. These uses of the *kgota* have generally passed away — in some villages only within the past two decades — though I was put up and entertained in the *kgota* in the old style in one particularly isolated village in Ngamiland. Today the *kgota* is just the council-place, the setting for the meetings of the *lekgota*.

Any man or boy may attend *lekgota* meetings, but only citizens of the village or visiting citizens of other villages, may contribute to the deliberations. Ideally only men legitimated by the payment of *bogari*, a bridewealth payment, may speak, but in practice this rule is not enforced. The older men, the *bagolo ba moze*, most of them family-group heads, have a particular duty to attend meetings, and while there is no quorum in the strict sense of the word, meetings may be postponed if some dominant members of the *lekgota* are absent.

The citizens are summoned to meetings by the counsellors, on the instructions of the headman. They are usually notified at least a day in advance of the time and the rough agenda of the meeting, though new issues may be raised at the meeting itself, usually by one of the dominant members. The meetings are traditionally chaired by the headman, assisted by his spokesman, the senior counsellor. Since the advent of the democratic District Councils, however, the District Councillor, with his special knowledge of the policies emanating from the District capital, and his influence there, has generally usurped the chairmanship when matters of policy are being dealt with. The headman usually comes back into the chair to deal with court-cases.

Until the election of the District Councillors, the bulk of the meetings were called at the instance of the headman. Today the headman and the District Councillor call more or less an equal number of meetings, accounting together for perhaps three-quarters of the meetings called. The others are called at the instance of the District Commissioner or other government and political party officials.

The *lekgota* meets on an average once every five days in most villages. In some villages there are regular weekly meetings on a certain day, but everywhere accidents affect the number of special meetings that must be summoned. Urgent and difficult matters may crop up which require the council to meet on several days running. Visits from officials may require the calling of the council, and if the District Commissioner is due for a visit at least one meeting is usually held to decide what matters should be brought to his attention. On the other hand, meetings may be postponed if important men are absent at cattle-sales or at meetings at the district capital, or even if an influential group of men for some reason stay away from the *kgota,* sulking in their tents.

Perhaps unexpectedly, seasonal economic activities do not seem to affect the incidence of *lekgota* meetings. When I made inquiries in 1964, a drought year when little agricultural activity was possible, informants suggested that in good years there were few *lekgota* meetings during the ploughing and reaping seasons. But my observations in 1966-7, a promising season with the best rains for many years, did not confirm this. There was no marked diminution in the number of sessions, though attendance did drop off, especially on the part of those whose fields were some distance from the village.

Meetings generally begin towards midday, after the men have finished watering their livestock, and may last from between an hour to five hours or more. The meetings always break up before sunset, and if the business of the day has not been completed another meeting may be called soon after. Towards midday on the appointed day, men begin to gather at the *kgota* where they sit about waiting, gossiping, tanning hides, smoking or dozing. When a number of men have collected, someone is sent to summon the headman and to carry his chair to the *kgota.* After sitting and chatting for a while, the headman instructs his senior counsellor to open the meeting. The senior counsellor then introduces the business of the day – he may lay a problem of policy before the assembly, present the preparatory facts of a legal action that must be judged, or raise any other question of public concern. The matter is then debated, men standing to speak in any order. Finally a counsellor sums up the debate and 'gives' the matter to the senior counsellor, who adds his comments and 'gives' it to the headman for his decision – a decision which usually reflects the sense of the meeting. The citizens then salute the headman in typical

Sotho style, *Pula! Pula! Pula!* (rain!), and disperse informally. In some villages, meetings may be opened and closed by prayers.

Of course, not all meetings run to type, but this is the general frame of a *lekgota* meeting. Particularly in contrast to a session of the tribal council in one of the Tswana capitals, one carries away an impression of informality. People often chatter while speakers are addressing the meeting; individuals leave from time to time to smoke or to relieve themselves; there are shouts and interruptions – heckling is generally tolerated; and there is a great deal of laughter. There is no formal seating plan, nor is there a marked tendency for members of the same faction to sit together. Office-bearers generally sit on the chairs, but some ordinary people may bring chairs rather than spend several hours sitting on the ground.

A few rules of conduct are enforced. One may not bring a stick or any weapon into the *kgota*; one may not smoke in the *kgota* during a meeting; one must be sober and decently dressed; and if one speaks one must stand and remove one's hat. One can ask the speaker to yield the floor, and although he is not bound to do so he will probably oblige if his status is lower, or if other participants call on him to do so. Finally, it is worth noting that conventional modes of behaving towards kin are submerged in the 'committee behaviour' proper to the *lekgota*.

Oratory is not generally far removed from conversational style, though some men embellish their speeches with proverbs and maxims, analogies, dramatic images and so on, sometimes delivered in an extremely theatrical manner. To quote one example, here is an extract from a speech by a man who objected to a report that the District Commissioner believed not enough children were being sent to the village school. He said:

'I am the man who preaches long sermons in church. I am Ramaseri [a local evangelist], I am the priest ... A person does not bear children like a dog – a litter of six or eight which all grow up at once! We cannot bear children like dogs and send them to school in the same year. White people are not good to us. We want to see the District Commissioner and explain to him that we are wilde-beast, and must be treated carefully ... [He complains of the authoritarian actions of the District Commissioner. Then:] If a teacher beats a child, the child cries and forgets the lesson. To beat a person is like sending him to prison.'

In the main the debates are informal, down to earth, and usually to the point. More typical than the speech I have quoted are the extracts from debates which I cite later, approximating in form more to ordinary conversation.

Finally, two distinguishing features of the *lekgota* should be commented on. First, there are no records of most of the decisions taken by the *lekgota*. The District Commissioners insist that the court-scribe records the main details of court-cases, and when levies are made collections are often recorded, but the decisions of the *lekgota* on matters of policy are not written up. Many citizens have commented to me on the need for such records, but their absence allows greater freedom in the making and breaking of political alliances, as well as permitting individuals to plead ignorance of decisions they disapprove of, advantages of which they are aware.

Second, and this seems to be most unusual in councils, there is very little lobbying and few 'deals' are made outside the meeting. Public issues are discussed informally outside the *kgota,* but continual probing on my part revealed no horse-trading and no active drumming up of support in preparation for a meeting, though tnis is, perhaps, a point on which no outside observer can be certain.

IV

The Kgalagari normally use few terms to distinguish the various activities of the

Table 1. Agendas for five *lekgota* meetings held in Kuli Village

Number	Date	Summoned at the instance of		Business transacted
1	18 Feb. 1964	Headman	(a)	Letters from District Commissioner read out;
			(b)	village branch committee of Bechuanaland Democratic Party discusses local progress and appeals for assistance;
			(c)	headman reprimands counsellor for missing meetings of the *lekgota* – threatens to fine him;
			(d)	assault case hearing begun.
2	25 July 1964	District Commissioner	(a)	Voting procedure in forthcoming self-government elections explained;
			(b)	revision of tax-register announced;
			(c)	cattle-sales discussed;
			(d)	school-feeding scheme discussed;
			(e)	famine relief measures: hand-outs for destitutes announced, and permission granted, on request of *lekgota*, to shoot a limited number of protected game;
			(f)	village water-supplies discussed;
			(g)	*lekgota* complains about transport difficulties and inadequate postal service;
			(h)	*lekgota* complains about prevalence of stock-theft by Bushmen.
3	30 Dec. 1964	Headman	(a)	Headman inquires into the smuggling of cattle in South West Africa – some village youths have been arrested there;
			(b)	case concerning a disputed sale heard;
			(c)	case concerning damage to property heard and settled.

87

Table 1. *(continued)*

Number	Date	Summoned at the instance of		Business transacted
4	4 Nov. 1966	Headman		Hearing on theft case begun and adjourned; discussion of how to organize the erection of a store for food being provided for school-feeding; government issue of seeds announced and discussed; T.B. vaccination programme announced.
5	11 Feb.1967	District Councillor	(a)	New watering fees announced;
			(b)	discussion of possible government move to post policemen in the villages – a recommendation made to be reported back to the District Council;
			(c)	discussion of race discrimination in the district;
			(d)	report made of a debate in the District Council on a territorial dispute involving the village – action here of District Councillor approved;
			(e)	applicants for labour permits for South West Africa registered by District Councillor for communication to District Commissioner;
			(f)	announcement made of impending visit by District Commissioner – outstanding court-cases must therefore be settled soon;
			(g)	forthcoming cattle-sale announced, and possibility of some unified sellers' strategy discussed;
			(h)	court-case announced and set down for future hearing.

Lekgota. A meeting is a *pijo* (cf. the more usual term, *pitso*) or a *puo*; but the term *puo* may refer even to meetings of smaller, less formal councils, such as the family council. A speech, a debate or a topic of debate may also be a *puo*. *Puo* is also one of the two terms used to distinguish the main tasks of the *lekgota*: *ritsheko*, legal actions; and *ripuo*, debates on other matters. This simple classification masks the multifarious functions which the *lekgota* performs.

Abstracting the matters dealt with in 41 meetings of Kuli's *lekgota* which I recorded during visits to the village in 1964 and 1966-7, I found that court-cases accounted for 21% of the items debated; discussions on policy and administration 32%; and dealings with external agencies directly or by a letter, including some further policy items, 47%. (A total of 112 items were dealt with at these 41 meetings.) This distribution does not, however, accurately reflect the time spent by the *lekgota* on these various categories of business. Unfortunately I did not consistently time debates on various topics, but I reckon that the *lekgota* spent well over two-thirds of its time on internal affairs — court-actions and matters of policy and administration.

Table 1 contains samples of the topics covered at *lekgota* meetings, where I set out 'agendas', abstracted from my records, of five representative sessions of the Kuli *lekgota*.

As these brief abstracts indicate, the *lekgota* directs and supervises the internal administration of the village to a large extent, judges legal actions, negotiates with outside powers, and disseminates information. Its central concerns are the maintenance of internal order and the 'developmental' needs of what is today, from the economic stand-point, a peasant community.

The legal work of the *lekgota* — even its occasional forays into legislation — has been carried over from the past with few modifications. The administrative and policy-making load of the *lekgota* and its functions in education and communication with the outside world have, however, expanded considerably to keep pace with the economic development of the Kgalagari. As a result the *lekgota* today grapples with problems different in kind from those of a generation ago. Should tribal labour be paid? How can the District Commissioner be persuaded to expand the school? If a local levy is raised, should rich men pay more than poor men? Should defaulters be handed over to the police if they disregard the judgements of the *lekgota*? In adapting itself to deal with novel issues of this sort the *lekgota* has carved out for itself a crucial role in modern local government.

A function which has dropped away with the development of the District Administration is the regulation of inter-village affairs. They were once characteristically settled by a joint meeting of the councils of the villages concerned. Even today, however, if a man is brought to trial before the *lekgota* of a foreign village, representatives of the *lekgota* of his own village (normally counsellors) will generally attend and participate in the trial.

In addition to performing vital governmental tasks, the *lekgota* has various secondary functions. First, it is a listening-post for the headman and officers of government, allowing them to gauge citizen reaction to policy-initiatives, and it permits the communication of criticisms and suggestions from the citizen body. *Lekgota* meetings give frustrated citizens the opportunity to let off steam, usually harmlessly and possibly even creatively. It is striking how vigorously men in *lekgota* criticize government officers in their presence, though they would hesitate to be forthright in a private confrontation. Second, *lekgota* meetings allow the bringing to bear of the pressure of public disapprobation on citizens who attempt to evade communal responsibility, a fact of some importance in a political community which has few means of penalizing the uncooperative. Third, in the absence of written records, meetings of the *lekgota* provide an opportunity for the public registration of personal commitment to policies, or for the public disassociation from them. And fourth, *lekgota* meetings allow the constant restatement, and perhaps adaptation, of communal values, and so, presumably, tend to reinforce and perpetuate them. Particularly as a court of law, the *kgota* is the stage for morality dramas and sermons; and political debates often involve the bringing out of certain key constitutional values.

V

Actions at law are first brought by the parties to the attention of the counsellors. A preliminary examination is usually carried out by the counsellors, perhaps with the assistance of the headman and a few other citizens who may be interested in the matter. Unless the matter can be settled out of court, or in a sub-clan court, the case is then presented to the *lekgota* and is heard and judged. Appeals from the *lekgota* to the District Commissioner's court or to the Supreme Court are extremely rare. The jurisdiction of the *lekgota* as a court is, however, limited. It has civil powers 'up to a subject-matter valued at pounds 25, ten bovines or fifty small stock, and criminal powers up to a sentence of imprisonment for three months, a fine of pounds 10 or five bovines or twenty small stock, and whipping up to four strokes' (Hailey, 1953: 227). Further, certain crimes such as witchcraft and murder and a few other matters are excluded from its jurisdiction. These limitations are sometimes evaded, and in practice almost every legal issue which arises within the village is settled in the *lekgota*.

The presentation of issues of policy to the *lekgota* is less straightforward. To begin with, a few fields of governmental action fall within the range of the headman's prerogative. This prerogative is not precisely defined. It usually includes such matters as the admission of new citizens, the appointment and dismissal of certain officers, etc., but even in these matters the *lekgota* usually exerts pressure on the headman. In exceptional cases – such as the sub-chief of Hukuntsi, who enjoys considerable direct police backing, or did until recently – the headman may even risk direct action on other matters. In general, however, administrative and policy matters which arise within the village are decided in the *lekgota*. Such issues include the enforcement of the *lekgota's* judgments and directives and the solution of local administrative problems – for example: the borehole mechanic goes on strike; what measures should be taken to restore the service? The village school-teachers demand better accommodation; what can be done for them? And so on.

In many cases the Administration virtually dictates action to the *lekgota*. On famine-relief, for instance, or new taxes, policy-decisions are taken at the national or district level, and the village *lekgota* is not even given a choice about the way in which the decision should be implemented. To stick to the example of famine-relief, the Administration decided in 1964 that such relief was necessary, and it delegated to the headman and *lekgota* the duty of registering 'destitutes'. Later it instructed the village officers to supervise hand-outs of food. The only choices open to the villagers were in the nomination of 'destitute persons' and even here they were limited by criteria laid down by the central government.

More commonly initiatives for community projects come about through a dialogue between the District Commissioner or other Administrative officers and the *lekgota* – or, since 1966, through negotiation with the District Council via the village District Councillor, who is instructed by the *lekgota*. The *lekgota* and the outside authorities generally agree broadly on ends. Everyone is agreed that better schools, improved water-resources, more efficient cattle-marketing methods and similar developments are in the public interest. Although villagers use their contacts with the authorities in the *lekgota* and through the District Councillor to press their particular claims, the final decision about the distribution of scarce resources between villages is made at the District capital or in the ministries, and not in the *lekgota*.

The *lekgota* comes into the picture once more when the authorities have made their decision. The Administration tries to involve village authorities in community-development projects, partly as a sort of character-building exercise, and partly in order to shift some of the financial and administrative burden. It may be agreed, say, that a village school should be extended. The District Commissioner (or today the District Council) offers to provide the building material and to supply extra school-teachers if the villagers themselves provide the labour and some of the capital for the project. In such circumstances the *lekgota* is faced with a series of issues which require decisions and action. The *lekgota* has to decide how the levy is to be raised and how labour is to be recruited. Should rich men pay more than poor men? Should parents of school-going children subscribe the bulk of the levy and provide most of the labour? Should the workers be paid, and if so how much? Further, a supervisor must be appointed by the *lekgota*, and the *lekgota* must keep an eye on progress. Many of these issues may be novel, even unprecedented in the experience of the *lekgota*. Nevertheless, agreed solutions must be found to the problems involved if the common goal is to be achieved.

Other outside bodies may also foist issues on the *lekgota*. The Botswana Democratic Party, for example, may ask the *lekgota* to elect representatives or nominate candidates for District or national elections. And many issues which arise within the village and are settled by the *lekgota* without consultation with outside authorities are dealt with in a particular way because of a fear that the authorities might intervene at some stage.

One may identify, then, three broad types of issue with which the *lekgota* deals. There are, first, the legal issues. They usually involve private parties, and the *lekgota* plays a neutral, judicial role. Second there are the issues of internal policy, which characteristically centre around conflict over power or competition for jobs. The *lekgota* then splits into factions. Finally there are the issues in which the *lekgota* unites in a confrontation with external authorities. These are, however, pure types.

An issue may present itself in different forms at different times, calling forth different structural responses; or the actual or possible intervention of external authorities may significantly affect the way in which the *lekgota* deals with a judicial matter or a problem of internal administration.

VI

An issue presented to the *lekgota* is debated fully – a grievance against many non-African District Commissioners is that they have no patience for the lengthy debates which the Kgalagari find necessary. If all goes well, an agreed decision emerges, which is gradually formulated and clarified by succeeding speakers. Dissentients voice their doubts and are persuaded to see the flaws in their arguments, or perhaps persuade the majority to amend their views. Ideally, as I have already said, the consensus is then summed up by a counsellor – ostensibly for the headman's benefit – and the headman seals the debate by announcing the formal decision or by adjourning the discussion. The headman's decision is usually a restatement of the popular view, but he may introduce variations in matters of detail.

Often, however, the members of the *lekgota* fail to reach agreement. The decision-making process in court-cases may approach the ideal, but policy decisions often create difficulties, and when factional interests are involved in an issue, conflicts may be too great to permit the emergence of any enforceable decision. One might say that there are several decision-making processes, characteristically initiated by different kinds of issues. I shall attempt to sum up this spectrum by presenting and analysing two cases, the first representing one of the simplest, the other the most complex and conflict-ridden decision-making which I witnessed in the *lekgota.*

The Case of the Cheeky Bushman

One night a Bushman named Sobe was badly beaten up while taking part in a Kgalagari drinking bout in Kuli village. He went to the headman for protection, and the headman summoned the *lekgota* early the next morning. Some villagers thought Sobe might die from his wounds. If he survived, he would have to go to the District hospital as soon as possible. In either event the police might take over the case, a possibility which moved the villagers to rapid action.

As soon as the *lekgota* meeting was opened, Sobe was asked to present his version of the events of the previous night. It appeared that Sobe had passed what was interpreted as a 'cheeky' remark about Kgalagari habits, and had been beaten up by his drinking companions. When his statement was over, cross-examination began. One of the counsellors took the major role, but questions were put to Sobe by a number of citizens present. Though the *lekgota*-men were clearly determined to establish the facts as fully as possible, they were impatient of any delays – 'If Sobe dies they will go to gaol. Rather try the case and judge it'.

The accused then made their statements and were cross-examined, questions once again coming from all round the *kgota.* The court tried to establish who had hit Sobe, and where. Soon it became apparent that two of the accused were guilty, and the interest was focussed on two others against whom grave suspicion rested.

When it appeared that no further progress could be made, a citizen summed up the evidence, noting where there was conflict and where the evidence was unsatisfactory. He concluded: 'The headman should be given the case to judge.' The senior counsellor then stood and related a precedent. A citizen urged: 'Counsellors, take time. You and the headman must take the case. The *lekgota*-men have not spoken much.'

Before judgment was given the two men against whom the evidence was overwhelming were asked to plead guilty. One hesitated, but eventually capitulated – 'You have given in to the *lekgota*' he was told. 'They will give you to the headman'.

In passing judgment the headman indicated that he thought all four accused were guilty. However, he could sentence only two of them, for he said, 'The *lekgota* has refused. The *lekgota* has said that only two men are guilty. Then, as he prepared to pass sentence, the court-scribe interrupted him and insisted on reading aloud and translating what he considered a relevant passage from the criminal code. The headman replied:

'When I judge, I do not judge as the white people do. The European judges for himself only. I judge my own people for myself in this country. The white place is at Ghanzi (the District capital) because their "camp" is there. The Bible says, judge honourably and blessedly. So I lead my people.'

He then passed judgment and sentence.

My concern here is with the decision-making apparatus, and I shall leave aside the legal issues involved. In this matter an agreed and known system of law is being applied according to set principles, if not, in this case, which was brought by a Bushman, completely without fear or favour. (However, when one of the accused asked for leniency on the grounds that he was a native of the village, he was told that this was irrelevant. A father could judge his own child.) Each party presents his story and is cross-examined on it, and if necessary witnesses are called by the *lekgota.* There is, then, a traditional procedure for getting at the facts, and a code, weighted with precedents, which guides interpretation and judgment.

A decision-making hierarchy is also evident. The ordinary citizens, under the guidance of the counsellors, reach a general decision. This is passed on to the senior counsellor, who adds his views, and then the headman pronounces the final judgment. In this case, as often, the headman accepted a decision with which he disagreed in part. He made clear his own belief that all four of the accused were guilty on the evidence, and not only two. The emphasis on consensus which appears here is carried further by the insistence, routine in Kgalagari courts, that the accused admit their guilt before the final judgment and sentence are handed down. Even in this extreme situation, the *lekgota* hesitates to coerce a minority.

An impetus to consensus which was obviously present in this case was fear of police intervention. This desire to settle matters within the village to avoid the unpredictable and often drastic results of direct uncontrolled intervention by the external authorities recurs in many contexts, and encourages the group to reach agreed solutions in a number of cases.

The Case of the Pumpers

This second issue provoked factional activity of unusual intensity. The 'Case of the Pumpers' also arose in Kuli village, where there are three factions, which have existed for the past fifteen to twenty years. There are two factions within the ruling Pebana sub-clan, one led by the headman, the other by one of his younger half-brothers, Mabote. The minority sub-clan, the Silebe, forms the basis of a third faction. There is a tendency towards the polarization of two factions on particular political issues. The third faction (Mabote's or the Silebe) sides with one group or the other, and their choice of sides usually determines the outcome of the conflict, though the influential neutral citizens also carry weight in such a situation.

The Pumpers' Case focussed on the government borehole in Kuli, for which the villagers are responsible. They should appoint and pay the 'pumper' who operates it, but here, as in many Kgalagari villages, the operation of the borehole has become a source of recurrent political tension.

The first pumper was the headman's son. He was dismissed in the late 'fifties by the District Commissioner, as a result of complaints from members of Mabote's faction. The incident occurred during a peak of interfactional tension. The *lekgota* appointed as his successor a man named Morimomong, who was a counsellor and a prominent member of Mabote's faction. In 1963 Morimomong left the village. He wrote a letter to the *lekgota* saying that his son, Sekoma, had succeeded him as pumper and should be paid his wages. The *lekgota* declined to consider the situation until Morimomong appeared before it in person. In 1964 Morimomong returned to Kuli, and Sekoma, who had worked unpaid all this time, precipitated a crisis by going on strike and hiding the crank with which the engine of the borehole was started.

The *lekgota* met quickly to discuss the crisis. The debate centred round two questions – by what right had Sekoma been made pumper, and should a new pumper be appointed? The headman pushed these questions aside and forced a decision on who should *now* become pumper. He said:

'The District Commissioner wants us to find another man for the engine. [This, I believe, was a piece of pure invention.] Sekoma is like Morimomong and deserts his post. I tell you, Pebana, you must look for a new pumper. I want a new pumper. I have no news and no case.'

Each of the two Pebana factions put forward a candidate for the post – Merahe, the headman's candidate, and Sekoma, Mabote's candidate. The Silebe were uncommitted and the *lekgota* waited to see whom they would support. A Silebe counsellor, a man who was often the Silebe spokesman in the *lekgota*, rose and called on the *lekgota*-men to express their opinions. They should not leave the decision to the counsellors. The headman's son tried to force the issue by suggesting a vote by a show of hands – a measure frequently suggested at times of apparent deadlock, but seldom, if ever resorted to. At length the Silebe counsellor spoke again. He would support Merahe's candidature, since a pumper should live near the borehole. This argument was unconvincing, for both candidates lived within a few hundred yards of the borehole. The Silebe were being tactful, but they had thrown in their lot with the headman on this issue.

The headman now spoke again. Mabote and his men had acted wrongly by appointing a pumper unilaterally. Mabote was absent today: he had sent word he was sick, but he said 'He is not sick. He is just against me'.

Morimomong, one of the protagonists, then spoke:

'I want to speak. It is not a strong word, so do not be afraid. I ask the *lekgota* not to be angry. These men [the citizens in council] are afraid to say yes. When the headman asks whether we agree, we men in *lekgota* do not reflect that if we say yes we will affect years of another man's life. We want the headman to appoint, and we will agree. Do not point to one man and say, you are the one who said yes.'

The discussion then moved on to the details of Merahe's salary, etc. and it appeared that the consensus had been achieved. A counsellor said, 'Headman, we have chosen Merahe'. Another man said, 'We are all sons of Ramoswane [the headman], we all know one another', in an attempt to stifle further discord. But there were echoes of Morimomong's speech. One man said, 'I am speaking because the men in *lekgota* will say they were speaking and I just kept quiet. When, tomorrow, something goes wrong with the engine, some men will say, *I* did not choose Merahe'.

Merahe worked as pumper for several months and then he went on strike, as Sekoma had done, and threatened to tell the District Commissioner, whose visit was imminent, that he had not been paid his wages. The *lekgota* met and soon recognized (as an influential independent citizen remarked) that Merahe had not been paid because Sekoma's supporters were not reconciled to his appointment, and were witholding their contributions to his salary. The dismissal of Sekoma was debated once more. Despite the fact that Mabote was present and argued Sekoma's case himself, it was soon clear that the majority would not accept Sekoma's claim. Mabote was vigorously criticised.

The debate was cut short by the arrival of the District Commissioner. After the District Commissioner had completed his business with the *lekgota*, the headman asked him to hear 'the case of the pumper'. But the only issue the headman put to the District Commissioner was Merahe's claim to the payment of his wages. The District Commissioner said that of course Merahe should be paid, and he instructed the court-scribe to see that anyone who failed to contribute towards Merahe's wages was banned from using the borehole.

95

This did not provide a permanent solution. In 1967 this and later resolutions had come to nothing. Due to the factional dispute, the borehole – after an anarchic period when a number of men operated it for the benefit of their own families – had become derelict. Even in the Kalahari, blood is thicker than water.

The question of the pumper had been a factional issue for years before the dispute I have described blew up, and factional activity dominated the *lekgota* debates. The headman's partisanship was particularly important – he forced the *lekgota* to make a rapid choice between the two candidates by invoking the name of the District Commissioner and he later brought in the District Commissioner in person to clinch his victory. He was in a position to take these steps only because he had the support of the Silebe and some neutrals in addition to the members of his own faction. He might not have risked his final move, despite this support, but for a threat from Merahe to appeal to the District Commissioner directly. This might have reflected on the headman's authority.

Despite the conflicts and the headman's authoritarian tactics, there was a clear concern for public agreement by the citizens in the *lekgota*. This emerged particularly in the speeches of Morimomong and the man who followed him, and indirectly, in the remark of the man who urged agreement on the grounds that 'We are all sons of the headman. We know one another'. (This is an argument based on the existence of multiplex relations!) What also emerged was the general reluctance to take responsibility for contentious decisions.

The opposition tactics deserve notice. Aside from their participation in some debates they influenced events by absenteeism. If one is absent one cannot be pressurized to concur in a decision, and one cannot commit oneself to its implementation. Mabote's absence thus left the way open for non-cooperation in the implementation of the decision – i.e. for the non-payment of Merahe's wages.

Finally, the role of neutrals and 'outsiders' should be mentioned. The District Commissioner was used to provide a sanction for the majority decision; and within the *lekgota* uncommitted groups and individuals brought delicate issues into the open, and significantly influenced the outcome by their choice of sides. Though detached from the factional confrontation, these men determined the immediate result.

The two cases I have briefly examined here offer examples of the two poles of decision-making procedures in the *lekgota*: on the one hand, the ordered, traditional mechanism of the legal case, where procedures, precedents and common interests unite to smooth the way to an accepted and enforceable decision; and on the other hand, the improvizations and conflicts of a factional issue, temporarily decided at last by majority pressure and the invocation of outside authority. Though representing extreme cases and not typical instances of the decision-making procedures of the *lekgota*, these cases illustrate most of the techniques of *lekgota* politics, and bring out the overriding concern with reaching a consensus. This last is a point which needs some development.

VII

The Kgalagari accept the value of consensus, and are quite explicit about the importance of persuading citizens not only to accept but publicly to identify themselves with a decision of the *lekgota*. As they frequently say, they are reluctant to force *(gopukeleja)* their fellows. In any case, everyone is well aware that in most matters of village policy the District Commissioner or police will not coerce dissidents. As Bailey has remarked, with similarly structured councils in other places in mind, 'Everyone knows that if the decision is not the result of an agreed compromise, then it cannot be implemented.' (Bailey, 1965: 8). The 'Case of the Pumpers' illustrates the fragility of a decision by majority, even when that decision is backed by the authority of the District Commissioner.

The main business of the *lekgota* is to reach, by consensus if possible, the decisions which will govern many of the public affairs of the village. The greatest danger facing the *lekgota* is that as a popular political institution operating within a small and closely-knit community it may provoke or exacerbate social conflicts, leading at last to the complete breakdown of village government. However, there exist various mechanisms which tend to dampen down conflict within the *lekgota*.

The most important of these mechanisms is perhaps the projection of the headman as the symbol of law, unity and shared values. When conflicts become too acute speakers in the *lekgota* complain that the headman's position is being threatened, that 'every man in this village thinks he is his own headman', etc. People hesitate to attack the headman directly. The chief councillor usually acts as the headman's spokesman, so protecting him from direct identification with any point of view. And the headman usually speaks only when an agreed point of view is emerging. As the 'Case of the Pumpers' illustrates, however, the headman may not always rise above open partisanship.

Other mechanisms tending to dampen down conflict are the discouragement of personal attacks in speeches; the use of the tactic of absenteeism, which allows tempers to cool and avoids direct confrontation in tense situations; and the use of scape-goats (always outsiders, and often school-teachers) to carry the blame for extreme conflicts. And finally shared interests, particularly vis-a-vis outside bodies, may be invoked. It is possibly unnecessary to add that these methods of reducing conflict are occasionally inadequate, and that the techniques the Kgalagari have refined are at times insufficient to ensure that decisions can be reached or enforced, particularly on matters of internal administration.

VIII

Contemporary anthropology with its functionalist and neo-evolutionist tendencies raises, at least implicitly, the question of the efficiency of institutions. This is a question of some practical importance where the *lekgota* is concerned, for this is a vital if somewhat neglected organ in modern local government. In 1964 my impression was that although the *lekgota* was irreplaceable as a court of law, and was very useful for purposes of instruction, publicity and general communications, it was failing in its role as a policy-making body. There were several reasons for this failure – poor communication (in every sense) with the District Commissioner's office; the weakness of the executive arm of the *lekgota* (the headman and the counsellors); and the difficulty of over-ruling minorities. It seemed possible that policy-making would become more efficient if the headman was strengthened, but this might result (as in northern Kgalagadi District) in a decline in the *lekgota's* influence, a loss which, particularly as Botswana's independence approached, would outweigh the gain.

When I returned to Kgalagari in 1966-7, after Independence had been attained, I found that this impasse had been broken by the creation of the democratic District Councils, with local representatives coming from each village. The District Councillor had generally displaced the headman as chairman of the *lekgota* when policy matters were debated. Chosen by his constituents for his political interests and comparative sophistication, and enjoying direct access to the District Council, the District Councillor is in a stronger position than the headman to negotiate agreement on problems before the *lekgota*. Further, he is generally free of factional commitment, though some District Councillors have formed steering committees of 'progressive' elements in the village. These more or less formal committees have great prestige and have initiated a number of far-sighted measures in various villages – consumer and producer cooperatives, bans on trapping near the villages, etc. The formation of these District Councils has also had the indirect result of broadening the horizons of the *lekgota*, and allowing greater exchange of ideas between the citizens of different villages within a District. (It is worth mentioning that the local government system was planned primarily with reference to the Tswana chieftaincies. The results of its application in the Kalahari State Lands were probably not foreseen by the planners.)

In northern Kgalagadi District the hereditary leaders are fighting back. They had been able in the past to rely on police backing to a greater extent than the headman in Ghanzi District, and today they are attempting to resist the new threat to their authority with the backing of the opposition Botswana Independence Party.

The *lekgota* may well gain in authority in the future, but many of the difficulties it has always faced as a policy-making body will be hard to overcome. Comparative research will perhaps show to what extent there are the irreducable complications of government by committee in face-to-face societies, where the committee must reach consensus before it can initiate effective action.

Notes

My first field trip in the Kalahari, in 1963-4, was financed by the Kalahari Research Committee. In 1966-7 I returned to the field with the assistance of grants from the H. Ling Roth Fund, the Horniman Bequest, and the Esperanza Trust. I am extremely grateful to these bodies for making my research possible. I have completed a full report of my study, published under the title *Kalahari Village Politics: An African Democracy.*

[1] See Schapera, 1956, for comparative material on the systems of government among various Southern African tribes. Material on tribal councils is provided on pp. 43 ff. and 141 ff.

[2] The position of Bushmen in Kgalagari society is discussed in Silberbauer and Kuper, 1966.

[3] The internal dynamics of Kgalagari factionalism can only be understood in relation to the kinship system. In brief, the death of a family-group head generally leads to the break-up of his family-group, accompanied by severe tension between paternal half-brothers, who may be in competition for power, position and property. Where a headman's family is involved, this usually leads to the generation of new factions, which are based on another complex of kinship ties. For an analysis of this problem see Kuper, 1969 particularly pp 297-300, and Kuper, 1970, ch. 5.

[4] It is common for councils to be associated, physically, and linguistically, with a council-place. Among the Sotho-speaking peoples there is also a further association. *Kgota* (or its cognates) is the term for a descent group and for the local unit associated with a descent group. It is also used to refer to the small assembly centre found in some local groupings within the village. A leading Botswana politician, the Hon. Q. Masire, has suggested to me that because the Tswana and Kgalagari think of a political community as being 'owned' by the descent group of the ruler, they use the same term for the central council-place.

THE CONCILIAR SYSTEM OF THE BEMBA
OF NORTHERN ZAMBIA

By Audrey Richards

The deliberative machinery of the Bemba is of special interest in the context of this volume and this for three main reasons. First it provides a good example of an elite hereditary council with specialist functions, working side by side with chiefs' court-councils of the common Bantu type. The Bemba polity consisted of thirty-four chiefdoms, of which three, that of the king or paramount, the Chitimukulu, and those of the two senior chiefs, the Mwamba and the Nkula, had a varying number of sub-chiefs attached to them. Each senior chief was in charge of political appointments and the associated ritual, and each chiefdom was virtually autonomous as regards the administration of justice, the keeping of law and order, the allocation of political appointments, and the collection of tribute in labour and kind required for the support of the personnel of government. In the nineteenth century there were even instances of major chiefs making raids into the surrounding areas on their own initiative. Each major chiefdom had its own court-council.

The sub-chiefs acknowledged the over-rule of the chief to whose chiefdom they were attached and sent him judicial cases on appeal.[1] They gave him some form of tribute such as ivory tusks, and military help on demand. Sub-chiefs were ritually installed by their senior chief's councillors and accepted the leadership of the latter in ritual matters. But otherwise these sub-chiefs were also autonomous in their own districts. They made their own political appointments, collected their own tribute, and had their respective court-councils. Below the chiefs were headmen ruling over small village communities, mainly composed of their kinsmen. These had no formally constituted court-councils either in pre- or post-colonial days.

The political structure of the Bemba has been called a kingdom, but this people had few central organs of government, and there was little joint activity co-ordinated throughout the whole tribe. The power of the king was based on his ritual supremacy, in that the Chitimukulu was believed to have supernatural powers which made him paramount over all the other chiefs, and that he was thought to influence the whole country by his right of access to the ancestral spirits of the royal crocodile dynasty, from which the senior and a number of the junior chiefs were drawn.[2] In the circumstances it was not surprising that the main task of the only body which could be called a tribal council for the Bemba, the *bakabilo*, was to maintain the sacredness of this type of divine kingship. It is this assembly composed of hereditary councillors with long lines of descent, which I believe to be of interest in this volume, because it is an example of an elite council which makes no pretence at being representative of the people in general, or of expressing their point of view.

Secondly, the Bemba material seems to me to be of value here since its conciliar system functions in an authoritarian society in which village headmen, sub-chiefs and chiefs were accepted without question, and political and legal powers were exercised according to a hierarchy based on age. Hence we have to ask which joint activities were achieved by the direct commands of the headman or some other authority, and which as the result of group discussions by which the participants were committed to carrying out the decisions reached by such assemblies. The same is true of legal cases and the functioning of formal or informal courts. How far was the settlement of disputes achieved by the direct intervention of some accepted authority, with or without advice, and how far were decisions given by a body of judges with more or less equal status? I shall try to show that in Bemba society some village activities were governed by the direct orders of the headman and some disputes settled by his decree alone. In other cases decisions were reached by the joint deliberations of the villagers. There might even be an alternation between the two methods, as in the case I instance later of a sub-chief intervening in a judicial case being heard by a group of judges, by striding up to the meeting and summarily telling an accused husband what he ought to pay to his injured wife for damages. (see p.113).

Lastly the Bemba data seems to me to be useful because the traditional deliberative machinery was functioning in something like its original fashion when I arrived in the area in 1930, whereas it is difficult in the case of some of the other selected societies to distinguish the traditional from the British elements in the council system. The British South Africa Company had established its first administrative centre at Kasama in the heart of the Bemba country in 1898. Its rural administration must have been very loose owing to shortage of staff, but it was 'direct'. Its officials acted as magistrates, hearing cases as they travelled through their districts. But native law was applied in civil cases according to a North East Rhodesia order adopted in 1900[3] and chief's courts continued to function, though without legal sanction, 'on sufferance',[4] until the Company rule came to an end in 1924. Indirect rule was introduced by the new British colonial administration in March 1929 as defined in a Native Authorities and Courts Ordinance modelled on that of Tanganyika Territory. By this measure thirty-four Bemba chiefs were recognised as Native Authorities. This Ordinance was only just being put into operation in April 1930 when I arrived in the country. The administration was not aware of the meetings of the *bakabilo*, the elite council, and it continued to function as before.[5] Government supervision of the chief's court-councils was only just beginning. Village meetings were too small to be recognised officially and must have continued very much as they had always done. This situation provided good opportunities for the anthropologists of the time, interested as we then were in studying peoples 'uncontaminated' by white influence. This interest in the reconstruction of conditions at the end of the nineteenth century, is no longer dominant in British anthropology; but observations made on a society at a time when conditions resembled those of the pre-colonial era seem to me to be of value here, since they widen the scope of our comparative survey. They also show clearly the dramatic changes in the whole conciliar system which had to take place before western ideas of welfare and development could be introduced.

On the other hand I was myself in a poor state to make the necessary observations. My knowledge of Cibemba was inadequate to follow the rapid exchange of council discussions during my first visit of fifteen months (1930-1) although it became serviceable during my second visit (1933-4), except in the case of some of the discussions of the *bakabilo* when an esoteric language was used (see p.105). No interpreter was available to help me at that stage of Bemba educational development. Tape recorders had not appeared on the scene.

Again I was engaged in a general study of tribal culture and structure, and such comprehensive observations were then common anthropological practice. It would have been impossible to combine this general type of study with continuous attendance at court-council meetings over a period of say a year. It must therefore be admitted frankly that much of my empirical data is of a very superficial kind. It might be described as a basis for further study rather than the adequate collection of data which would make a complete analysis possible. I have often had to rely on casual observations noted in my diary, but never followed up with systematic study.

I re-visited the Bemba country for a few months in 1957, but had little time to make a special study of the changes that had taken place in the council procedure. The material given at the end of this section comes from district note-books. I know still less, unfortunately, about the further changes which must have been introduced by the newly independent government of Zambia. I have therefore used the past tense throughout my descriptive account of the Bemba deliberative machinery.

The nature of conciliar activity in Bemba country

In traditional Bemba society a court or a council meeting seems to have been regarded as an activity in which the older men engaged from time to time rather than as a permanent institution with an accepted name and a fixed composition. It was a verb rather than a noun. Even the elite council of Bembaland, composed of the king's hereditary councillors, had no name until the colonial authorities insisted it should be given one when they adapted the institution and gave it new functions (1948).[6] Conciliar activity is described as *ukuteka icilye. Ukuteka* means 'to place or put in order', but also 'to keep control of', as a man speaks of herding livestock or a chief is described as looking after his people *(ukuteka abantu)*. The paradigm of a council is that of a chief, or some other person in authority, advised by a group of men. These were, in the capital, *bafilolo* or heads of divisions, and some of the *bakabilo*. In the ordinary chiefdoms they tended to be men holding ritual offices, and old and respected men who had long been resident in the village.

The composition of the king's *bakabilo* council was fixed by rules of descent, but in the case of other chiefs' court-councils membership was determined by exclusion rather than inclusion. Strangers, women, and young people might not take part, though boys could listen to proceedings. Heads of divisions could be summoned peremptorily by the chief to attend, but the rest of the councillors seemed to select themselves from the ranks of those who were willing to help and were thought eligible. [7]

Kinship was not significant as a basis of a chief's council in Bemba society. Schapera and others have stressed the importance of the chief's male agnates, often his father's brothers, as the inner ring of advisors among the patrilineal peoples of the Southern Bantu,[8] but in the case of the matrilineal Bemba there was no such corporate group of male kinsmen of the chief available at the capital.

This fluctuating group of councillors advised the chief, or other authority; provided him with knowledge of past precedents and of the views of his subjects; and commented in practical fashion on the ease or difficulty of any course of action the chief wanted to pursue. They supported or restrained the ruler according to circumstances. They shared in his onerous duty of deciding on the guilt or innocence of criminals, or of finding a solution to a quarrel between two individuals or groups. Both these were duties conceived by the Bemba as being of the essence of chieftainship and as being the most dangerous and difficult task authority had to carry out. A wrong verdict left either a permanent grievance or the possibility of further hostilities between two groups – dangers expressed in the Bemba belief that a dead man unjustly accused returned as an evil spirit *(ciwa)* to punish those who injured him in life. Only a chief of great power, advised by wise and just men, dared to take this risk and cases of special difficulty were sent from headman to sub-chief, and sub-chief to chief, chief to paramount chief,[9] and sometimes from chief to district commissioner and then from district commissioner back to paramount chief.

It is important to grasp the traditional Bemba concept of conciliar activity from the outset. A council was not considered to be representative of different groups in a chiefdom or in the country as a whole. There was no expectation that the members of a village, of a district or of a descent group should have someone to speak for them at a council meeting. Schapera writes of the South African peoples 'But among the Bantu as among the Hottentots, the chief has a formal council that includes the heads of all local groups; these men are the representatives of their followers and through them the views of the whole community can be expressed'.[10] This is emphatically not the case among the Bemba. In fact I never heard a Bemba discuss the question of representation at all, except in the case of men who had been instructed in British political ideas and this was during my third visit in to the country in 1957.

Nor were council meetings based on democratic principles in any of our many uses of the term. African politicians often tell us that political problems were solved in the 'good old days' in democratic fashion by groups of old men sitting under trees. In Bemba society the men under the tree were essentially a group of people clustered round an authority, the king, a chief or sub-chief, or even a headman; a group of varied composition which helped the ruler to do what he wanted to do, or dissuaded him from doing disruptive or unpopular things. I think this concept of conciliar activity will be found to have been more common in Bantu chiefdoms in pre-colonial days than is admitted now.

It follows from this that the place of meeting was usually a space in front of the ruler's house. This was commonly an ant-hill or other eminence on which he usually sat, though a case might be taken to the hut of any eminent visitor passing through the village and who might be asked to give a verdict in a legal case.

How then was a council meeting distinguished from any gathering of men come, for instance, to bring news to the chief or to drink beer with him? What is the difference between a formal meeting of the *bakabilo,* when they are described in respectful terms as holding a council *(bateka icilye)* and the deliberations of small groups of these councillors forming a series of little meetings which fill the day and a large part of the night during a time of ritual activity at the capital (see p.119). The difference lies in the behaviour of the councillors, in the seating arrangements they follow, in their stance and demeanour, and in their speech patterns. Seating is inevitably more casual when meetings take place on the open ground, according to the traditional Bemba practice, than when a council or court is held in a building with fixed seats. Nevertheless it was subject to definite conventions.

When a court case was heard the appellant and the defendant faced each other at the bottom of a chief's anthill, with their supporters and witnesses near them. Those hearing the case tended to sit in a semi-circle with the chief, often with a small pot of beer in the middle. During my second visit in 1933 clerks had been appointed to chief's courts and they stood rather than sat, since the British administrators had taught them that it was respectful to stand in the presence of a higher authority, whereas the Bemba considered, and still consider it, respectful to sit. During council meetings of the *bakabilo,* different seating patterns were adopted according to the matter in hand, whether it was a succession case or a ritual matter (see p.119). I never attended any meeting in which arrangements were discussed. Men simply went to the place appropriate for that type of discussion.

Councillors sat alert at a meeting and did not lounge or drink beer, although the chief himself might do both these things. In court cases men often stood to plead while women sat with downcast eyes or knelt in a supplicant attitude. It was proper for both to maintain completely expressionless faces at a court session or before an authority. The court itself might rock with mirth, and the provoking of laughter was one of the devices by which a skilful chief might try to break the hostile mood between two complainants and so get them to agree to a solution of their conflict; but the appellant and the defendant were expected to remain grave.

Speech patterns at a court or council were distinct from those of every-day life. Speakers who used ancient forms of speech, rich with proverb and allusion, were admired as were those who were described as speaking 'Cibemba of under the ground' *(Cibemba ca panshi)* or Cibemba rich in hidden meanings, as distinct from the Cibemba of every day. This was specially the case at meetings of the *bakabilo* when highly allusive terms of phrase were used with the express purpose of preventing passers-by from understanding what was going on. I even heard phrases said to be in Ciluba, the language spoken in the Congo, whence the Bemba claim to have come. This type of speech, more common in council than in court meetings, was thought to demonstrate a man's knowledge of the past, and hence his ancient connections and status. A good memory was also much admired and court cases often required the recitation of a long series of ancestors and their relations with the predecessors of the man accused, as well as the speaker's own dealings with the same person. The speaker who wanted to make his hearers *au fait* with these complicated relationships required considerable skill as well as a retentive memory.

Fluency was also demanded. A man was expected to speak in a steady, almost monotonous voice without the slightest hesitation. Fluency was in fact thought so important that special words were used as fillers when a man was stuck for a fact or an argument. By convention speakers repeated the meaningless phrase *kabinge na kabushye* as many times as necessary to fill any unfortunate gap in the stream of words. This type of speech had become less common when I returned in 1957 to find many more literate councillors, clerks and pleaders in court. In fact two young men speaking to me in English referred rather scornfully to some old councillors as 'those old *kabinge na kabushye* boys'.[11] The difference in qualities needed for the old type of conciliar activity and the new is discussed later.

Women were not expected to perform such feats of memory, nor to be so aggressive in their statement of their rights. They spoke kneeling, in a high-pitched sing-song voice and their weapon was usually a fine and sophisticated irony delivered in a completely expressionless tone.

Finally I was surprised at the complete lack of demagogy in Bemba council meetings. Speakers were not, after all, trying to rouse an audience to feel or to act. They were more often than not recalling precedents and previous transactions in order to persuade a chief and his councillors to accept their claims, or they were referring to the past in order to encourage a chief to modify his actions. Attempts to use oratory for moral suasion came with the Christian missionary sermon, and I suspect that the demagogic tradition only dates from the beginning of political parties in Zambia – that is to say about 1955.

Levels of conciliar activity

Court-councils exist at three different levels of Bemba society – that of the village, the chiefdom and the tribe. In each case the functioning of the council depended on the sphere of joint activities which required discussion and decision-making and the type of disputes which had to be settled.

The village level

Bemba villages were small, largely autonomous and isolated in the thirties, and the absence of 45–60% of the men at the mines made the organisation of local activities difficult in many of them. My observations on conciliar activity were therefore made in one or two villages which happened to have a full complement of young and middle-aged men. [12] Villages were probably larger in pre-colonial days, as a result of the unsettled condition of the country which made small communities defenceless against raiders. They were certainly very much smaller at the time of my third visit in 1957, owing to the colonial government's decision in 1936 to introduce the 'parish' as a political division in order to allow individuals to settle alone with their families anywhere within this area. I describe conditions in 1933-4 which are intermediate between these two types, and I am therefore referring to communities of about thirty-five to fifty huts.

The composition of the village is obviously a determinant of its conciliar activity. How far did the villagers accept a common plan of action as the result of joint discussion, and how far were they merely following the orders of a headman or a group of elders who were standing in a position of grandfather, father or mother's brother to them?

Bemba villages were composed of relatives of the headman, the matrilocal family group consisting of his own household and those of his married daughters, with other kinsmen and women who chose to live with him. He was the permanent centre of village life, either because he had succeeded to the headmanship, or because he had managed to acquire a sufficient following to enable him to claim permission from his chief to start a new settlement. [13]

The villagers were united by a variety of kinship ties to the headman and if they were unhappy under his rule they could leave him. The village itself changed rule every four to five years and this made a convenient opportunity for dissident groups to break off. There was no property owned in common, such as land or cattle, to keep the villagers together for land was plentiful, and the people were shifting cultivators. Livestock survived with difficulty in this tsetse-ridden country, and this form of property was limited to the occasional goat, sheep or chickens. Those who remained permanently part of the village did so because they wanted to, and in these circumstances it is not surprising that they accepted the orders of the headman with whom they had elected to live. Moreover in this matrilineal, matri-local, or rather uxorilocal, society, there was no corporate group of male agnates persisting from generation to generation. The husbands of the village girls were

106

strangers who had come from other communities, and many of them wanted to return to their own villages in a few years time. This type of marriage, plus the absence of permanent economic assets meant that groups with conflicting interests, permanent feuds or sectional opposition, which are so characteristic of the structure of many other African societies, were not noticeable in Bemba country. Nor was the intense desire for lineage representation in councils at village, chiefdom or tribal level which is evident in other societies. It may seem curious that council procedure should be thought to depend on the type of property owned in the society or the lack of such capital assets, but I think it will be found that this is the case. I should expect that the desire for representation of groups or villages on higher councils would be found to appear in Bemba society when the colonial government began to introduce native treasuries with funds for distribution which could be spent on one project rather than another (1936). I think there is some evidence that this has been so.

Let us turn now to the joint activities of the village which require organisation and decision-making. These were the following:

(1) The co-ordination of agricultural activities such as the selection of the annual area of land for clearing, and the signal for the firing of the piles of lopped branches at the future sites for gardens. This latter activity has to be synchronised since a man who fires his branches before the rest of his fellows risks starting a forest fire which might destroy the garden sites of his neighbours before they had finished piling their own branches. Sowing and first-fruit ceremonies were performed by the headman. Hunting drives had also to be organised jointly as well as fishing parties.

(2) The collection of tribute in the form of beer or flour to be carried to the chief, or the nomination of men to go for their annual three or four days labour for their chief, which were both obligations which fell on villages as communities.

(3) Reactions to an emergency such as the arrival of a district commissioner; the collapse of a bridge over a nearby river; an accident to a villager such as a fall from a tree; or to the news that a curse had been put on the village.

(4) The organisation of some village ritual such as the rites for founding a new village, or those carried out for purification after a contagious disease or a death; and in pre-colonial days ordeals for the detection of a witch, before the suspected culprit was taken to the chief to be subjected to the *mwafi* poison ordeal.

It will be realised that most of the joint economic activities of the village were of a familiar and repetitive kind. The headman had to set them in motion by performing the necessary rites of prayer to his ancestors which preceded the annual tree-cutting, branch-firing, sowing and harvest. He also made a direct announcement to the people by shouting from his hut door, usually in the early hours of the morning, about dawn when the village was quiet. 'My friends we are going to stretch the nets today' would, for instance, give notice of a hunting drive. No formal council seemed to precede such an activity. It is true that the men of the village sat in their shelter each evening, gossiping, sharing their meals and often engaged in making bark-rope, baskets or mats. No doubt they would discuss the plans for the coming day, and the headman would probably be aware of their views, but these men were never said to be holding a council and the formal signal-giving was the headman's responsibility.

Emergencies such as I have listed were also mainly of a familiar nature. The visit of a district commissioner for instance was preceded by a regular series of activities such as the clearing of his camp site, the building of his latrine, and the grinding of flour for his carriers. The headman made the public announcement giving formal acknowledgment of the emergency, and he might proceed to select one or other of the villagers to do a particular job, but the visit did not seem to require a long process of decision-making. The headman acted on his own, sometimes after private discussion with some of his contemporaries. At other times he took the initiative on the request of a villager. I heard a woman beg for a headman's intervention when a neighbour had put a conditional curse on her pumpkins, which had been stolen. After talk with the complainant he shouted at sunrise next morning 'She who put a curse on her pumpkins, let her have mercy. It might be a child without any sense who took the food and this child might die.' After a stirring and a murmuring and an opening of doors it was announced that the curse had been removed. This was another example of a familiar technique set in motion by a headman.

These then were small villages in which both men and women were constantly in touch with each other. They were communities based on kinship but not on property-owning groups of kinsmen fighting for their own interests. The basis of their recruitment was relationship to a headman voluntarily acknowledged at the building of the village on each new site. They accepted his commands, or at any rate his signals, either because of the size and composition of the community, because of the importance Bemba attached to the ritual which they believed that only the headman could do for them, or because the range of alternative actions was small and there were few new situations to discuss or changes to be planned. It must be remembered too that the colonial government of the 1930s was not engaged in the welfare and development measures which were later to become one of its most important preoccupations. It was issuing direct commands on a few issues such as the building of latrines, or the siting of houses and roads. Like the headman the district commissioner, the medical, agricultural or education officer issued his orders direct to the villagers during his tours of inspection. The people were called together to hear the announcements, but not to discuss them. One chain of command went from the government officer direct to the headman and so to the villagers; another from the district officer to the chief and via the latter's messengers to the headman. Other commands went from the chief direct to the headman.

Are we then to conclude that the ordinary villager merely received instructions from above and took no part in the decisions taken? This is plainly not a democratic society in the sense that Kuper uses the term of the Kgalagari[14] but of course in practice the headman was fully aware of what the villagers were thinking and what they were ready to do, and this is possible in a small community. If he was wise, he would seek the advice of the older men. An elderly or weak headman was in fact, very dependent on their counsel. Thus the headman's orders were not surprising to the villagers. They often consisted of a formal announcement of views commonly held.

The villager, and especially the older villager, was also identified with community politics and activities by the fact that he stood constantly ready to act as a substitute for his senior in the decisions of everyday life, and to replace his superior after his death by the Bemba *ukupyanika* installation rite, a form of positional succession which is performed for every man or woman who dies, and by which the successor to the dead person adopts the latter's name, status and kinship terms. Apart from this belief in the equivalence of men and women in the same kinship category, there was substitution of one man for another on a basis of seniority in age. It is a constant surprise to a European observer in a Bemba village to note that each individual knows exactly how much older or younger he is than his fellows, with the date fixed to the nearest season. In terms such as 'The year of my birth, but in the rainy season, or in the hunger months' a man will describe his neighbour's seniority. This system allows for automatic substitution without discussion. A sick headman was immediately replaced by the next in seniority, just as the head of any group of carriers I had, was replaced without a word if substitution was necessary. Both the ranking of the community by age and the system of personal replacement within the descent group make for a type of participation in community decisions by each villager.

Does this then mean that there are no deliberations at a village level of the type we have defined as conciliar? On evidence that is admittedly inadequate I believe that such meetings occurred, but only in the case of a limited number of situations. The long discussions preceding the moving of a village were once described to me as *ukuteka icilye* (to hold a council). This was a decision demanding agricultural judgment and knowledge of the soil; ritual experience necessary to order and interpret omens and to conduct the village warming ceremonies; and memory of the history of previous moves in the area. On such occasions the company sitting and chatting in the men's shelter or on the verandah of a headman's house would adopt a serious mien, speak in formal tones, and conclude with some kind of pronouncement. It became, in other words, the 'village in council'. I would expect the same type of council to take place before some ritual of village purification, or in the case of the choice of a successor to a dead headman, though I never attended such discussions. In brief the village met in council before events which required the pooling of memories of precedent and succession histories, and of knowledge of the geographical environment and of the rules of ritual. It met also, I believe, when a formal description of a social fact or situation was required. On one occasion a Bisa travelling through a Bemba village had announced in the men's shelter that his ancestors had preceded the Bemba in that country. A bitter quarrel followed which ended with the foreigner announcing that he would 'throw a lion' at the village, the famous cursing by a lion which is much feared by the Bemba. Next morning there was a formal statement by the village men assembled in the shelter to the effect that they recognised that their ancestors had come second on the scene – an end to a conflict publicly announced. Similarly the villagers sitting in their shelter became a council for the public announcement that a child had begun to sit up and was considered ready to be admitted to the society, which was done by ritually feeding it gruel at the shelter.

Finally we must consider the settlement of disputes at village level. Quarrels within the community seemed to me to be frequent – quarrels over broken pots, marital misdemeanours or points of status. When angry shouting broke out, the immediate reaction of the headman was to try to stop the noise. He was not concerned with the rights and wrongs of the case, but merely in preventing a disturbance in the village, in securing at least a cooling-off period. 'Silent you two! Get back to your huts! We don't want fighting in the village. Stop your words'. This was the sort of admonition I heard and in this authoritarian society the headman often succeeded in stopping a quarrel. On this occasion the two young women went sulkily indoors. More serious quarrels involved the older relatives of the combatants, very often the heads of matrilocal family groups, who sprang to the defence of a daughter involved in a fight. Even such shouting matches were sometimes forgotten next day, and people faced with the prospect of walking fifteen or twenty miles to the nearest recognised court, often managed to compose their differences. But where the dispute was still more serious and bitterness continued, the conflicting parties either had to make use of some visiting authority to decide the case, try to settle the matter with the aid of local judges, or take the matter to the chief's court. I heard a legal case tried with all the formality of a chief's court in a small village in which one of the *bakabilo* happened to be spending the night. This royal counsellor, the Chitikafula, was of great seniority, and of royal descent. He called himself a chief. He was immediately asked to try a marriage case.[15] I have myself been asked to act as a judge in a village case. Outside arbitrators were preferred, and this was natural in a village in which all members were linked by kinship ties of some sort or other.

I consider my data on the settling of village disputes inadequate, but it is my impression that, as in the case of the organisation of the village activities, the direct command of the headman was the first mechanism used, but that recognised court procedures came into operation on occasion when a visiting judge became available.

In brief, the regular court-council procedures with its definite behaviour conventions was rarely called into operation, but was used when some public recognition of a social situation was required, such as the formal admission of a child to the village society; when the village was to be moved after the headman had done the necessary rites; or when acknowledging that a man was guilty of an offence. The difference between secular and religious ritual is here a close one. It is my contention that in villages of this size and composition the court-council functions more often to obtain a public expression of views and attitudes than as a means of reaching decisions as to action. This is a hypothesis that requires much more testing than I have been able to give it. It should be possible to list for a series of villages the number of times the men could remember having adopted the necessary conciliar behaviour described as *ukuteka cilye*, and also the number of cases taken to the chief's court each year.

The chiefdom level
By the 1929 Native Authorities Ordinance chiefs were recognised as native authorities, four of them chiefs, the Chitimukulu, Mwamba, Nkula and Makassa,[16] and thirty of them sub-chiefs dependent on the chiefs. The changing status as between chief and chief which the history of the nineteenth century depicts, was therefore ended and the dependency of a particular set of sub-chiefs on three or four chiefs was fixed. The constitution of the council was not defined by the ordinance but native courts were separately recognised, again without any defined constitution.

In the 1930s legal judgments and political decisions were actually made by the same court-council, and many different issues were brought before the chief one after the other and quite at random on any one day. The division I make here between the treatment of legal cases and of all the other different affairs brought before the court-council will seem rather artificial to anyone who has sat for a few hours on the mound where a Bemba chief transacts business.

The chief and his councillors as a court
Court cases were heard in the place where the chief usually sat. No special building was erected for the purpose, but the spot where the court sat was always fixed. For instance in the 1930s both the Chitimukulu and the Mwamba spent the day lying on mats spread on the top of high ant-hills overlooking their respective villages while the Nkula heard cases on a big verandah surrounding his hut.

The composition of the court varied according to the issue discussed. The decision taken was in theory that of the chief and during a hunger year (1933) when Chitimukulu found it impossible to feed many councillors, I have known cases decided by himself and the clerk provided by the Colonial authorities, the latter introducing the 'pleaders' and recording the chief's judgment. This seemed to be the method followed when the case was a very simple one, such as that of a man who claimed he had been promised before witnesses a certain sum for making a garden hedge, but had actually received half the agreed figure. In more difficult cases the Chitimukulu sent for the *bafilolo*, the heads of the capital divisions, *(fitente)* to help to judge the issue. These men always claimed that it was 'their work' to sit in court. In cases involving some dispute concerning the succession to an office, or the right to perform a public ceremony, some of the hereditary councillors, the *bakabilo*, were sent for from their villages. Memory of past events was here essential and I have known a very old councillor, the then Chimba, carried two hours in a litter to give his evidence.

The Bemba chiefs had no fixed panel of judges to help them, but operated an elastic arrangement by which men of status known to have a good memory of the transaction under discussion could be drawn upon. Chiefs feared to give unjust decisions because of the supernatural sanctions involved and it was my impression that they valued the support of councillors and wanted as many suitable people as could be mustered to help them.

Cases heard by Bemba courts were judged according to a well accepted code which most adult informants could recite glibly. They would also give the damages which were claimed in actions between two parties in case of bodily injury, theft, damage to property, marital misdemeanours, sex offences, insults, defamation of character or ritual injury.

The procedure in any civil action was for the appellant or his headman to plead his case and the respondent or his headman to reply. After each statement the councillors quizzed the speakers, challenged their witnesses and attacked the evidence. It was perhaps the councillors' duty to ascertain the facts. But it was up to the authority in charge to sum up the evidence which had been given, perhaps over many hours, and suggest a solution and fix damages or penalties. The man in authority whether he were chief, headman, or man-of-note, was said 'to cut the case', and would possibly have been responsible for persuading the parties to accept it. The Bemba status system makes for ready substitution of older by younger, headman by elder, chief by councillor as we have seen, but this duty of cutting the case is considered as the real expertise of a chief. I was constantly surprised by the way in which a chief who was old and appeared fuddled by beer would sum up a case involving negotiations which went back fifty years or more and that he was often able to do so with greater exactitude than I managed to produce from the entries in my note-book.

This is again a case of judgment by authority with advice, rather than a ruling reached by consensus in a court of equals. According to his temperament, status and the difficulty of the case a chief might decide a case on his own or he might consult his councillors as an equal and ask some such question as *'Bane'* (my friends or mates), 'shall we decide like this?' This is understandable where there is a fear of supernatural punishment in the case of an unjust judgment. Also when a court has no power of enforcing its decisions it is vitally important to get a solution that is accepted by the majority. The councillors often backed up the chief by shouting to the plaintiff and defendant to accept the judgment, but it was the chief who announced it, and it was to him that both sides had to acknowledge the rightness of the verdict, by giving the traditional subjects' salute, that is to say by rolling on their backs and clapping.

There was also a category of crimes which could only be punished by the chief and which could not be brought before any other authority. These were murder and witchcraft, both reckoned as crimes against the chiefdom.[17] All deaths had to be reported to the chief and in case of homicide he arranged the compensation to be paid to the bereaved family. Preliminary tests for witchcraft were done at the village level in pre-colonial days, but only the major chiefs could preside over the final *mwafi* poison ordeal. I was told that *bafilolo* or *bakabilo* would be summoned to help the chief in his judgment in witchcraft cases or to be informed of it.

Lastly outside the schedule of torts and crimes recognised by customary law, were offences against the chief's honour or ritual status, against his person, his property or marital rights, *lese-majeste* in fact. In such cases the chief himself acted as prosecutor and judge, and sentenced the man who had, for instance insulted him obscenely *(okutuka nsele)* or stolen his wife, to brutal mutilations, blinding, the cutting off of tongue, lips, ears or hands. Mutilation seems to have been limited to the greater chiefs, the Chitimukulu, the Mwamba and the Nkula and to have become common when the present dynasty came into power in the early eighteenth century. Praise songs of past Chitimukulus described as hacking and blinding their subjects date from about that time.[18] The punishments evidently became more standardised since there was a definite concept of what was reasonable or unreasonable in the way of mutilations; but chiefs acted on their own with their own executioners. Their councillors were apparently informed of the judgment and could put brakes on a chief who was behaving outrageously by a form of silent opposition known as 'looking dark'.

Besides the main body of customary law known and observed by a chief and his assessors and cases against the king's person in which he inflicted his own penalties at will, a new category of offences was introduced by the colonial administration. These included infringements of regulations such as tax default, failure to build latrines and the use of unlicensed guns. Such offences seemed to be dealt with by the chief and his clerk alone, either because it was becoming increasingly difficult to muster councillors for court work, in a country with such a high emigration rate for males, or because guilt was easy to establish. The penalties, usually fines, were defined, and there were no conflicting parties to reconcile to a judgment given. The most likely explanation of why such offences were dealt with by chief and clerk alone is that chiefs were afraid of the colonial administration on which they were dependent for their position and their salaries, and did not trust their councillors to give the verdicts which the district commissioner wanted. The views of the colonial administration also affected the hearing of cases, and chiefs who were in a better position to know these views than the councillors sometimes intervened personally when cases were being heard by an informal group of *bafilolo* at the capital. In 1933 I saw Sub-chief Luchembe striding across to a group of elders hearing a case brought against a man accused of beating his wife, and summarily imposing the damages he thought advisable. He said to me in explanation 'The Europeans don't understand wife-beating. They will be angry with me for allowing the case to get into the records. I had to finish it quickly.' The situation was new, but the combination of decisions made by a group of elders with those of a chief theoretically with power to 'cut' all cases, was traditional.

The chiefs' council

Political issues to be decided by a chief's council were relatively speaking few. Native treasuries were not established by the 1929 Ordinance, and therefore the native authorities had no decisions to make as to the allocation of funds. No specific schemes for welfare or development were then being administered by the chief and his councillors and hence discussions followed a more or less traditional pattern. Messages came and went between the chief's capital and his villages, and these seemed mainly to be concerned with the state of the harvest of different crops and the general economic situation of the country. These reports were mainly of interest in relation to the availability of tribute and tribute labour, on which the position of the chief and his power of organisation depended. The political issue on which decisions were most frequently made was that of the allocation of headmanships. Men had to apply to their chief for the right to build a village or to succeed to an old headmanship. The colonial government had made the chief's right subject to a proviso that a man could not claim a headmanship unless he could prove that at least ten taxpayers were ready to join him. Some of the decisions on this type of case were made by the chief alone. In 1934 I heard four headmanships granted by the Chitimukulu, here acting as head of his own chiefdom, Lubemba, and these issues were decided in about fifteen minutes each, in the presence of the court clerk and any *bafilolo* who happened to be present. More difficult questions such as the transfer of a village from Chief Makassa's territory to Lubemba, that of Chitimukulu, were heard more formally and by a group of *bafilolo*. Two or three headmanships involved disputes over a succession or were associated with the succession to a liturgical office, such as that of the Mukosa (see p.121). This latter case the Chitimukulu refused to hear without the presence of some of the *bakabilo* and the two contestants had to wait for the arrival of the latter.

Other issues considered of political importance to Bemba councils were the organisation of the chiefdom rituals for sowing, tree-cutting, and first-fruits, and the care of any shrine to dead chiefs which might lie in the area. Such ritual duties were of supreme importance in the case of the Chitimukulu's capital, but each chief, senior or junior, was responsible for organising the ritual required for his own territory and had the help of his councillors for the task.

There were no economic activities carried out on a chiefdom scale with the exception of the collection of tribute at the capital and the organisation of tribute labour for the chief's fields, though I have heard councillors summoned to hear news of a famine in another part of a chiefdom. The military force gathered for raiding purposes seems to have been collected from villages near the capital, or from amongst the followers of specially loyal headmen. There was no military levy from every village in the chiefdom.

Legislation in the sense of discussing and framing new rules of behaviour was not a function of the chiefdom councils although such conciliar activities have been reported by Schapera and Wilson in the case of some South African tribes which had been long in contact with Europeans.[19] Written records of Bemba council meetings however date from recent times only, from the late 1930s and 1940s.

There was no attempt to link the small and dispersed villages together by means of representation on the chiefdom council and indeed such representation was hardly required when common action was not involved.[20] In brief, a chief's council was a body of advisers of no fixed composition, summoned according to the nature of the case discussed. Its function was to allocate positions of authority, to organise the rituals of the chiefdom, to receive messages from different parts of the chiefdom and from the Chitimukulu and other chiefs; and to 'teach', that is to say to remind and advise the chief.

The tribal level

The only Bemba council which existed at a tribal level was the assembly of the king's hereditary councillors, the *bakabilo*. This body had special duties and its debates were governed by a special procedure. It functioned quite apart from the court councils of individual chiefdoms just described including that of the Chitimukulu himself who had his own chiefdom council like any other chief. The *bakabilo* council had no legislative or administrative functions in regard to the tribe as a whole, and it was never a court of appeal from lower chiefdoms. However the term 'tribal council' is, I think, properly applied to the meetings of the *bakabilo*, because they were responsible for maintaining the sacredness or 'divinity' of the Chitimukulu and his ancestral relics and on this the people's whole sense of tribal unity depended. The *bakabilo* acted as ritual specialists responsible for organising the ceremonies connected with the kingship. They examined and judged cases of infringement of the rules which guarded the divinity of the king, whether the errors were committed by commoners or by the Chitimukulu himself. They dealt with questions of succession to the different chieftainships in the country or to the ritual offices at the capital. They listened to disputes between the chiefs of two territories and judged points of status between them. They admonished the king and his royal relatives if they seemed to diverge from the tribal concept of chiefship.

The bakabilo council composition

The composition of the *bakabilo* council was fixed, in marked distinction to the fluid membership of the other Bemba councils. Each senior *mukabilo* had in fact his own drum rhythm used to call him formally to the meetings. The rhythm was beaten on a special type of wooden gong drum kept at the capital.[21] This custom is of interest since drum language was not an important feature of Bemba culture.

All *bakabilo* were of hereditary descent, mainly in the patrilineal line, from former chiefs or their followers. Some could claim up to twenty predecessors in their office whereas the king himself could not reckon more than thirty-three at the most. For instance five called themselves sons of the first Chitimukulu, Chitimuluba, who is said to have led the first group of Bemba from the Congo in the middle of the seventeenth century, and two were reckoned as his paternal grandsons. The total number I listed was ninety-seven but these varied very much in status and only the senior members seemed to be essential when council decisions were required.

The *bakabilo* were divided into groups based on historical precedence and liturgical functions, and these groupings determined their seating at council meetings. There was for instance a division into 'houses' between those responsible for the care of the relics of Chitimuluba, kept in a separate house (eight *bakabilo*); those in charge of the relics of Katongo, a Chitimukulu who succeeded later, after a break in the line (thirty-seven *bakabilo*); the house of the *bashika*, those who had been appointed by Chitimukulus from among their favourites as war lords (thirty-eight *bakabilo*). There was a further subdivision according to ritual function into the *bafingo*, the embalmers of the king's dead body (fourteen); the carriers of the corpse to its grave; and the purifiers of the king and the man in charge of his sacred fire. There was yet another grouping into those entitled to wear plumes, and those not. These overlapping categories determined the seating order at council meetings of different types. They made for a tightly structured, highly institutionalised assembly.

The bakabilo council-procedure

The procedure of the council varied according to the matter in hand. As a court of arbitration the *bakabilo*, or some of their number, could act as a court of inquiry into differences between two chiefs. In such cases the Chitimukulu acted as judge and conciliator and the *bakabilo* functioned as advisers and as remembrancers of the king, reminding him of previous incidents between chiefs of similar status. For instance on 24 May 1933 Lombe, a small chief from Makassa's territory and Shiluipa, a headman with royal connections, were sent to Chitimukulu by their district commissioner because they were continually quarrelling. Lombe, a 'son' of the Chitimukulu's immediate predecessor, Ponde, held the chieftainship, but Shiluipa reckoned himself genealogically senior since, by the Bemba system of positional succession, he was the 'son' of a previous Chitimukulu, Makamba. He claimed that he should be given the labour of several villages as a consequence. In other words the case, as so often in Bemba courts, hinged on a point of status.

Chitimukulu Kanyanta heard the case for an hour and a half on 24 May, but postponed it till the arrival of some of the *bakabilo*. However on 26 May he called for Lombe and scolded him publicly on his court mound, for not honouring his elder — another instance of the common Bemba practice of combining direct action by an authority with a procedure of joint discussion.

On 28 May some of the *bakabilo* arrived and a formal court was opened. It began by a traditional historical mime in which a member of the reciprocal clan of the royal crocodile totem, danced up to the royal mound, threatening the king with his broad-bladed fishing spear. The *mukabilo*, known for historic reasons as the king's dog, defended the Chitimukulu in an imitation of a barking dog. The praise names of *bakabilo* were shouted as they stepped on to the mound and various historical instances were recalled. A formal session of the *bakabilo*-in-court had begun.

Chitimukulu sat on top of his mound with his clerk standing in front of him. Lombe with his followers sat below on his right, with Shiluipa and his men below on the left. The *bakabilo* sat apart in a group – nine or ten in number, under the leadership of the senior present, Lupombwe Chiti, who had status as a 'son' of Chitimueuba, the first ancestor, and Kaseke, one of the hereditary war captains who often acted as the official remembrancer of the king. Chitimukulu made constant appeals to him on questions of history.

To decide the question of status the history of the occupation of the whole of Makassa's territory was teased out. Councillors remembered as children seeing elephant tusks carried as tribute to this chief and that. The relation of the Makassa to all his sub-chiefs was discussed. The case aroused much heat, and Chitimukulu called for a break to let the participants' hearts 'get cool'. Finally with much appealing to the *bakabilo* for support,[22] Chitimukulu gave his judgment. He confirmed that Shiluipa was the genealogical senior and in fact that he had the status of 'father' to Lombe. He then appealed to Lombe to honour his 'father' and to give him the labour of one little village. (The *bakabilo* supported him by murmuring 'Eya! Eya!') Chitimukulu reminded Lombe that he himself was of a junior line which had succeeded to the kingdom. 'God just gave it to us'. Yet nevertheless he, Chitimukulu, gave a village to the *mukabilo* Chimba, and others who came from older lines. He did it out of respect. Lombe should do the same.

Lombe looked sulky, and Chitimukulu started the work of reconciliation by making the whole group laugh. He reminded them of one of his ancestors who, as a young man, refused to honour the Chitimukulu. The latter took arms against him and forced him to flee. Later the young man wanted to return to his home, and went to the Chitimukulu with a child on each shoulder to avert his maternal uncle's wrath. He rolled on the ground in the subjects' salute, which was very difficult to do with the children he was carrying. The court rocked with laughter at the king's graphic account. The king of the legend was so much touched that he gave the young prince back his land. This was apparently taken as an example of a ruler who. forgave although he was not obliged to do so.

Chitimukulu then told Shiluipa that he was not to mind if his 'son' was unruly; and that he would learn manners 'when you have taught him'. Shiluipa must get on with Lombe or it would spoil the land. Laughter broke out again as Chitimukulu told him not to be like the madman who broke his child's arm, a reference to a proverb in which a stupid man felt his child kick him, and reacted so violently that he broke the boy's arm. Shiluipa, mollified, did the salute of acceptance and left. Lombe, more reluctantly, did obeisance too, while Chitimukulu continued to give him practical advice saying 'You only have to allow him to sit on a mat in your presence and give him a bit of cloth. You have got the land. You only have to give him respect *(mucinshi)*.' This example shows how the *bakabilo* support and advise the Chitimukulu in judging an inter-chiefdom dispute and help in the work of reconciliation by laughter and cries of encouragement.

The bakabilo and the maintenance of the kingship

The full council of the *bakabilo* met on several occasions during my visit in 1933-4. It met to arrange for the purification of the Chitimukulu before his prayers to the ancestral spirits at the opening of the annual tree-cutting (March 1933); and to plan and arrange for the ceremonies which precede the building of a new capital. The Chitimukulu had been living in grass huts near his old village site for nearly a year[23] and on 4 April (1933) he announced that he wanted to build his new capital, and sent messengers to summon the *bakabilo*. In the event however, the new capital was not founded till the end of June 1933 owing to a ritual calamity, and to a series of minor succession ceremonies, which had to be carried out before the building of the new capital *(kusokola umushi)* could be begun. The way in which the *bakabilo* dealt with these emergencies and the procedures they followed illustrate clearly the functions of this elite council in maintaining the sacred nature of the kingship on which they believe that the welfare of the whole tribe depends. The length of the discussions was also, I think, typical since the number of liturgical councillors is so large and the possibility of an infringement of ritual rules is so great that one crisis after another seems to occur. Not only the king himself, but any one of the *bakabilo* may be at fault and the chances of a conflict between the letter of the ritual law and the dictates of common sense and political convenience give a particular character to decision-making at this level.

The ritual disaster that faced the *bakabilo* as they assembled at the king's old village site was however no ordinary one. It was suddenly announced to the senior councillors (24 May) that the *mukolo*, or head-wife, of the Chitimukulu, the 'wife of the land', was pregnant. This was most alarming news. The *mukolo* of the king plays an absolutely essential role in the ceremonies by which he is purified before approaching his ancestors in prayer before the founding of the new capital.[24] In order to play her part the head-wife of the Chitimukulu must never have a child. She must perform a ritual act of intercourse with her royal husband before his purification ceremony, but otherwise she should live apart. For this reason it is usual for the king to select an older woman for his *mukolo*, and often one past child-bearing. This Chitimukulu Kanyanta had refused to do. Some six years ago he had chosen, against all advice, a young and very attractive woman as his queen, and it was this wife who had become pregnant – an event thought to put the whole land in extreme ritual danger.

The case was typical of the category of problems with which the *bakabilo* have to deal. The taboos which protect the kingship are so elaborate that infringements are frequent, and they are most often committed by the king himself. It is the duty of the *bakabilo* to establish whether or not a rule has been broken and this is a task of some delicacy when the culprit may be the divine king himself. It is also their task to estimate the degree of danger to the land which is involved, and the best methods of combating it, and finally to conceal the negotiations as well as possible from the ordinary people. On the occasions I mention this was done by long, entirely private discussions by a group of four or five senior councillors who had to decide whether the facts could be brought into the open or not; then there was a court of inquiry into the facts, one form of *cilye;* and finally recommendations for action.

Events in the case moved quickly. The head-wife's pregnancy was announced on 24 May and on the morning of 25 May five senior *bakabilo* sat discussing the matter alone over a pot of beer. They were the Chimba, head of the *bakabilo* and of the 'house' of the buriers of the king, with a royal descent as long as that of the Chitimukulu and the man chosen to succeed him temporarily after his death before the new heir had been selected; the Munuca, 'son' of Chitimuluba and head of his 'house'; the Chitikafula, 'grandson' of Chitimuluba and head of the royal buriers; the Katenda, 'son' of Chitimuluba, and in charge of special relics, and on this occasion the Chikutwe, the senior of the king's hereditary war captains, the *bashika.*

By 29 May the main body of the councillors had arrived and a meeting was called. Though assembled to judge the king and to save the kingship, yet they opened with formal and respectful greetings to him as he lay on his ant hill. Each senior *mukabilo* was hailed by his praise name and the pageant of the mock attack on the Chitimukulu by the head of his reciprocal clan took place, as it did before the Lombe trial (p.117). Having thus made a public representation of their descent, status and prestige the *bakabilo* betook themselves to an open space in front of one of the ritual huts, the *kamitembo.*[25] Here the seating differed from that adopted at the Lombe trial. The 'big four' sat on a mat in the centre with the addition of a fifth, the Nsenshi, while the members of the other 'houses' were seated in groups round them. Chimba sat alone just out of earshot with his followers.

Munuca started in the usual manner by announcing publicly in a sing-song voice the things that everyone knew, but which had not been lifted from the sphere of gossip into that of high politics. 'My friends there are three things which have become difficult: the affair of the royal wife and those of the succession of Mwana Bwalya and Mwangata' (two essential officials whose offices had been made vacant by the breaking of other taboos). He said 'It is time that these things should be brought out into the sun. They have been boiling in our hearts for a long time'.

What everyone knew, did not exist as a tribal issue till it had been announced at a *cilye* meeting. This announcement was carried to the Chimba by one of the traditional messengers, the Mulombelwa (of the king's reciprocal clan and head of the house of Katongo), the Kanungwa, and the Nkolemambwe, one of the chief embalmers of the king. The messengers play an important role in these negotiations. They 'carry words', which may well be offensive, to the Chimba and to the king, but these high personages cannot be angry with them, because they are merely carrying other people's words.

The Chimba was the main interpreter of the ritual situation. After a twenty-minute pause he sent word that he was puzzled and could find no solution. The *mukolo* had performed the purification rite for the king and touched his sacred pot. He did not know who would take 'the chieftainship' back from her person.[26] Perhaps a grandson of the king would do. The whole thing was outside his experience. The *bakabilo* were much concerned and felt the conflict between the desire to get the best ritual solution and the practical difficulties of the occasion. Munuca said 'Here we are with our minds flying one way and another, but the Europeans are hurrying us to make the new capital'. Chitikafula added that they were a great crowd with little to eat as it was a hunger year; they could not wait for long but there were many difficulties. They couldn't nowadays burn the *mukolo* as would have been appropriate. They could send her away but they must first find out whether the woman was pregnant by a lover or, which would have been much worse, by her royal husband.

The *bakabilo* then became a court of inquiry. They sent a messenger to the Chitimukulu to ask whether the child was his, and they interviewed the *mukolo*. The meeting lasted two and a half hours during which time the discussions were carried out in 'Cibemba of under the ground,' or with proverbs and legendary references, for fear passers-by should hear. 'How are we to know the king hasn't thrown the grass over his back?' said one councillor, referring obliquely to a former Chitimukulu, caught in the same predicament, who had smuggled his erring wife out of his enclosure in a bundle of grass cut for thatching his hut. Far from being a council designed to represent the common people, to express their views or to inform them, the *bakabilo* were much concerned with preventing other people from knowing what they were doing.

The *bakabilo* finally decided to accept the evidence that the *mukolo* had committed adultery and declared that she must be sent away. They continued in endless discussions as to the best methods of removing the shadow of the chieftainship from her, and of taking back from her any royal insignia she might have. Such problems, part ritual and part personal, were a constant preoccupation of the councillors. The meeting ended in the early afternoon.

In order to be able to complete the ceremony for founding a new village the *bakabilo* had also to decide who should succeed to the important post of Mwana Bwalya, the man who precedes the king on to the new village site and warms it by

120

sleeping with his wife there; and also to the Mwangataship, a post connected with the ritual purification of the king. The offices of Tompwe and Mukosa were also vacant. Each case involved long discussions between the senior *bakabilo*, the heads of the clans involved and the Chitimukulu. Naturally with a liturgical council of ninety, such succession cases are frequent.

A second meeting of the whole *cilye* took place on 31 May when the Munuca again made a formal announcement, this time that the *bakabilo* would disperse for a fortnight on account of shortage of food. 'We don't want to decide things in a hurry – any old way' *(pambilibili)* he said. Again everyone knew of the decision to postpone the meeting, but it had to be formally announced in order to become an act of the council.

The bakabilo and the organisation of ritual

The same type of procedure was followed when the councillors reassembled to build the capital at the end of twenty-four days. There were still many issues to be settled. According to Bemba belief ancestral spirits can only be approached for help after an act of ritual intercourse by a man and a woman and, in the case of important chiefs, between a man and a special ritual wife. The position of the Chitimukulu is even more complicated, since he must be purified before access to the tribal spirits by means of a simultaneous act carried out in three ritual huts by the king, the Chimba and the Chikutwe, the head of the war captains. Hence, at all important religious ceremonial at the capital, each of these three dignitaries must have a 'wife' in the right ritual category, to go through the ceremony with him. The 'wife' problem seemed to involve endless discussion of, and search for, suitable partners. Again, for ceremonies of succession to a *mukabilo*ship two women might be involved, the widow of the dead man must have the 'death' taken off her by sleeping with his brother or some kinship equivalent, and the successor once selected, must be provided also with a wife suitable for ritual purposes. Hence the number of secondary decisions to be taken in relation to any part of the royal ritual. Lastly shortage of funds, and the unwillingness of the Chitimukulu to spend his government salary on rewarding the *bakabilo*, led to further anxious discussions. Which of the liturgical specialists were absolutely vital to the performance of the ritual in time of money shortage? The *bakabilo* were constantly involved in difficult decisions based on precedent, in conflicts over precedent, and often in a kind of battle of memories between two antagonistic councillors, ending with some kind of compromise between the paradigm of the royal ritual and the stark realities pro-duced by shortage of money and time.

The conciliar procedure was in all cases similar, that is to say there were private meetings of the three or four senior *bakabilo*, with or without the Chitimukulu, followed by formal, almost ritualised statements made by the Chitimukulu to his *bakabilo*, or by the head of the *bakabilo* to the main body of the councillors. Until a formal statement of the problem was made, the council could not go into action.

Thus on 24 June (1933) the Chitimukulu began to summon his *bakabilo* for the final rites for the new capital. He had chosen, but not revealed, the name of his new head wife. The important office of the Mwangata had been filled. There remained the question of Mwana Bwalya, the official warmer of the new capital, who had not yet been chosen although the 'death' had been taken off the widow of the last holder of the title. Again there was one of the endless delays which hold up Bemba ceremonial. On 25 June it was announced that no-one would succeed to the office of Mwana Bwalya since the previous holder had been gored by a buffalo! People were afraid of bad luck attaching to the office. The inner ring of *bakabilo* was called to the chief's house to be informed of the difficulty and after discussion it was agreed that the head of the special group of men responsible for 'warming' the new capital should be sent on a two-day journey to force a man to take the office. In the intervening delay all senior *bakabilo* spent part of the day (25 June) sitting with the king, discussing the past, remembering the doings of past Chitimukulus, and particular events such as a plague of locusts in one king's reign and its probable supernatural causes. Such discussions were thought valuable in themselves, and are in fact necessary in a system in which political authority is so largely based on long lines of succession and the keeping, or failing to keep, of a very complex series of ritual rules.

On 27 June four senior *bakabilo* were again called to the chief's house to discuss the payments to be made to those in charge of lighting his new fire. Shortage of money was the issue, and it was suggested that the number of ritual specialists involved was too large. It could be cut by half so that everyone could have a few shillings. Here was a typical conflict between practical necessity and the ideal of ritual perfection which occurs in a system of royal ritual as complex as that of the Bemba. It was solved in a way which is common in pre-literate societies, by accusing someone of falsifying history. Someone said that it was only the Chimba, the ancient head of the *bakabilo*, himself absent at the moment, who insisted on so many ritual specialists being present. He was always 'spoiling the past' *(Ukuonaula fintu fya kale)*. Where there is no written record of past precedent, one way out of a practical difficulty is to deny the validity of a particular version of precedent.

By the evening the Chimba was carried in on a litter, and the Chitimukulu summoned him and the other three senior *bakabilo* and merely made a formal request in the singsong of ritual to have his capital built.

On 28 June a meeting of the whole *cilye* was called. The Chitimukulu's request was formally announced to the assembly, now some forty or fifty strong. The request was carried by the messengers to the Chimba, again sitting apart and for twenty minutes violent vituperation was heard in the distance. The messengers brought back a suitably edited version of the Chimba's views which was taken to mean that he had accepted, with reluctance, all the many compromises proposed. 'The affair is finished' shouted the Chitikafula, and everyone got up.

Later in the morning the Chitimukulu called the Chimba and the official messengers and explained formally the delay over the Mwana Bwalya. The Chimba scolded him violently for breaking rules, for choosing the wrong head wife, re-instating the wrong Mwangata, and for showing meanness over his rewards to the *bakabilo*. The then Chimba was a cantankerous old man, but it was the duty of his office to fight against the breaking of ritual rules, and perhaps his custom, after abusing an erring sovereign, to consent as he did on this occasion.

In the afternoon Chitimukulu again summoned the Chimba and the messengers and announced the name of the new head-wife, a suitably elderly woman. The party began to discuss the order in which the men of the house of Katongo should greet the Chitimukulu after his night of purification – one of the duties of this 'house'. I was implored to write the order down in my book so that there would never be quarrels again! On 7 July, forty-three days after the first council called to consider the matter, the building of the new capital began.

I have chosen one particular set of ritual activities to illustrate the functioning of the Bemba tribal council, but I could have selected a number of others, such as the organisation of the Chitimukulu's tree-cutting rites, the burial of the king, or the installation of his successor. All such ceremonies require long discussion and organisation, an aspect of ritual to which Firth has frequently drawn our attention. Even the feeding of large bodies of men is difficult in an area where all loads have to be carried on the head. In the hunger year of 1933 I described a ceremony postponed for a month because of food shortage, and my diary records constant discussions over the division of beer and other forms of food. Again, the large number of ritual specialists involved in the transactions caused complications and delays – delays while men and women were fetched by messengers on foot;[27] while succession ceremonies for lesser luminaries had to be waited for; while men were purified; while substitutes were looked for in the case of illness or refusal to act. The very complexity of the ritual is also a difficulty in a preliterature culture like that of the Bemba. Mistakes were made, and endless discussions followed as to their possible rectification. It was, for instance, remembered at the last moment that the newly installed *mukolo* could not emerge from the ritual hut in which she had spent the night until she stepped over a sacrificed sheep. The king had forgotten to provide a sheep so that she had to remain incarcerated for twenty-four hours!

But the numbers of the *bakabilo* of course increased the survival rate of the royal ritual since so many people gained status and prestige by continuing to perform it. Some ninety to a hundred important political personages were thereby committed to the ideology of kingship. The ceremonial greeting of the king, the recitation of praise names and of events in tribal history (see p.122), and the historic mimes, became symbolic expressions of a whole system of political values. Individual ceremonial acts became impossible for practical reasons, were forgotten, modified or omitted, but the pageant went on because so many actors were involved.

From a practical point of view the ceremonial also strengthened the position of the *bakabilo* when they felt it necessary to criticise or oppose the Chitimukulu; an alarming task, one supposes, in the days of the powerful kings of the nineteenth century. Their numbers increased their hold over the Chitimukulu and I watched his increasing submission to their demands as they assembled in the capital. The very procedure of the council gave gathering confidence, with its preliminary meetings of senior *bakabilo* in secret sessions, followed by formal statements to the full meeting of the facts which it had been decided to bring into the open; then the sieving mechanism of the reference to and from the Chimba, the ritual specialist on whom the Chitimukulu depended so much for the divinity of his kingship; and finally the 'carrying of words' to the king himself.

I have called the *bakabilo* a tribal council because they existed to maintain the paramountcy of a king who had, until the arrival of Arab guns in the middle of the nineteenth century, little other support in the form of wealth or arms. The *bakabilo* corrected the king but protected the kingship; they opposed the Chitimukulu, saluted him and covered up his mistakes.

It is appropriate also to speak of a tribal council when a body of men act as regents for a dead king, choose and install the new heir, decide on succession cases in all the lesser Bemba chiefdoms, and hear disputes between chiefs as in the case of the Lombe–Shiluipa case described earlier. The *bakabilo* also perform the installation rituals for chiefs and for other *bakabilo* all over the country.

Finally I have used the term tribal council because the *bakabilo* regard themselves as such. They call themselves 'we the Babemba' and speak of the interests of the tribe as a whole, and it was this fact which impressed me so strongly during my first and second visits and which I attempted to describe in a paper prepared for the then colonial administration.[28]

But of course the *bakabilo* council, as it was then constituted, provided for no participation by other members of the tribe. Commoners, and even headmen were purposefully excluded from its deliberations. Its language was secret; and there was no attempt to represent the views of the villagers at its meetings. This was not a need felt in pre-colonial times since in the dispersed population of small villages there were no common activities to be organised or new legislation to discuss. The commoner participated in the organisation of village activities through his position as a kinsman of the headman and a potential substitute for his immediate senior in the local community, but the decisions taken at his own chiefdom council or by the *bakabilo* were not his concern. He visited the capital as a tribute labourer or a litigant. He was interested in the happenings in the chief's enclosure, and anxious that the public ritual should be correctly performed, but he referred to the appointment of a new Chitimukulu or a new chief as an event of great importance to him, but over which he had no possible control. Even in 1957, after all the political stirrings that had been caused by the controversy over the Federation of the two Rhodesias and Nyasaland, headmen of villages seemed amazed when I asked them whether they thought they should be represented on their chiefdom council. 'We are only villagers' was their immediate reply.

The Bemba conciliar system had obviously to be radically changed if it was to conform to the British pattern of local councils as bodies allocating funds raised locally, controlling social services and passing local by-laws, with territorial units large enough to make such activities economically feasible.

Modern developments of the Bemba conciliar system

The Native Authorities Ordinances of 1929 and 1936

The British administration which was set up in Northern Rhodesia in 1924 proceeded to recognise the existing African authorities and to fix the boundaries of their territories. The Native Authorities Ordinance of 1929 constituted Bemba chiefs as 'native authorities', but it did not define the constitution and functions of their councils; nor was the existence of the *bakabilo* then suspected. Native treasuries were not constituted at the time and therefore the authorities had little stimulus to start to finance new enterprises. Legislation had never been a function of the Bemba councils, but district commissioners began to encourage chiefs to make by-laws. Native courts were established by a separate ordinance in the same year. The jurisdiction of the courts was defined, but there was no attempt to separate the judiciary from the executive, or to prescribe the composition of the courts. Court records were inspected by district commissioners but a European judicial adviser to the courts was not appointed till 1948. Cases continued to be heard by chiefs' court-councils with the elasticity of composition characteristic of the traditional system. The judiciary began to be separated from the executive at the central level when a judicial sub-committee of the Bemba government was set up (1955) and much of the hearing of court cases at the capital had been devolved onto a special official, the Secretary Councillor, or *Mwanangwa*, by 1957 when I last visited the area.

By the 1936 Native Authorities Ordinance, native treasuries were introduced, although they had then very small funds available to them.[29] The authorities were however, given power to levy local taxes. But the salaries of chiefs were to be paid by the treasuries and those of some other officials. These included some of the senior *bakabilo*, the Chimba, Katenda, Chitikafula and Chipashya who were thus recognised as part of the Bemba government for the first time. In fact they became minor civil servants as well as being ritual specialists. The importance of African councils was recognised in this ordinance in that it was decreed that a 'native authority' was to consist in future of 'chiefs with their councils',[30] rather than chiefs alone. The functions and composition of the chiefdom councils were still not defined.

The administration was, however, concerned to develop an effective central tribal council which, according to the colonial policy of the time, was to elect members to an African Provincial Council, in this case the Central Areas Council which included the Kasama, Mpika, Chinsali and Luwingu Districts, and this council in turn was to elect two members each to an African Representative Council set up in 1946 with power to appoint two members to the Central Legislative Council of Northern Rhodesia by 1948.

An effective tribal council was therefore seen as an essential step in the building of this pyramidal structure. It was also considered an important means of centralising tribal government. The difficulty was however obvious. Was the British government to use the *bakabilo*, the ritual specialists who formed the existing tribal council, or to appoint a new body? They had to choose between a group of councillors who were uneducated in the modern sense of the term, but were experienced in the traditional tribal administration and had a real sense of tribal welfare; and younger and more educated men without this experience, and often without these attitudes. Moreover men who were educated, or even literate, were rare at this point in Northern Rhodesia's history. The administration's decision was a compromise, as in other parts of Africa. The senior *bakabilo* were appointed to all the council bodies set up by the government, but so also were Africans with specialist knowledge of one kind or another, and representatives of the African Welfare Association, a group composed mainly of the lower grades of African civil servants.

Attempts to centralise Bemba government

The administration had worked for some years to build up the position of the Chitimukulu as a superior authority and to turn him from a divine king into a territorial administrator with considerable powers. He was encouraged to tour the whole country, which would have been ritually impossible in pre-colonial days, when two chiefs were not allowed to meet owing to the belief that 'one chiefship threatens another'. The senior *bakabilo* sometimes went with the Chitimukulu to hear judicial cases on appeal – another innovation. In 1956 the Chitimukulu was even asked to hold an inquiry into the maladministration of a senior chief, the Nkula, who was formerly a nearly autonomous ruler. He was also expected to deal with the prophetess Lenshina [31] and her followers on behalf of his whole country.

Centralisation proceeded rapidly after the 1936 Ordinance. A meeting of all Bemba chiefs from the Kasama area and five outlying districts was held in 1938. This meeting of chiefs was another revolutionary step, although it was one which was welcomed by many of the younger chiefs who said it was a pleasure to meet brothers whom they had not been allowed to see for so many years!

In 1948 the legislative powers of the subordinate authorities were withdrawn and the 'Superior Authority' became the sole legislative body for the area. It was reconstituted in 1949 to include six *bakabilo* and eight departmental councillors with specialist knowledge of different aspects of the work.

Experiments in the formation of a new tribal council seem to have begun in 1949. There is a record of a meeting of chiefs, hereditary officials and others in

126

1954. It discussed such practical matters as court fees, marriage regulations, nutrition and a Bemba national school. In 1955 it met again under the new title of *Lilamfya* (see note 6) when thirteen chiefs, 'numerous' hereditary councillors and nominated members were present. In 1956 it appointed sub-committees on judicial affairs, administration and natural resources, and it discussed such matters as self-government, land, forest reserves, and salaries – that is to say political as well as administrative issues. Meanwhile the Chitimukulu had been made chairman of a small 'cabinet' composed of six *bakabilo*, seven departmental councillors, and the Secretary-Councillor. It was known as the *Ncenje,* a word meaning a pointed thing or apex of a hut. It was formally constituted in 1951 and was to meet 'regularly every Friday' and to have power to make decisions between the yearly meetings of the *Lilamfya* council. This was centralised government indeed!

Were the *bakabilo* any use on a new type tribal council and executive committee? The administration seemed pleased with them. They were, after all, trained to manage the Chitimukulu and other authorities, and this experience was useful. A government report of 1938 refers to them as 'men of marked ability and while these survive and retain their wisdom and tact, the Paramount's dealings with his subjects will remain cordial'.[32] The superior authority was said to have 'a flair for central government' (1952). This was of course an authoritarian society and measures decided at *Ncenje* or *Lilamfya* meetings, chaired by the district commissioner had, not unnaturally, a good chance of being put through with the help of hereditary councillors. African peoples, in the first stages of the introduction of local government, have often advanced more quickly in the case of monarchies with trained personnel than in the case of segmentary societies. They tend however to fall behind when it becomes necessary to enlist public support.

Did the new organisation develop any contacts with the villages, which played no part in traditional tribal politics? The administration tried to inaugurate a parish system in 1947. This was designed to allow men to move out of their villages and cultivate on their own. There were one or two attempts to hold meetings for the headmen of parishes by Chikwanda in 1956 and by Chipashya in 1957, but the parish system made small villages even smaller, and the administration evidently gave more thought to tribal administration than to village representation.

Did new conflicts develop in chiefdom councils when these were given control of their own treasuries? My evidence is not good enough. The funds available were small and the possibilities of development limited in this barren province of Northern Rhodesia, so it is difficult to answer the question. In any case the administration of the Bemba country has been changed and rechanged so often that the picture is confused. The government's strong move towards centralisation after 1936 began to be criticised in 1957 and reversed in 1958. In 1961 all native authorities were placed under a Ministry of Local Government at Lusaka and chiefs and hereditary councillors ceased to be paid. The *bakabilo* will presumably continue to act as a council of ritual experts as long as the Chitimukulu remains as a symbol of Bemba unity. The funerals of the last two holders of the title were attended by President Kaunda and other officials and well reported in the local press. But it is difficult to discover whether the Paramount and his subsidiary chiefs are still performing any local government functions. If their former duties have been taken over by the political party officials and they have no salaries or other sources of income for the reward of their councillors, the traditional elite council will certainly disappear.

Notes

My thanks are due to the Wenner-Gren Foundation for generous help towards secretarial assistance on this and other projects.

[1] It is likely that the practice of sending to higher courts cases that have proved insoluble at a lower court became much more systematised when the British authorities gave formal recognition to chiefs' and sub-chiefs' courts in 1929.

[2] See A.I. Richards, 1969.

[3] The North-Eastern Rhodesia Order in Council. See L.H. Gann, 1958, p.92.

[4] Ibid. p.92

[5] See A.I. Richards, 1935.

[6] The title the Bemba chose was *Lilamfya*, the name of an ancient war oracle, a horn which moved in one direction or another when the blood of a human victim was poured on it. This rather inauspicious title was defended by the councillors whom I visited in 1957. They said the British administration had insisted they chose a name of something that existed in the past, and this oracle had not been used for many years!

[7] A large court-council is a mark of a chief's popularity and sagacity.

[8] I.Schapera, 1956, p.42.

[9] In Great Britain the parties to a case can appeal to a higher court against a judgment given in a lower court if they think the first decision is unjust. In Bemba country it was not the plaintiffs who appealed, but the lower authority himself who lost confidence in his own judgment and appealed to his next superior to take the risk. The word used was *twafilwa*, 'we have failed' or been unequal to the task.

[10] Schapera, 1956, p.210.

[11] The current British practice of inserting 'you know' at the end of each sentence is somewhat different since it is often intended to make speech sound less formal, grammatical and elitist.

[12] Kasaka and Kampamba in the Chinsali district.

[13] A comparison of the headmanships in two chiefdoms in 1934 showed that 49% and 42% respectively of the headmen were newly appointed, whereas 51% and 58% respectively had inherited their offices. See Richards, 1939, p.412, Table D.

[14] Kuper, 1970.

[15] At the village of Canda we Eiya in April, 1933.

[16] A 'son' of the Chitimukulu and not a member of the royal clan, but reckoned a senior chief by the British since he ruled over a large territory.

[17] Under the 1929 Ordinance, murder and witchcraft and cases involving Europeans were removed from the jurisdiction of Bemba chiefs.

[18] Mutilation is said to have been introduced from the Mambwe country in the time of Chitimukulu Chileshye whose accession is roughly dated as 1750.

[19] I. Schapera, 1970; M. Wilson (nee Hunter) 1936: 165, 396.

[20] Sub-chief Chikwanda had started a meeting for headmen in his chiefdom in 1957 as the result of a course in local government he had attended in Torquay. It was considered a most

extraordinary activity by the people concerned.

[21] Also at the capital of Chief Mwamba who was claiming equal importance with the Chitimukulu at the time of the arrival of the first missionaries in the country. I heard these drum beats used at Mwamba's village to call the councillors whom he also referred to as *bakabilo* in 1934.

[22] In such phrases as 'Am I not right, my friends?'

[23] Because he had angered his councillors who refused to do the necessary rites for the founding of a village.

[24] See A.I. Richards, 1969.

[25] The sacred store-house of the king. See A.I. Richards, 1969 p.29.

[26] When a man or woman dies some individual reckoned as their kinship equivalent must sleep with the surviving spouse to take the presence of the dead person off him or her.

[27] For instance the two days' journey to fetch a new Mwana Bwalya held up proceedings for four days (see p.122).

[28] A.I. Richards, 1935.

[29] £1,303 to be divided among six districts in 1938 according to the Report appointed to inquire into the financial and economic position of Northern Rhodesia, 1938, p.114.

[30] Annual Report for Native Affairs, 1936, p.29.

[31] Alice Lenshina was a Bemba prophetess who broke away from the Church of Scotland mission in 1953 and founded the Lumpa Church. Her followers came into conflict with the colonial authorities before Zambia became independent. In 1964 they waged a holy war in which 700 people were killed.

[32] Annual Report for Native Affairs, 1938, p.45.

THE DEVELOPMENT OF TOWN COMMITTEES
IN AHAFO,WESTERN GHANA [1]

By A. F. Robertson

In the development of modern centralised states it seems inevitable that the elabor-ation of a detailed constitution for central authorities should precede the growth of a uniform system of local authorities. It is salutory to recall that whereas the establishment of our British parliament is lost in myth, our Parish Councils are of very recent origin and are by no means fully developed constitutionally. This unevenness in political growth is not solely a logical progression over time from central to local control. The organisation of local government confronts a basic dilemma: there is the need for a system which is nationally uniform, but to be effective the system must accommodate to the exigencies of local variation.

In Africa, this problem has been heightened by the experience of colonial rule and the transition to independent statehood. British authorities often found it more expedient to govern the various peoples of a territory discretely, through their own leaders and indigenous systems, than to press for integral local government with a national identity. Constitutional development came piecemeal to the various region-al units, and when coalescence within a unified national system became imperative at independence, their disparity was often uncomfortably obvious. In the Gold Coast (now Ghana) it was not until 1946 that Ashanti joined the Colony in a single legislative council, and as late as 1954 when elected representatives from all regions first sat together in Accra.

The late 1940s and early 1950s were years of economic and political unrest with profound consequences for the constitutional development of Ghana. Hostility to colonial government and its close association with traditional authority fostered a new idealism, particularly among the younger and better-educated, which found expression in the growth of political parties and a vigorous independence move-ment. In 1948 the government was obliged to take rigorous measures to contain an outbreak of cocoa disease. This triggered off rioting which, in turn, obliged the colonial authorities to undertake a critical appraisal of the constitutional develop-ment of the country. An all-African commission of enquiry was appointed from among Legislative Council members, and its recommendations were published in 1949. On this basis a series of reports, plans and ordinances subsequently sought to translate the new ideals of democracy and nationhood into practicable constitutional terms.[2]

It was intended that a new local authority system should be established, which would 'penetrate' to the towns and villages of Ghana, allowing ordinary people to participate in the choice and control of their own community services and amenities. It was hoped that eventually this system would subsume pre-existing institutions in a nationally uniform way. However, the constitutional changes of the 1950s could hardly be accomplished by revolution. Much compromise was necessary; democratic idealism had to be tempered with a recognition of the enduring authority of the chiefs and the continuing need for local political officers. While a modern, integrated system of government was essential to independent statehood it was incumbent upon planners and legislators, in the face of great regional and tribal diversity, to seek formulations which were the lowest common denominators of local variation. When it came to organising the town, village and area Committees the government was prepared to offer only the most general formal framework, anticipating that they would grow where there was sufficient local enthusiasm, spontaneously accommodating themselves to local circumstances.

The single, secular local authority has not yet appeared. Instead, government in the Districts of Ghana remains vested in an historical accumulation of three separate but interrelated structures. Originally, in the Akan states, there were the chiefs and their traditional councils; in colonial times they were obliged to yield much of their authority to the District Officers, and again, in the 1950s, both had to adjust to the new Local and District Council system. For a short but momentous period local government generally was subsumed by the political party organisation. In this complicated share-out it seems that the town Committees have been obliged to glean whatever authority they could find.

In this essay I shall describe the development of town and village Committees in Ahafo, a District in western Ghana. (see Fig.1). In the circumstances, it is the extraordinary vigour of their growth which calls for some explanation. Statutory specifications and official encouragement have been relatively weak, nevertheless Committees have become firmly institutionalised in all the towns and larger villages of Ahafo. What are the reasons for this rapid progress? How and in what form have the Committees become established? What tasks do they perform, and how?

In attempting to answer these questions it would seem inadequate only to pursue a series of static, institutional specifications of what a Committee is and does. I believe it is more fruitful to examine such a decision-making body in the widest political context, and to understand the various limitations which constrain its organisation and operation. Taking this point of view, it is less relevant to define the Committee in terms of its own internal structure and immediate actions than to understand its status and role in a much wider political system.

I shall label the organisational and operational features of the Committee respectively as its *legitimacy* and its *competence*. As two aspects of the same thing they are interdependent, and changes in one can certainly be related to effects in the other. A change in the legitimacy of a Local Council will, for example, alter its competence. To understand the legitimacy of the Committee we must know the authority it has to make decisions and execute its consequent responsibilities. A decision-making body derives its legitimacy from its formal relationships within a wider political system, ranging from the 'public' which it serves, to the limits of the polity in which it is involved – for example, the state. In some societies the authority derived from superior political levels may be very limited, in which case it would be advisable to pay particular attention to the other side of the coin, the relationship between the council and the community to which it is responsible. Authority, let us remember, is as likely to be conferred 'from below' as 'from above'.

I have felt obliged to view the development of town Committees in Ahafo in the context of Ghanaian government at large, a political compass with which the social anthropologist is not altogether familiar. In the course of the essay I shall consider the Committees in terms of their statutory specifications and their relations with central authorities, as well as with the Local Councils, political parties, and so on. When it comes to discussing the Committees vis-a-vis the townspeople we shall encounter the complex question of representation and the conflict of interests which animates decision-making. Essentially as a product of these considerations of legitimacy we may eventually come to understand something of the limitations on the internal organisation of the Committees, their *composition.*

Perhaps the most apt vernacular (Twi) translation of *legitimacy* is *tumi,* a common word with a wide semantic range. It is not entirely appropriate in that it is more associated with power than with authority, and in a more absolute than relative sense. I have often heard it used with reference to the state, the District Officer and the higher traditional authorities. Within the town, I have occasionally heard it applied to the chief, but the fact that it is rarely used of the Committee may be a just reflection of its political significance. *Competence,* with its inherent notions of rights and duties, could well be rendered as *adwuma* in Twi. Although the Committee may lack a full measure of *tumi,* no one would deny that it had *adwuma.*

To persist, a decision-making body must have recognised rights and duties, there must be issues over which it has accepted *competence.* It may be useful to distinguish internal and external competence: on the one hand the Committee is concerned with issues raised by community members and with making and executing decisions on their behalf; on the other hand it makes and transmits community decisions to other, external authorities and, reciprocally, passes on instructions from outside to the people. Here, at length, we are concerned with Committee activities, and in a final section I shall examine matters of *procedure.* Again I shall avoid limiting attention to the Committee itself and attempt to see the

132

decision making with which it is concerned in a comprehensive frame. As a guide I shall refer to three typical phases in the decision-making process: the raising of the issue, the making of the decision, and means of assuring that it is put into effect.

Taking such a wide conspectus on the development of Ahafo town Committees poses certain problems of presentation. I shall begin with a brief introduction to Ahafo and then outline the formal legal specifications of the Committee. At the same time I shall indicate in very general terms the ways in which these specifications have been interpreted in reality in Ahafo. I shall then discuss Committee growth in terms of relationships with central authorities, the District Officers, the Local Council, the traditional authorities, the political parties and, finally, the townspeople at large. I shall then examine the decision-making procedures. I am aware that readers who are unfamiliar with the government organisation and recent history of Ghana may find the various names and events mentioned somewhat confusing. As a guide I have included two tables, 1 is a brief chronology of central and local government affairs, and 2 a diagram of government structures in Ahafo, roughly as they were in 1968.

Finally, it seems appropriate to comment here on the timing and management of the research on which this essay is based. I lived in Goaso, Ahafo (see Fig.1), for a year, 1968-9, some two years after the coup d'etat which ousted the government of Kwame Nkrumah, and during the inter-regnum of the police—military National Liberation Council. Although I was unable to observe party politics in action the atmosphere of candour and self-criticism prevalent in Ghana at the time provided many useful insights into problems of government. I was very fortunate in securing the friendship and co-operation of the well-informed and very professional District Administrative Officer of Ahafo, Mr. E. C. Kotey. He provided me with introductions to the people and the Committees of Ahafo, and they in turn bore my intrusions with remarkable good-will. I also enjoyed the advantage of liberal access to local government documents.

Perhaps the greatest problem in studying the Committees was my own inadequacy in the vernacular. Another difficulty was that every community is a complex world of its own, and an adequate understanding of the issues, procedures and personalities at a particular meeting depends upon more intricate knowledge of local affairs than can be acquired in the limited time available for research. At the same time, it seemed essential to visit as many Committees as possible, and in this I encountered many practical problems. Communications were, at times, extremely difficult, and often it proved impossible to get sufficient notice of a meeting. It was extremely frustrating to arrive shortly after business had been completed. I tried to overcome some of these problems by concentrating my efforts on Goaso, my home town, by using tape-recorders and two assistants, by talking at length, before and after meetings, with the participants, and by including questions about Committee affairs in the interviews I held throughout the District. I visited all the main towns in Ahafo and tried to get some idea of the extent of organisational variation, but I

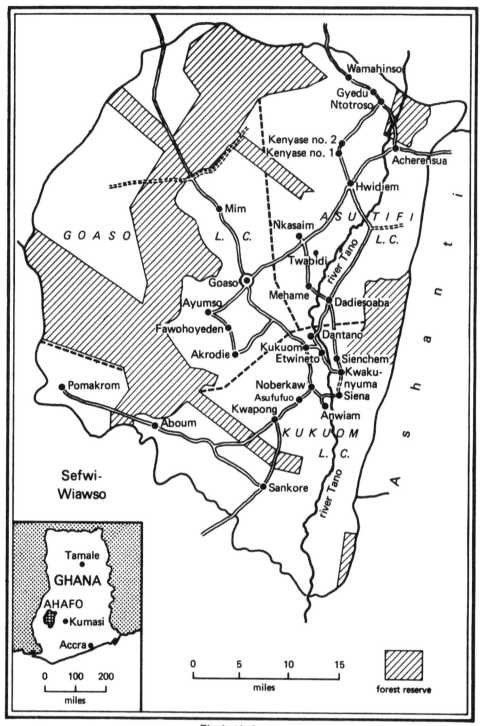

Fig. 1. Ahafo

am certainly aware of the limitations of my knowledge. My main complaint must be that no sooner had I begun to understand some of the complex problems of Ahafo, than I had to take my leave.

The Committees in Ahafo

Ahafo is a heavily forested, cocoa-producing District in western Ghana. It was part of Ashanti until 1959, when it was included in the new Brong-Ahafo Region; this is 'the rural boom area of Ghana' (Caldwell, 1967: 128), its population young, heterogeneous and increasing at a rate far in excess of the national average. Today, Ahafo is a distinct Traditional Area, an Administrative and Local Authority District, a Regional Planning Area, and an organisational unit for most Ministries, government

Table 1. Chronology of developments in the government of Ghana

Central government	Local government	Ahafo affairs
1901: Ashanti annexed		1898: Ahafo chiefs sign British protection treaty
		1912. Commissioner's office established
	1924: Native courts established	
	1925: Provincial councils of chiefs established	
	1935: Ashanti Confederacy estd. Native Authorities set up	1935: Ahafo comes under Kumasi N.A.
1946: Ashanti and Colony united in one Legislature	1944: N.A. Finance Boards set up	
1948: Riots over cocoa disease		
1949: Convention People's Party estd.		
1951: 1st C.P.P. government elected	1951: new Local Authorities estd. Local and District Councils, separate judicial system	1952: 1st Ahafo Local Council estd.
		1953: 9 town Committees registered
1954: C.P.P. government re-elected		
1956: C.P.P. government re-elected		

Table 1. *(continued).*

Central government	Local government	Ahafo affairs
1957: INDEPENDENCE	1957: Greenwood report: further L.A. changes	1957: Ashanti allegiance terminated: State Council of chiefs established
1959: Separate Brong Ahafo region cut out of Ashanti		
1960: Ghana becomes a Republic	1961: Local Govt. and Chieftaincy Acts; separate traditional and secular councils	1961: Now 28 town/village Committees
1964: Ghana becomes one-party (C.P.P.) state	1962: Party-appointed District Commissioners	1962: Ahafo L.C. divided into Asutifi and Asunafo Local Councils
1966: Police-military coup d'etat: C.P.P. govt. overthrown, National Liberation Council takes over	1966: Local government system suspended, management Committees appointed. Civil servant Admin. officers appointed	1966: Asunafo L.C. divided into Goaso and Kukuom Local Councils State Council of chiefs abolished
1969: New constitution approved New (civilian) Progress Party government elected	1969-70: preparations for establishment of new Local Authority System	(1968-9, duration of research project in Ahafo.) Now 69 town/village Committees

agencies and voluntary organisations. It also comprises two parliamentary constituencies.

Within Ahafo the most distinctive socio-political unit is the town. This is a nucleus of permanent settlement varying in population from less than 100 to as much as 7,000 (Mim, see Fig. 1). Goaso, the administrative centre and the town to which I shall refer most frequently, had a population of 3,554 in 1959. Settlement in Ahafo has built up around 28 of these nuclei, each of which is a politically distinct unit referred to in traditional terms as a *stool (akonnua).* Each stool has under its control a specific area of land, including several villages and temporary farming camps. It has its own traditional Council consisting of the chief and between three and twelve elders (see App. B). Today, the stool Council is expected to concern itself with the spiritual welfare of the people, with matters of land tenure, and with the maintenance of peace and progress. The subject villages of each stool also have their own headmen and 'elders' but their authority in traditional affairs is more restricted.

Each town and village is entitled to form a Development Committee consisting of seven to eleven representatives chosen from the community, with the chief or headman as chairman. It is a non-judicial body and has important practical tasks to perform. The Local Councils have been unable, mainly for budgetary reasons, to develop intensively the amenities in all the towns and villages in their charge. If a community requires a new school, or road, or better sanitary service, it can ensure more speedy provision by collecting money and doing the job itself by communal labour. Achievements have been considerable; from time to time the Ghanaian press reports communities which have installed pipe-borne water or an electricity generator. However it is clear that Committees in some parts of Ghana have been more active and successful than in others, and that only part of the explanation for their growth rests in the official prescription of their functions.

Provision for the establishment of Committees was first made in the Local Government Ordinance (no.29) of 1951. I shall quote the relevant sections in full:

44. (1) Subject to the provisions of this Ordinance and of the Instrument, and with prior approval of the Minister, a [local] council may appoint such town, village, or area committees within the area of its authority as it may deem necessary or expedient, and may delegate to a town, village, or area committee so appointed, with or without restrictions or conditions, as it thinks fit, any function exercisable by the council with respect to the area of authority of the town, village, or area committee, except the power of making bye-laws, approving annual estimates, levying a rate or issuing a precept, or of borrowing money.

(2) The number of members of a town, village or area committee appointed under this section, their term of office and method of selection, and the area within which the committee is to exercise its authority, shall be specified by the council.

46. Every committee or joint committee appointed under the provisions of this part of the Ordinance shall report its proceedings to the council ... appointing such committee.' (Laws of the Gold Coast, vol. II Cap 64, Accra, December 1951.)

The Ordinance also specified that the Local Councils could lay down standing orders governing the place, frequency and conduct of Committee meetings.

Goaso formed the first Committee in Ahafo in October 1952, an early start attributable to the location of the Administration and the Local Council in the town and to the interest and energy of the semi-literate chief. He summoned 'A Meeting of the Inhabitants of Goaso Town', took the chair, and supervised the drawing-up of a Committee:

'Messrs A. and B. were asked by the odikro [chief] and his elders to find out suitable candidates who could run the town. These two headmen presented 8 men to the meeting this evening. The composition was found to be bad as most of the candidates could not read or write. This technical objection was raised by Mr T.N. Baidoo [the Local Council Chairman, a Goaso resident] seconded by Mr. C. . . . The meeting retired into consultation and the following candidates were elected by popular votes: [6 men, plus 3 nominated by the chief and elders]. It was found that the composition of the Committee was quite in order. It was also agreed in principle that the Chairman of the Ahafo Local Council would be invited whenever possible to give some advice to the Committee on the duties and limitations of such a Committee.' (Goaso District Office Records.)

This meeting was important as it set a precedent which the other Ahafo communities were quick to follow. In this short extract several of the features which were to characterise Committee growth are apparent: the patronage of the chief, the guidance of the Local Council, the need for educated members, and the ad hoc selection procedure with its distinctive way of reaching final agreement ('the meeting retired into consultation'). The model of the Local Council was followed, with appropriate quotas of popular and traditional representatives. It is interesting to note that the chief initiated the selection of the former by placing the onus upon the 'headmen' *(asafoakye)* the traditional spokesmen of the interests of the common people.

Within three years the Local Council had registered twenty-two Committees, and was obliged to form a development committee of its own to attend to their affairs. This mainly involved the supervision of the 'special rates' they had agreed to levy, either a surtax of two to five shillings per load of cocoa or an annual rate of £2-4 per man, £1-2 per woman. The sums involved (in excess of £1,000 a year for Goaso) brought the Council-Committee relationship under severe strain, with accusations of abuses on both sides. Committee affairs came more and more within the purview of the District Officer, whose correspondence frequently suggested the ambivalent attitude of officialdom: 'As I have pointed out several times before although the Mim Town Committee is not officially recognised, it is a voluntary organisation playing at least the role of a consultative machinery, I am willing to give it rather unofficially all the support I can.' (Goaso District Office Records.) The problem was that the Committees had come to assume rather more authority than government was prepared to concede. By the late 1950s they had become more than the Local Councils could handle and in subsequent legislation most of the responsibility for registration and control was transferred to the District Officer and the Ministry of Local Government.

Section 34 of the 1961 Local Government Act (no. 54) stated that the Minister could, by legislative instrument, regulate the appointment and recognition of village, town or area Committees, and the delegation of their functions within Local Council areas. In December 1962 a cabinet decision that every town, irrespective of its size, should have its own official Committee led to the promulgation of the first comprehensive regulations (Legislative Instrument no. 119 of 1962.) Each District Officer was to keep a membership register of all the Committees in his area and representatives of the Department of Community Development were to attend all meetings. The Committees were to assist local authority revenue officers in rate collection, to organise sanitation and local cleanliness, discuss community problems and make general recommendations on appropriate subjects to the Local Council. Otherwise they were rather unhelpfully charged to 'take over all the duties and functions hitherto performed by Town and Village Committees'. Finance was to be firmly controlled; the Local Councils still supervised rates, grants and loans, but the levying of 'special rates' was subject to cabinet approval and – a caveat to the Councils – were strictly for the use of the towns concerned. Ministerial instructions gazetted in March 1963 (LI. no. 262) further specified that Committees should consist of up to eleven members and a chairman, who should be the chief of the town. The quorum was to be one third of the members plus the chief and the community development officer, and meetings were to be held fortnightly.

After the police-military coup d'etat of February 1966 which overthrew the government of Dr Kwame Nkrumah (see table 1), the Committees, which had served the interests of the proscribed Convention People's Party very well, were suspended along with many other government institutions. Just three months after the coup, however, the National Liberation Council (N.L.C.) instructed that provisional committees be established consisting of the chief, four of his elders, the

Table 2. Government structures in Ahafo.

Territorial basis	Chiefship	Local authorities	Administration
Region * (Brong-Ahafo)	House of chiefs		Regional Office
District/ Traditional area * (Ahafo)	[State Council, abolished 1966] Association of Ahafo chiefs (since 1966)	[From 1970, District Council]	District Officer
Local Council area * (Goaso, Asunafo & Asutifi)		Local Council	
Town/ stool * (e.g. Goaso)	Chief & stool Council	Town Committee	
Village *	Village headman & elders	Village Committee	
T H E P E O P L E			

* Also: from c. 1957-66, local organisation of the Political parties.

139

Council clerk and the Community Development Officer. In Ahafo a District Association was set up to encourage the re-establishment of the Committees. In March 1967 the N.L.C. laid down regulations which empowered the new District Officers to control the appointment of members, and obliged the Council clerk to register them.[3] Significantly, the chief was recognised as the final legitimising authority in the town: for example, only his endorsement was required on expenditure authorisations.

Under the provisions of the new Ghanaian Constitution the future of the Committees has been assured,[4] but as yet there has been little formal elaboration of their organisation and functions. There have been two very recent developments in their official financial competence; not only are they to be entrusted with the collection and control of their own funds, they are also to be charged with the collection of Local Council revenue.[5]

The Committee and the Government

So far I have considered only the formal, legal development of the Ahafo Committees. Table 2 indicates the alignment of the various institutions with which I shall be concerned in discussing the legitimacy of the Committee in the government of Ahafo. I shall describe in turn the involvement of each of these structures in Committee development, and then consider briefly the momentous but shortlived influence of the political parties.

The Committee, of course, enjoys a relationship with government in the widest sense, beyond the confines of Table 2. It is now generally recognised that a town or village without a Committee is lacking a governmental institution as essential to the state as to the people themselves. People are keenly aware of the strength of central government *(aban)*, however obscure their understanding of its operations may be. I have heard many times such expressions as *'se wo yi nyame aban na owo tumi'* – 'next to God, government is most powerful'. People realise that the authority of the Committee derives ultimately from the state, and only in an immediate sense from the Local Council or District Officer. The Committee has come to play an important part in the relationship of the individual to his *aban,* and vice versa. It is clear that the member of parliament, the Local Council, even the indispensable District Officer, do not offer the individual such an immediate and appropriate means of expressing his interests. The Committee has come to serve as a valuable nexus of communication, enabling the central authorities to inform the people in the most distant rural localities and mobilise their energies for local and national purposes – a facility which the Convention People's Party in its heyday was not slow to turn to its advantage. From the individual's point of view, the onus of establishing mechanisms for this delicate process of communication rests in the first instance upon the state; as one Ahafo chief instructively put it:

'Ansana wobeka biribi no na aban aye kuo, no moako hia adwendwen ho akoto aban anim.

140

Before you can put your problems before the government it must make an organisation for you'. (Chief of Kenyase no.I – interview.)

Representatives of the principal government Departments are stationed in Ahafo, and for them the Committees afford a valuable means of establishing and sustaining contact with the people. In their various capacities they encourage and advise in the development of educational, health and other amenities. Committee meetings are usually too frequent to enable the Community Development Officers to attend as regularly as they are expected to, nevertheless they are closely concerned with the activities of the Committees and have done much to encourage their growth.

The Committee and the District Officer

From a local point of view the District Officer provides the most important political articulation between Ahafo and the *aban*. It is essential to recognise the extent of his authority in understanding any aspect of local decision-making and government in Ahafo. Councils and Committees everywhere repeatedly make decisions in terms of 'what prior authority will tolerate'; in Ahafo this usually implies, in the first instance, what the District Officer will tolerate. Most of the decisions taken locally which have to be referred to the Regional or Central authorities must pass through his office. During my stay I was struck by the frequency with which Committee – and Council – decisions were made expressly 'for Mr Kotey'. From their inception the Ahafo Committees have developed to a large extent by the District Officer's sanction. He has been in a position to influence their relationships with the Local Councils and the traditional authorities and since the mid 1950s he has had authority to convene and dissolve, to supervise the selection of members, to regulate competence and provide guidance in matters of procedure.

The District Officer is as essential today as in the years before 1957, and is certainly not simply a relic of colonial government. Nevertheless, an important aim of local government reorganisation in the past, and doubtless in the future, has been the devolution of much of the authority that is vested in his role. One of the constitutional changes of the early 1950s was the redesignation of the District Commissioner as 'Government Agent'; it is interesting that this should have reverted to 'D.C.' in the heyday of the C.P.P., the post acquiring new significance as an important party appointment. After the 1966 coup this title had again acquired unpleasant connotations and new 'District Administrative Officers' were appointed, technically sharing authority with a senior police or army officer, but in fact performing nearly all governmental functions in the Districts themselves. With the rehabilitation of civilian government some attrition of the authority the D.A.O. has enjoyed in the three years of national crisis can be expected, but local administration without the supervision of a highly-trained, resident Officer has become almost unthinkable. Perhaps his importance rests not so much in his routine functions, great as these may be, but rather in his capacity to intervene in almost any contingency. In the uncertainties of colonial and post-colonial government the role has been very much that of a *deus ex machina*. In 1951 Sir Sydney Phillipson concluded a schedule of the District Officer's multifarious duties with the ominous entry: 'Fires and Occurences' (Gold Coast, 1951: 203).[2b]

To the people of Ahafo, the District Officer has always been 'D.C.', regardless of changing nomenclature.[6] In spite of the change from European to African officers and alterations in their official functions, popular perception of the role seems to have remained surprisingly constant. An important reason must be the long-standing public adjustment to it; a District office was established in Ahafo in 1912 and seems to have been regarded locally as one of the few stable institutions in the recent years of drastic constitutional change. The most conspicuous modification in the District Officer's role came during the C.P.P. government. New party-appointed D.C.s took charge, although much of the work continued to be performed by civil-servant administrators. The D.C.s were frequently local men, rarely as well educated as their predecessors, and often ebulliently partisan. It is significant to note, however, that the Ahafo people do not seem to have regarded them as in any sense *'proper* D.C.s', and find in the present-day District Officer something much closer to their expectations. His potency was described to me in terms such as these: 'At the moment the most important man in Ahafo is the D.C., who is representing the government, for all the information from the government is sent through him. Because the power is in the government's hands he is more powerful than any of us here *[enam se tumi wo aban nsam nti owo tumi kyen yenyinaa]*.' (Chief of Kenyase no.I – interview).

The Committee and the Local Council

As we have seen, the principal political affiliation of the Committee was initially to the Local Council.[7] By the mid 1950s it was apparent that the Councils were unable to contain the Committees within their own authority and that the relationship had fallen far short of the ideals expressed in the Ordinance (see p.137). The Committees had become institutionalised and independent to the extent that much of the responsibility for their control had shifted to the District Officer; in 1961 central government itself took charge of several aspects of Committee affairs, 'special rates' being levied at the discretion of the cabinet. The Council's inability to control the Committees is attributable in part to the general laissez faire attitude adopted towards their growth and in part to organisational problems of its own.

Foremost of these has been the repeated reorganisation to which Councils have been subjected. Since 1952, Ahafo has experienced local government by a mixed traditional/elected Council (1952–9), by a Council elected on a competitive party-political basis (1956–62), by Councils appointed by the local organisation of the ruling Convention People's Party (1964–6) and, for fully one-third of the time, by small government-appointed Management Committees (1959, 1962 and 1966–70).

The wheel now seems to have come full circle, for by the provisions of the new Ghanaian constitution Local Councils with one-third traditional and two-thirds elected membership are to be established, as in 1952. Another debilitating product of these changes has been the frequent turnover in Council membership: once in 1958, twice in 1959, twice in 1962, once in 1966 and again in 1967.

The forms of representation employed have been a major weakness in Local Council organisation. One man was obliged to stand for a *ward*, a new political unit consisting of several towns and villages with little meaning for the people. In terms of inter-community rivalry, the Asutifi Local Council ward 1 combination of Mehame, Dadiesoaba, Twabidi and Sienchem must have rendered its representative almost powerless.[8] So much of the Local Council's business is the allocation of limited available resources among the demands of the individual towns and villages, and so far no system of representation has provided a satisfactory basis for this economising. In a rather negative way the Committees have thrived on these deficiencies. The inevitable suspicion of the Councils' financial activities has encouraged the communities to seek more immediate ways of acquiring and maintaining amenities; in the years before 1966 the Councils' control of funds and budgeting became manifestly fallible, prompting the townspeople to take the initiative themselves.

Initially the Local Councils lacked the experience and confidence to view the establishment of a secular political force in the towns with much enthusiasm. In March 1953 the Council clerk reported apprehensively to the District Officer that he had received applications from nine Committees[9] for formal recognition:

'You will be pleased to hear that all over the Area, both towns and villages are anxious for authority to form village committees.'

'The snag in it, I am sure, is that it will give room for unnecessary pressure to be brought to bear on the Council.' (Ahafo District Office records.)

The District Officer reassured him that the Ministry of Local Government's policy was that formal recognition should be sparing. The Council's attitude was equivocal; the Committees could exert pressure but where they functioned well they could greatly assist such vital operations as rate collection and the conveying of information to the public. The Council has certainly given considerable encouragement to Committee growth, not only through its staff but also, as we have seen in the inauguration of the Goaso Committee, through the activity of its chairman and members. An example of this interest was their decision in March 1961 that:

'As the town/village Committees form an ARM of the Council in its administration: a FORUM be established whereby these Committees would know their scope of activities to promote a more organised service to the people' (Brong Ahafo South Local Council minutes, It. 19, 1961).

The following month 91 delegates from 30 Committees attended a conference at Goaso, and were addressed by the Council chairman. He defined the Committee as 'a body of persons appointed for the progress of the town' and found it necessary to stress its distinctness from traditional authority: 'To be a member of a Committee is no chieftaincy, but rather to serve as a servant'. (Goaso Local Council records.) The delegates were advised by several speakers about rates and revenues, market control, self-help schemes, youth organisations and the need for education. It was agreed that the meeting should be convened annually, and it is clear that the main product of the exercise was the generation of enthusiasm.

Perhaps the most penetrating influence of the Local Council has been the extent to which it has served as a model for the internal organisation of the Committees. In the beginning, as we have seen, it provided a key for their composition; it is also tacitly assumed that their procedures should follow as closely as possible the style of the Local Council. When advice is dispensed to the Committees it is usually no more than an interpretation of the standing orders and regulations of the Council. Nevertheless, there is ambivalence in such authority as the Committee derives from its Local Council affiliation; the secretary (whose contact with the Council is most direct) of the Goaso Committee confessed:

'I am often puzzled... often [the Local Council] lays all their burden upon us... but the town Committee is only supposed to supplement where [the Council] is weak. The Council is a government arm, we can't force it... they are our bosses, I would say they are our government from whom we take our inspirations. The townspeople expect us to oppose inimical regulations from the Local Council... they expect us to petition the Local Council. But if we don't also take care we fall into trouble with the government. We are to help the Local Council with the administration of the place, but we are not to interfere. We are between and betwixt, you see...' (Goaso Committee Secretary – interview.)

One thing is clear; in no sense is the Committee simply an extension of the Local Council into the town. Rather, its rapid growth and its problematic relations with the Council reflect the extent to which the Committee has come to belong to and serve the interests of the townspeople.

The Committee and the traditional authorities

The growth of the Committees and their acquisition of legitimacy have been radically affected by the traditional authorities in Ahafo, particularly within the towns and villages themselves. It may be useful to trace briefly the changing role of the chiefs in the government of the District as a background to the more detailed consideration of their involvement in Committee development.

The first major formal involvement of the chiefs in the colonial government of Ashanti was the establishment of four grades of Native Court in 1924, whereby the most important traditional Councils were accorded official judicial powers. The chiefs of Mim, Noberkaw and Kukuom (see Fig.1) each administered justice in one third of Ahafo with Kukuom, recognised as Paramount, having appellate privileges. In 1935 the government reorganised and centralised the various states in the region into an 'Ashanti Confederacy' modelled on the Union of pre-colonial times. The

Confederacy Council at Kumasi was the most senior of a system of traditional Councils officially recognised as 'Native Authorities'; the three Ahafo Divisions were ranked equally and placed under the aegis of the Kumasi authority, Kukuom appearing to lose its paramount status in the process. The Authorities were empowered to assist in the maintenance of order, to make certain rules and regulations, to establish treasuries and to undertake such development projects as road building, the provision of water supplies, and so on. In the Districts there was little structural innovation, new functions and authority being allocated to pre-existing bodies. According to his traditional status the town chief was a Native Authority councillor in his Division; government and matters of development within his town remained in the hands of his stool Council.

The chiefly hierarchy remained when the new Local Authority system was introduced, but beyond its involvement in the Local Councils its competence was restricted to such 'customary' matters as land tenure and ritual. At the same time the chiefs' tribunals were abolished and most of their judicial functions transferred to a new system of magistrates courts. The division of labour and authority between the chiefs and the Local Councils became a cause of great contention in Ghana, one side frequently accusing the other of trespassing on its competence. Attempts to segregate and circumscribe traditional and secular authority culminated in the twin Chieftaincy and Local Government Acts of 1961; however, the division was neither complete nor enduring, and by the provisions of the new constitution chiefs and laymen are to share authority in the Local Councils once more. It is notorious that the C.P.P. did not permanently diminish traditional authority; in Ahafo as in other parts of Ghana party conflict tended to become another dimension of pre-existing inter- and intra-stool rivalries.

These rivalries have characterised the political history of the relationships between Ahafo communities and, strangely enough, have contributed to Committee growth. There is an important connection between the physical well-being of an Ahafo town and its moral and political welfare, an idea deeply rooted in Ashanti tradition. Today as before, a chief manifests his goodness in the quality of his regalia, his 'palace' and his town, and in the prosperity of his people. Official roadside boards proclaim the extent of each Committee's authority, and an imposing tarred mainstreet is a sine qua non for any community hoping to compete in the fierce politics of aggrandisement. In retrospect, the spread of Ahafo Committees was predictable according to the long-standing political alignments in the District; it would be an affront to Mim if Goaso had a Committee and it did not. Kukuom could not let its arch-rival Mim take any advantage over it and the rivalries continued more or less ad infinitum.

If the establishment of Committees became involved in inter-stool politics, it also opened the way for new political activity in the relationship between town and village. In a traditional context the villages are subject to the twenty eight Ahafo stools, but in secular terms their Committees are on a par with the towns, both being responsible in the first instance to the Local Council and District Officer (see table 2). This has enabled villages to join forces irrespective of their stool allegiance, and, on certain issues, to confront the authority of the towns on equal terms. Recently Goaso convened a gathering of Committees within the stool area to persuade them to contribute to the extension of the town Middle School; the debate was vigorous and wide-ranging, but after an injudicious reminder from a Goaso delegate that the villages were, after all, finally subject to the authority of the Goaso chief, negotiations broke down. On this subject the villagers claimed the right to think otherwise.

The establishment of Committees has changed substantially the government of the Ahafo communities, and inevitably the stool Council (in the villages, the headman and his elders) has been profoundly involved in this process. In speaking of the development of Committees it would be incorrect to speak of replacement, addition or even adaptation; what is appearing is a new system of authority in which the Committee has come to play quite an important part. The roles of the chief and his stool Council have also changed; in 1948 Fortes observed: 'The crucial point is that while Ashanti feel very strongly that no community can exist without a chief they have no clear-cut unanimous ideas as to what a chief should be and should do, and they have lost the sense of the chief's belonging to them as the representative of their will.' (Fortes, 1948: 25) Twenty years later the enduring importance of chiefship is manifest in many ways – not the least of which are the frequent depositions and the strenuous competition for office (Mim has had eight chiefs since 1938). A town without a chief and Council is almost unheard of. For over two years Acherensua (see Fig.1) had neither, allegedly because of the 'socialist pressures' from the C.P.P. Youngmen there. It is significant, however, that a complaint was made to the Local Council that this was making the selection of a town Committee impossible. After the 1966 coup the government was anxious to ensure that the chief and Council of Acherensua were reinstated.

I was told: 'A town without a chief becomes a public [sic] town; as there is no respect everyone just speaks as he likes'. (Goaso chief – interview). Writing of the endurance of traditional authority, Apter has described the chiefs as 'integrational integers' (Apter, 1963: 105); Busia, less abstrusely, has pointed out that the chief was traditionally 'the axis of the political relations of the different elders and their subjects' (Busia, 1951: 22). Today, the chief still exerts an essential, ancestrally-sanctioned influence on the affairs of the Ashanti community. He is obliged by oath to resolve conflicts among his subjects, to respect them and to foster their spiritual, political and physical well-being. In all things he must act in consultation with his elders in the first instance and then, if necessary, with his subjects at large. Rattray has emphasised this repeatedly, e.g.

'To all outward appearance and to superficial observers, who included the populace, the Chief was an autocrat. In reality every move and command which appeared to emanate from his mouth had been discussed in private and been previously agreed upon by his councillors, to whom every one in the tribe had access and to whom popular opinion on any subject was thus made known. Such, at any rate, was the ideal; serious departure from this custom would eventually lead to destoolment'. (Rattray, 1929: 82).

People 'speak well' of a successful chief, and his reward is honour *(animuoyam)*. Formerly, and to a large extent still, issues were brought to his attention by his elders; this acting as intermediary is still an important Ashanti principle, and one frequently hears such expressions as *'obe dwantua mpaninfoo'* – 'he is petitioning through the elders'. When an issue *(asem,* or *asembiba)* is brought to his attention a chief customarily consults first his senior elder, the *Gyasehene* or *Krontihene,* and his *okyeame* ('spokesman') to decide on an appropriate means of seeking a solution. As we shall see, this control over public decision-making remains an important function of the chief. As chairman of both bodies he is a direct link between the Committee and the stool Council; his authority, however, derives immediately from the latter, which has power to appoint him, the former being obliged to accept him *qua* chief. He therefore has political responsibilities to his elders which supercede his responsibilities to the Committee, and which thus affect his priorities in the management of town affairs.

The competence of the chief and his stool Council in matters of ritual, land tenure, etc., is recognised statutorily. When, for example, the Biaso Committee requested the Local Council to promulgate a by-law banning dogs and goats, obnoxious to the local fetish, from their village, the Council promptly replied: '. . .that this is a matter within the competence of the traditional leaders of the village and not of this Council' or, for that matter, the village Committee' (Goaso Local Council minutes, It. 9/1968). It is generally asserted, however, that the stool Council must take a direct interest in the improvement of services and amenities within the town. Frequent references to this in deposition charges suggest that it is not just a privilege but an obligation, e.g. 'CHARGE 1. THAT since Nana K.S. was enstooled there has not been any improvement in the town. This proves that he does not love the town' (Kukuom Ahafo State Council record book: May 1966). I was repeatedly told 'the elders help the town to progress'; in this they enjoy supernatural authority:

'We [elders] lie down and dream *[ye da na yaso daye]* and so we know what is good for the town. Those who represent us do not lie down and dream – they only think about their money. Just now I know the needs of the town because I pour libations [to the spirits and ancestors] and lie down and sleep, then I know that when I dress everything will be all right because of the [protecting influence of the] stool. When I pour libation I usually pray that government developments can come to Goaso and make it a fine town'. (Goaso chief – inverview.)

The Committee and party politics.

Even after the 1966 coup d'etat Kwame Nkrumah is popularly accredited with the considerable feat of bonding the interests of individual Ghanaians to the state in terms of the Convention People's Party organisation. From the C.P.P. point of view, the town Committees provided a useful foothold for the extension of the party organisation into the rural communities; from the point of view of the Committee, the party did much to mobilise public participation and established an important precedent of modern political organisation. Initially, party involvement in local government affairs was viewed with apprehension; although Local Council seats were contested on a party basis the spirit of rivalry was not supposed to be taken from the hustings into the Council chamber, and was considered wholly incompatible with the functions of the Committees.[10] The influence of the parties did not gather momentum in Ahafo until shortly before Independence (1957), but thereafter politics were taken up with great vigour. Committees were usually deemed to be wholly C.P.P. or United Party (rarely a mixture, apparently), and complaints of bias were frequently made to the administration by one side or the other. The idiom of party politics became very noticeable in Committee transactions: for example, in September 1958 the chief 'met the masses of Goaso for a discussion of the town Committee' and 'threw it to them to select nominations' (Goaso District Office records). In a climate of intense national political activity, Committees were set up and toppled all too frequently. Town interest groups were subsumed by the C.P.P.–U.P. dichotomy, and even chiefship passed back and forth between partisans.

Inevitably, these influences generated some confusion, reflected, for example, in the appointment of officials. In 1959 Kukuom had a 'chaplain', and the Sankore Committee a mysterious 'Potter' (porter?). There were treasurers, sub-treasurers, assistant treasurers, internal and external auditors. Sometimes the townspeople's desire to establish a truly 'modern' organisation ran riot. Rather than following the example nearest at hand – the Local Council – the town of Dantano (population 789) took a lofty governmental model and in 1962 appointed Ministers of Education, Finance, Health, Transport-and-Communications, until the District Officer was prompted to enquire if they proposed to declare independence.

After 1961, as the C.P.P. organisation gradually took over local government, Committee meetings became party meetings. When Ghana became a one-party state (1964) the people were informed by the C.P.P. District Officer: 'That Osagyefo Dr Kwame Nkrumah had instructed that a town or village Development Committee should be made of the chairman and the secretary of the town or village Party Branch and five other appointed members . . .' (Goaso Local Council records.) The influence of the traditional authorities was thus severely curtailed, and the chief was grudgingly allocated a nominal, presidential role. This does not seem to have improved the efficiency of the Committees: there appears to have been little consideration of local amenities and services, and latterly a pattern of lethargy, infrequent meetings and poor attendance set in.[11] In 1964 Asutifi Local Councillors were exhorted to attend Committee meetings, not to advise on organisation and procedure but to 'educate them on Party Ideology' (Asutifi Local Council minutes, It. 36, 1964).

Perhaps it is surprising that the demise of the C.P.P. did not also extinguish the Committees. It is surely a good indication of their basic importance to the townspeople that they were being re-established spontaneously only a few weeks after the coup. The·C.P.P., it is generally acknowledged, had the virtue of drawing all the interests of the community into a single arena, and stimulating public involvement. After a poorly-attended public meeting in Goaso in 1968 I was wryly assured by a former District Officer that 'in the old days the Party saw to it that everyone attended'. Although it generated much mistrust and confusion it also went far to educate the people in a modern idiom of political behaviour.

The Committee and the community: composition and legitimacy

'The smaller the society the more complex the issues: the hostilities and alignments in a parliament of six hundred are more easy to follow than those in a parish council of twenty'. (V.S. Naipaul, 1967.)

If the legitimacy of a decision-making body is derived from its relationships within a wider political system, we must not only consider the formal status conferred 'from above', but also the effective recognition of its authority by the public it serves. Social relationships within small communities are 'multiplex', the same people interacting regularly with one another in terms of different roles. Different political interests are associated with these roles and may be deployed in various contexts of public decision-making. The extent to which the Committee can fairly represent the various interests of the townspeople and villagers of Ahafo is an important measure of its legitimacy.

In the course of general socio-economic change the organisation of Ghanaian communities has altered considerably, and there are new interests which the traditional authorities cannot claim to represent. This is where the Committee has come to play an important part in public decision-making. Representation is still problematic and, as we shall see, this limitation of its authority has a marked effect on its competence and the procedures it is obliged to adopt. I shall outline the seven most important and most common interest groupings which may become involved in public decision-making in Ahafo towns and villages. The sets are not, of course, mutually exclusive and an individual's association with any particular interest is contingent upon the various issues which may arise.

Most closely associated with the organisation and competence of the stool Council are the *kin groups*. The basic structure of the traditional Ashanti town depends upon a set of family groups or matrilineages from each of which specific town leaders may be chosen. Lineage elders consider likely candidates from their 'royal' family and submit their choice to the town chief and stool Council for approval. This pattern is followed in even the newest Ahafo communities; the chief normally comes from a 'founding family' and elderships are reckoned to have been vested in other families arriving subsequently. Traditionally this constituted an effective system of representation on which several writers have commented, e.g.:

> 'The chief communicated directly with his elders, they in turn with the headmen of the villages under them and they with their subjects. When the system functioned well it was democratic. There was an aristocracy of rulers, but they were constitutionally elected, and they were under popular control by the right of the destoolment vested in the electors. Everyone was represented on the council through the lineage system'. (Busia, 1951: 22).

In Ahafo, where such relationships often lack the sanctions of long-established tradition, there is much scope for inter- and intra-familial conflict over rights to elderships and chiefships, and the associated rights in property. Such disputes would normally be dealt with by the stool Council but on occasions the Committee has acted as mediator; the second meeting of the Goaso Committee in 1952 arranged 'the settlement of a dispute between Goasohene and the Akuranza family' (Goaso Local Council records).

Political intrigues about chiefship are endemic in Akan political organisation, and the stool disputes in Ahafo are notorious. When such activity is rife it tends to paralyse all public decision-making, including the activities of the Committee. *Leadership factions* may be distinguished as a second kind of interest grouping, as they quite frequently do not correspond with the kin groups. Townspeople may divide simply for or against a particular chief (or elder) or chiefly candidate. During my stay, in the complex period of post-C.P.P. restitution, this was the most significant and the most common conflict of interests in the Ahafo communities; I was frequently told that there is not one town without a pair of factions, one supporting the chief and the other seeking his deposition. The strength of these sentiments is at least an indication of the revived political significance of the role of chief.

Another by-product of traditional leadership is the contraposition of *elders* and *Youngmen;* much of the impetus for Committee growth has derived from this distinction. 'Remember', one Ahafo chief told me, 'even if you are grey haired but not a chief, you are called "Youngman".' Perhaps 'commoner' is therefore a more accurate if less conventional rendering of the Twi *aberantee.* The Youngmen were, as we have seen, represented on the stool Council by their family representatives the elders *(mpaninfoo),* but they also had a leader of their own, the *asafoakye,* [12] through whom they could voice their opinions on certain occasions. It is significant that the *asafoakye* is now a recognised office in the town Committee, charged with overseeing communal labour, and sometimes referred to as 'foreman'.

An important feature of traditional decision-making was the soliciting of the Youngmen's support at public meetings on certain major issues. Quite clearly, this is the precedent for the public meetings which today play such an important part in issues involving the Committee. Describing the general meeting usually held to approve the appointment of a new chief, Busia has noted that 'On the announcement of the name [of the proposed chief] demonstrations of approval or disapproval were unmistakably given by applause, grunts, hisses, laughter or silence' (Busia, 1951: 11). At the secular meetings I have attended the public has been a great deal more explicit.

When the new town Committees were introduced, with the official assurance that they were to stimulate popular participation in local government, they inevitably came to be regarded as being 'for the Youngmen', while the stool Councils were 'for the elders'. Youth is certainly one of the distinguishing features of Youngmen; more education is another, something which has made them better attuned to participation in the new bureaucratic government system. To some extent 'scholars', 'Youngmen' and local development have become confused ideas in the growth of the Ahafo Committees, e.g.: 'We have formed the town's improvement Committee, bearing the name "The Akrodie Scholars Association" and our aim is to improve the town at large.' (Ahafo Local Council records). The elders have been quick to contradict any proprietary claims by the Youngmen, pointing out that if the Committee is to represent the town as a whole it must also represent the elders (see App. A). The fear that it can harbour a rival leadership faction has prompted the elders to maintain an active interest in the Committee — sometimes too active for the Youngmen's liking. In 1955 the Youngmen of Mim complained that the chief had arbitrarily appointed a Committee of his own, and retaliated by forming separate Town Improvement and Town Youth Associations.

With the high rate of immigration to Ahafo, the distinction between *Townsmen* and *Strangers* has been very important. Being a townsman *(kromeni)* in Ashanti means being a committed resident, owning property, being related to other townsmen, being recognised officially by the chief and stool Council and thereby being inextricably involved in the competition of interests within the town. The stranger *(ohohoo)* has not yet acquired the status of townsman; the term is not necessarily pejorative, it is said that 'not all the people who establish a town arrive at the same time', and that 'strangers develop a town' by working there, contributing land dues, paying rates and eventually adding to the numerical strength of the community by settling there. The 'resident stranger' *(ohohoo omanifo)* may eventually be recognised as a townsman by a formal presentation to the stool Council; he will cease to pay land dues but must undertake to share town debts and profits and other community responsibilities.

It is necessary to distinguish further between strangers from other parts of Ashanti and 'foreigners' from other tribes and other countries. The latter provide the labour force for the cocoa farms and constitute the majority of the 'resident strangers' in town. They live in a specific quarter called the *zongo,* often distinguished from the 'Ashanti-town'. The *zongo* has its own headman *(serikin)* and tribal sub-chiefs, but has no direct representation on the stool Council. They are, however, residents, benefitting from local amenities, and they seem to contribute disproportionately heavily to community development, particularly in labour. The *zongo* people are diffident about entering the political arena of the town, and it is often necessary for government officials to hold special meetings to encourage their participation in the discussion of certain local issues. It is becoming customary for Committees to have at least one *zongo* representative (see App. A), appointed by the *serikin* in consultation with the tribal sub-chiefs.

The diffidence of the foreigners is matched by the vociferous politicking of the Ashanti strangers. These are townsmen from other parts of Ashanti whose interest in Ahafo extends little further than the cocoa farms they have established there. They face much local hostility on the grounds that they carry the wealth of Ahafo out of the District and contribute insufficiently to its progress. For their part the strangers complain that they enjoy no representation on the stool Council or town Committee and should not arbitrarily be required to pay for amenities in towns and villages which they do not regard as 'home'.

In 1956 a number of them formed an association and complained to the District Officer and the Ministry on this score. They protested that they were being denied a say in the levying of town 'special rates', but the Local Councillors dismissed this as 'a wicked plan by the non-native farmers to prove. . .that they had supporters', and branded them as 'a section of the community who . . . always deprecate *[sic]* the downfall of the state [i.e., the stool] and feel loath to support any attempt to improve the town'. (Ahafo Local Council minutes, It. 71, 1957.) Eventually the District Officer was persuaded that on such issues the Committee was not adequately representative and that final approval should henceforth be sought at a public meeting. The Local Council clerk accordingly sent out a circular requiring that issues of rating should deploy the entire decision-making capacities of the community:

'Before the final discussion of the Local Council estimates, towns and villages are requested to forward their proposals for inclusion in the current estimates. The Chief, Elders and the Voluntary Town Committee on which the neighbouring villages have representatives, hold a mass meeting to discuss the issue. Having come to a decision they discuss how much cocoa tax they wish to collect and the project they intend to put up. They embody their resolution in the form of a mandate signed and thumbprinted by the Chief, Elders and Representatives of the Town or Village Committee.' (Goaso Local Council records.)

Modern *occupational* differentiation has introduced a range of competing interests to the community. The most common distinctions are made between farmers, storekeepers, market vendors, labourers and 'clerks' – i.e., schoolteachers, letter-writers, government employees and other 'white-collar' workers. Occupational groups are often very well organised, and government bodies are likely to consult with the 'chief farmer' or 'chief market woman' of the community on certain issues. Even the sanitary labourers in larger towns have something akin to a guild, and such groups take it amiss if their interests are not reckoned with in public decision-making. Occupational interests become involved most notably in the organisation of communal labour; the Committee has to establish which groups are able to work at which times, and to negotiate a fee for those unable to attend. They can also mobilise considerable pressure in favour of or against a particular project – more market stalls, the construction of a feeder-road, or the improvement of school facilities.

Religious groups are becoming increasingly diversified in Ahafo. In Goaso alone there are some ten different churches and several mosques. Traditional belief has its staunch adherents too; in Goaso the fetish *Bonsam* is regularly celebrated by functionaries of the older generation, and there are few people in the town who would discount its influence absolutely. The gods and fetishes are closely identified with the corporate welfare of the town, or sometimes with a specific kin group, and they do much to sanction the authority of the stool Council. Moslems are nearly all non-Ashanti *zongo* dwellers and are most likely to express their interests through the *serikin* or the Committee representative. The identities of the various groups are clearly advertised, notably in the colourful, uniformed religious parades and fund-raising activities, and there is a good deal of proselytising. Rivalry is normally good-humoured, however, and as far as the Committee is concerned it can affect such things as spending on educational establishments or the allocation of building plots. Again, the holy days of the various groups have to be reckoned with in the planning of communal labour.

Finally, it is necessary to note the important political distinction, part traditional and part modern, between *men* and *women.* Conjugal role segregation in Ashanti is very marked and women have considerable economic independence, particularly in their capacity as petty traders. The recent military government recognised this by requiring that a 'woman representative' should sit on the Local Council management committees, an example which many town Committees have followed (see App. A). Every stool Council has an influential female representative in the queen mother *(obaapanin),* who has important traditional duties regarding the welfare of women and girls in the town. Although they are normally quite passive in discussion the women can assert their interests with tenacity, having consolidated their opinions beforehand in such places as the market.

During my stay I attended the selection of a few of the sixty-nine Committees currently operating in Ahafo. Most, but not all, were convened by the District Officer and Local Council clerk, and Legislative Instrument 540 (see p.140) was punctiliously explained to the public meeting. Nominations were called for, and if these were not at once forthcoming certain categories were suggested by the District Officer: a literate member to act as secretary, an elder, a *zongo* representative, a woman and so on. Sometimes he intervened to prevent a single interest group being obviously over-represented. With each nomination, assent was taken when a convincing-looking number of people raised their hands in support; this, I was assured, was very much how a chief ran Committee selection in the past. It is a sequential consideration of seven to eleven individuals, with votes being solicited but rarely counted, and the results being recorded as 'unanimous', obviously in the sense of 'without explicit dissent'. Judging from the discussion at these sessions the two main, ostensible criteria for election are 'good-mindedness' *(adwene ye paa)*, and whether or not the candidate 'can speak'. The former seems to imply notions of altruism, sobriety and fairness, and the latter not just good oratory but also the capacity to represent expediently some interest or group of interests within the town. There is some conflict of ideals here, however, for it is strongly felt that representation on the Committee should be implicit, not explicit. While all interests are concerned to 'have a voice' on the Committee, their expression is ideally contingent only upon issues as they arise, and conscientious Committees try to maintain a corporate, non-partisan approach to business.

The diffidence with which some candidates accept nomination is striking. There are, of course, two sides to representation, who has the right to be represented and who has the right to be a representative?

Duncan Mitchell (1952) has discussed these problems of legitimacy with regard to the growth of Parish Councils in Devonshire. In the terms of Max Weber he has observed that the change from the traditional authority of the squirearchy to the new 'rational-legal legitimacy' of the Councils has engendered a feeling that:

'Despite the legal right there is no belief in a social right to stand for election and no recognition of the present machinery of government'. . . 'In some parishes. . . quite suitable people would regard it as a joke if it were suggested they should sit on the Council and, few having the requisite personal prestige to be able to carry it off, there is as a result a shortage of people considered by their fellows eligible to be representatives.' (Mitchell, 1952.)

This reluctance does not constitute such a problem in Ahafo, and as one conspicuous reason I would single out the penetrating influence of party politics. After the demise of the C.P.P. in 1966 the District Officer often experienced difficulty in persuading suitable people to join the Committees. One Goaso member described the cajolery he had experienced:

'I was in the house one day when I got a letter from [the District Officer]. He wanted to make me a town Committee member – in fact I didn't like it. . . He says: "don't worry, in fact I have contacted some people and they say you are the only man for the job". Well, he is my senior, I have to take his advice, so I said I'd do it. The chief himself came to me and told me everything was all right, and I told him that as I was a citizen of this town I have to do it. I will sacrifice and do it. . .' (Interview, English.)

The selection procedures reflect this diffidence; people do not normally 'stand' for election, or promote themselves, candidature is by nomination in public and there is no competitive vote. The choice is finally legitimised by the chief, the clerk of Council and the District Officer.

No-one is more apprehensive about his right to Committee membership than the *zongo* representative: 'We here are all foreigners and we came here to work as labourers. If I can get money I shall take my money and go off. When I set out, I never told my father that I was coming to be a chief. What can I gain from being a chief?" (Interview, Goaso *zongo* representative). To him, authority in the town, traditional and secular, is all one, but certainly not his. He is disturbed, too, that his 'chiefship' lacks a clear mandate from the *zongo* people themselves:

'I discuss matters with the *serikin zongo,* I am his representative on the Committee. In the Committee they see the scars on my face and know that I am the *zongo* representative. The *zongo* people are all my masters and I do not want to work for someone who will not praise my efforts. If all the *zongo* people came to me and told me: "we have elected you to represent us" – then I would be prepared even to die for the *zongo.* But they just sent a letter, and if I had torn it up I would have offended the D.C. But I have respected him and that is why I am on the Committee. ' (Ibid.)

Probably the most demanding, necessarily neutral role in the Committee is that of secretary. It is a position of considerable responsibility and in many towns a measure of personal prestige has come to be associated with it; otherwise, financial rewards are only nominal. It is the secretary who has the most frequent dealings with the Local Council, the District Officer and other authorities; he is, as it were, a political 'bridge' to the Committee. At meetings he is very active, introducing business, guiding discussion, recording decisions and bearing the brunt of members' frustrations – he is *de facto* chairman. I also noted that he rarely votes or offers a personal opinion. The secretary is usually a prominent local schoolteacher and therefore quite commonly a 'resident stranger'. This can provide a useful sense of detachment; protesting that he was not involved in town interests, the Goaso secretary reminded me that he was a 'stranger' (resident more than eight years) and anyway was 'just doing a job'. Clearly, the Local Council clerk provides the basic model for this role, nevertheless there are strong parallels between the secretary and the *okyeame,* the chief's spokesman in the stool Council. The latter also controls, but does not participate in discussion, and divergences from what one might conventionally expect of a Committee secretary can often be explained with reference to the *okyeame* model.

Decision-making procedures

Part of the legitimacy and competence of the Commiteee is statutorily prescribed on a national level; part is derived from its relations with other authorities in the District; and part, as I have just described, is derived from its relationships within the town or village itself. Ultimately, then, the Committees are idiosyncratic; just as Ahafo generally differed from other Districts with regard to Committee development, so the 69 Committees within Ahafo differ, sometimes quite substantially, from one another. By choosing to focus on their growth at the District level I have mainly been concerned to describe the limits of this variation. Decision-making procedures are a kind of ritual, and rituals, as anthropologists know well, tell much about the organisation of a community. Variations in the conduct of meetings I

155

attended in Ahafo were sufficient to remind me that the distribution of authority in which the Committee is involved is not uniform in the Ahafo communities. In discussing matters of procedure I again seek a District norm, but resort in matters of detail to the particular case of Goaso.

Townspeople do not seem to have any fixed idea of the competence of the Committee, beyond the fact that it 'develops the town'. Normally there is only one procedure for raising an issue formally, either by townsmen or outside authorities, and that is by reference to the chief. The enduring recognition of his role as moderator in town affairs is one good reason for his appointment by the government. as Committee chairman. A chief and his elders are supposed to be readily available to their people, and to be able to decide quickly on an appropriate course of action. In this regard, one Ahafo chief compared his role with that of the Local Councillor:

'To the ordinary people, the chiefs are the most useful. . . because people dislike the order of the Local Council. Sometimes they go about saying ill words against the Local Council: "what I am after is this, but because there is no funds the Local Council won't do [it]". But the chief, who is supposed to be the father of all people, he can be easily touched and asked why this is not done. Even this morning people have come to me to ask: "look, the Local Council, when you go there you won't meet the chairman and the members are also scattered away to their own places and you can't get in touch with them". So they prefer the chief to any other people.' (Chief of Mim, interview, English.)

The chief has responsibilities to his people, to his traditional overlords, to the Local Council in his capacity as Committee chairman, and in a general sense, to the District Officer; these allegiances may not always be easy to reconcile, but chiefs are normally in little doubt about their priorities in the handling of town affairs. Presented with an issue, the chief will usually discuss the matter with his senior elders before calling either a meeting of the stool Council or the town Committee. Each of these will in turn consider the need to hold a public meeting:

'Before I discuss developments in the town with the Committee I discuss things with the elders. . . The Committee represents the Youngmen in the town but I discuss matters with the elders before I submit it to the town Committee, and the gong is beaten to arrange a meeting of the people . . . If I discuss something with the Committee without informing the elders it is difficult for me to tell the people of the town about it.' (Chief of Kenyase, no.I – interview.)

The effect of this chain process is that the issue becomes progressively modified, reduced to a set of practicable alternatives and ultimately presented cut-and-dried for a final public decision. This reduction of issues constitutes an important part of the Committee's work, in addition to those matters it has the competence to resolve itself.

Only the chief may authorise the beating of the town gong,[13]. The official and binding signal for the people to assemble. He thereby controls the calling of public meetings which, as I have pointed out, play an important part in the settlement of more weighty issues. Apart from these 'steering' functions the chief's role in decision-making is what I would call 'terminal'; he controls the manner in which an issue is presented at the outset and he endorses the final decision, but he takes virtually no part in discussion. Unimpeachable impartiality within his community is a fundamental expectation of the Ashanti chief. When his people are firmly behind him, the chief is an important and at the moment very active spokesman for the town.[14] There is an Ashanti tenet that a chief is never wrong; he is therefore not given the opportunity to be wrong. He should never participate in a discussion in a partisan fashion, and as safety-measure he is obliged to communicate through his spokesman *(okyeame)* on all official occasions. In the Committee and at certain public meetings the secretary has come to serve as surrogate for the *okyeame*. Busia has pointed out that before his installation a chief is obliged to settle all outstanding disputes, particularly those involving his kinsmen (Busia, 1951: 11 and 25). The Ahafo chiefs, still smarting from their involvement in recent party political schisms, tend to labour the need for impartiality, to the extent of avoiding regular attendance at one particular church or selling their cocoa to a single buyer.[15] As one Goaso Committee member put it: 'before they make you a chief you must be a friend of everyone'. This restriction on the chief's role in public debate causes some equivocation about his Committee chairmanship; eighteen of the twenty-eight Ahafo chiefs approved of their participation, saying their presence was a restraining influence in discussion and diminished the likelihood of corruption. The seven who were against their chairmanship felt that it was at odds with their role of final sanctioning authority in the town: 'The chief should be the one to whom the Committee reports the proceedings of its meetings. If the chief is there in their midst — what is the sense of it?' (Chief of Akrodie — interview.) 'What I would like is for a common man to be elected as their chairman so that after their meeting he can report to me. If I don't understand, I shall call the townspeople and put the matter before them. But if I go and meet with them to discuss the matter — how can it be advanced?' *(ebe ye den ako soro?)* (Chief of Ayumso — interview.) Whatever the decision, and wherever it is made, the chief will be expected to claim it as his own. When the due processes have been followed his authority cannot be gainsaid, it is the authority of the community: 'If you offend a chief a sheep will be slaughtered and you will get a big [law] case... The people are careful with their words. If you offend a chief you offend the whole town'. (Goaso Committee secretary — interview, English.)

Public decision-making in Ahafo towns can thus be regarded as a single process involving a set of institutions sharing the authority to resolve and execute matters. An issue is settled by the stool Council, the town Committee or the public meeting, each according to its competence; in this process the Committee has acquired the authority to make decisions mainly concerning the material welfare of the community — e.g., selecting contractors and materials, planning expenditure and organising labour, to prepare decisions on levying and major undertakings for reference to the public, and to arrange for the execution of all such undertakings. It also has wide consultative capacities, and the elasticity of its competence is suggested by its occasional arbitration and mediation in community disputes.

Although they may be seen as participating in a single decision-making process, the Committee and the stool Council ideally operate as quite separate institutions. As a Goaso Committee member put it: 'when the elders have finished their discussion then, if they wish, they can put the matter before the town Committee. . . When the elders have their meetings they do not allow the town Committee members to attend, for it is up to them to inform us about what they have discussed. They have their meetings, and the town Committee has its meetings.' (Goaso town Committee member – interview.) Although the conduct of the meetings of each body reflects its involvement in community decision-making there are, nevertheless, important procedural differences which may be regarded as the enactment of distinct ideals about their respective legitimacy and competence.

The stool Council meets 'when an issue *(asembiba)* crops up' (Hwidiem chief – interview), summoned. by the *okyeame* at the chief's behest. The elders gather at his official house *(ahenfie)* and sit around him in rank order on special chairs and stools. The chief inaugurates most stool Council meetings by pouring a libation to the ancestors, gods and fetishes, praying for guidance in their deliberations; the remaining liquor, perhaps provided by a supplicant, is then consumed and enlivens the discussion. The Chief of Fawohoyeden explained how his Council discusses an issue:

'I have to summon the elders and put the matter before them, as it is they who express their feelings first. They state their opinions one by one. When each has had his say I will think which of them has the most support and judge accordingly. If they all agree I shall confirm their decision. If they say something I disagree with I shall ask them to explain again. They say: "I have taken this stand for this or that reason". I tell them if I find their explanations faulty and we consider the whole issue again. Then, when I am satisfied, we decide the matter." (Fawohoyeden chief – interview.)

Discussion usually opens with a statement of opinion from each in order of rank, sometimes starting with the most junior sometimes with the most senior. Thereafter 'talking-it-out' is considered essential; discussion tends to be cyclic and repetitive, particularly as the proceedings have to be interrupted and summarised for the benefit of the frequent latecomers. Much value is placed on good rhetoric, and resolution is sought by continual re-statement and rephrasing. Anterior preparation of decisions is less obvious than at Local Council or Committee meetings, where agendas are drawn up, motions proposed and questions tabled. There is an insistence that all dealings should be on a face-to-face basis, and the settlement of many issues turns on matters of character, motive and morals. For most of the meeting the chief sits impassively, and the *okyeame* regulates proceedings on his behalf.

There appears to be a 'mystique', as Bailey would put it (Bailey, 1965: 2), about consensus in Ahafo; 'consensus', however, is a blanket-term for various non-voting systems of decision-making, so perhaps it is more accurate to say that there is a dislike in Ahafo for the overt, majority vote. A vote is very rarely recorded in the minutes of the now defunct Council of Ahafo chiefs (1957-66) where decisions are usually 'unanimously decided. . .'. It should be pointed out that 'unanimously' seems to have acquired the sense of 'with good will' — judging by its frequent application to majority votes in the Local Council minutes. Only very rarely has a chief attempted, or expressed the desire, to 'modernise' stool Council procedure; the literate chief of Mim, for example, favoured free discussion and voting, which he supported with his favourite motto: 'life is mathematical'. In Ahafo, and I imagine in many similar situations, sub-group activity plays an essential part in attaining 'consensus'. It is quite in order for petitioners and groups of elders to withdraw politely from a stool meeting to consolidate their opinions.[16] At larger meetings, intermediaries may pass between sub-groups seeking coalescence. When they return to the meeting a spokesman will present their views. 'Walking out' has another function, however. When a person or group has expressed an opinion which is clearly outweighed they may withdraw from the meeting while the decision is being taken, at once sustaining their protest and allowing 'consensus' to be expressed. If they are few, the decision does not appear to be any less valid, and if there is further business the abstainers usually return to the meeting. I cannot recall a single 'traditional' meeting I attended in Ahafo where 'walking out' was not evident in some form. There is good reason to suggest that devices such as this make 'consensus' possible at gatherings larger than the fifteen-person limit suggested by Bailey (1965: 2). More probably it is our understanding of decision-making procedures generally which is unclear.

Although statutorily they should be convened monthly, town Committees do not normally meet more than about eight times a year — less frequently than the stool Councils. In procedure the Committee quite consciously follows the Local Council model. In recognition of its distinct, secular functions it meets in the local school or courthouse and, unlike the stool Council, tends to exclude spectators. This is undoubtedly associated with its desire for 'consensus'; a Goaso member told me: 'the Committee should speak with one mind to the Local Council and the townspeople'. Ordinary Committee members usually wear European dress but the chief (and his stool Council) almost invariably wears the traditional cloth and sandals. Dress is the most obvious distinguishing feature between elders and Young-men, and is clearly a symbol of the contraposition of tradition and modernity. The importance of this symbolism is suggested by an amusing but significant passage from the minutes of the Ahafo chiefs' Council. At a meeting in December 1962 the Regent of Hwidiem (whose status as a chief was clearly equivocal) was cautioned by the Paramount for his 'improper attire':

'He further emphasised that every chief or regent should put on a Native attire during any Council meeting, before he be allowed to take part in the Council's proceedings. [The Regent] agreed to the chairman's remarks and also suggested that the secretary to the Council [a layman] should put on full European attire during the Council's meetings.' (Ahafo State Council minutes, 28 December 1962.)

At Committee meetings the chief sits at a table beside the secretary, facing the members. The seating of the Committee can betray major schisms of interest; the meetings I attended in Goaso were disturbed by a leadership dispute and it was conspicuous that the pro-chief faction gathered at the right of the courthouse, the anti-chief faction at the left and the two or three neutrals, including the Community Development Officer, centrally and to the rear. Meetings invariably open with a Christian prayer from one of the members. Drinking and smoking are prohibited, punctuality is stressed, and there is a sense of urgency to complete the schedule. Nevertheless, there is considerable freedom to raise issues casually with the secretary's approval, in spite of such formal constraints as the agenda. By virtue of his greater familiarity with Local Council business and in the preparations he makes for each meeting, the secretary can exert considerable control over the admission and conduct of business and the 'setting-up' of decisions. Ideally, discussion is linear, repetition being considered a waste of time. Efforts are made to minimise private consultation and 'walking out', which at the Local Council level are interpreted not as efforts to resolve an issue but as detrimental to democratic procedures.[17] Nevertheless, it is interesting to discover Local Councillors over-coming an impasse with such devices as 'a brief recess'. Like the Local Council the Committee is expected to decide by a show of hands on a motion put up by a member (Nsarkoh, 1964: 152). In both bodies, however, a vote is taken only when consensus fails, and then a secret ballot is preferred. For the Committee the dilemma is this: they are expected to vote, but thy process inevitably draws attention to the presence of factions and damages the affective interest in corporate action. Moreover, the Committee has important executive functions which, as Bailey asserts (Bailey, 1965: 13), disposes it to consensus. One of the greatest crises in Committee and Local Council alike is the use of the chairman's casting vote. The District Officer told me that he always tried to ensure that Committees had an odd number of members to diminish the likelihood of the chief ever being placed in the untenable position of having to make a second, decisive vote (see App. A.).[18]

The chief summons the public meeting and, *qua* chief, takes the chair. The tenour of these meetings is a complex blend of traditional and Committee procedure, and apparent anarchy. Some elders and Committee members usually attend, and the main speaker is normally the secretary. The meeting is held in the lorry park or a convenient shady street and is characterised by much coming and going, noise and boisterous behaviour. The meeting may open with a short preamble by the chief, almost certainly setting the tone for consensus: 'the town belongs to all of us, let us put our minds coolly to improving it'. Once the secretary has put the issue to the people, 'Talking it out' is again encouraged: 'We allow everyone to talk, to express himself. We are never tired. We have time for that — that's why we start the meetings earlier and close them late. . . Everybody is allowed free expression'. (Goaso Committee Secretary — interview, English.) People do not complain if their opinion is overruled, but they are indignant if they are not allowed a say.

The public forum offers the greatest opportunity for 'walking out'. I told the Goaso secretary that I found these meetings very fluid and confusing; he explained:

'When the actual meeting is going on we find two or three people grouped outside the meeting, discussing the issue, just something like being in the committee stage. . . I'll call you, as my friend, we stand aside: "look, this is the issue they are telling us, don't you think that if we go on like this, this will be the result. . .?" They try to, probably, make up their minds and you get something like disorderly behaviour. You get some who think on the line of the Committee when you meet like that and they will be defending, supporting the Committee, while you get individual groups expressing opposing minds.' (Ibid.)

Very rudimentary minutes are taken and speakers are apt to come up to the secretary if he is holding a notebook and demand that their names be recorded. As I have explained, the chief exerts an essential restraining influence: 'Before they allow you to make a statement to the chairman, the chief, then you have to behave yourself, you know, because if you don't you will be sacked from the meeting.' (Ibid.) Finally the debate simmers down:

'After so many discussions you will notice that I say: "this is the opinion of this side, and this is the opinion of that side; the Committee say this, and this is what the Youngmen are saying, we get another group saying this; which of these groups do you support?" You will hear a great deal of noise. . . We count, just like that. I think you saw me counting occasionally. . .' (Ibid.)

The Goaso secretary upholds the virtue of voting, but 'counting' is indeed occasional, seldom necessary, and never recorded: 'The people say "yes" or "no" quite clearly. I write down in my book: "approved — ¡unanimously", (Ibid.) The chief rises, much as he does at the Committee or his stool Council, and states the matter simply, e.g.: 'we shall dig the drain by communal labour, starting next month'.

The decision has been made.

Conclusions: the development of town Committees in Ahafo

In this essay I have attempted to account for the development of a modern government institution in the towns and villages of Ahafo. The town Committee was born of strong, national democratic ideals but with relatively little formal planning; in its growth it has been obliged to accommodate itself to the reality of existing authority structures, nevertheless it has become firmly institutionalised in the government of Ahafo. I have attempted to account for some of the ways it has acquired legitimacy, not only by statute but through its relations within the community and within the District. I have suggested that this legitimacy is reflected in the competence of the Committee to perform certain functions within the community and within the political system at large.

However humble it may seem, the Committee can only be understood in the full context of the wider political system. I have singled out the relationships it has had with the central government of Ghana and its Ministries, with the District Officer, the Local Councils, the traditional authorities and the political parties. I have indicated how the statutory and other relationships have changed as the Committee has consolidated its authority in the communities; originally it was sufficient to delegate control of the Committees to the Local Councils, but gradually this was transferred to the District Officer and then to the Ministry and the cabinet. This growing importance of the Committee can be traced to the role it has acquired in community affairs, the tasks it performs and the way it performs them. The pivotal role of the chief is essential to an understanding of the legitimacy of the Committee *vis-a-vis* the traditional stool Council and the townsfolk; he 'manages' most of the community decision-making, steering an issue through his stool Council, the Committee and the public meetings, his endorsement providing an essential final ratification. However, I have been concerned to interpret the 'intrusion' of the Committee not as implying the eradication or even the supplementation of traditional authority, but rather as part of a series of changes in the government of the Ahafo communities in which the chief, the stool Council, the Committee and the public at large are all systematically involved.

Much of my argument has concerned matters of political scale, the government of the community in the context of the government of the state. It seems necessary to draw attention to certain differences associated with scale which may be over-looked; central political institutions tend to be characterised by a more formal, rigid organisation which therefore can be more simple for the anthropologist to describe. Local political institutions tend to be more complex and characterised by organisational variation from community to community which can make the recognition and portrayal of some normal type a difficult task. Pragmatically we set limits in our descriptions of such variation, balancing our ability to speak authoritatively with our desire to make useful sociological generalisations. In choosing to generalise about Ahafo I am aware that I am stretching my resources very far; we are right to be sceptical of detailed descriptions of local institutions which purport to be standard in large polities. My concern is not simply methodological. I would argue that the local political variation, so often ignored or obscured in anthropological description, has essential functions of its own. In particular, it is the means whereby the norms, ideas and practices of a single political system at the highest unitary level can adapt to the social idiosyncrasies of local communities. The growth of new institutions such as the Ahafo town Committees can provide a useful insight into these processes. By corollary, it seems that if we are to understand the organisation and operation of local decision-making bodies we should not seek rigid formulae, we should rather seek to specify the political limitations on their authority and competence.

Notes

[1] This paper is based on research carried out in the Ahafo district of Ghana between April 1968 and April 1969, under a Research Fellowship from the Social Science Research Council.

I was privileged to examine, and have reproduced here short extracts from recent Local Government records. I do not take lightly the great freedom I enjoyed in this respect, and must record here my great indebtedness to the then Commissioner for Local Government Dr A.A.Y. Kyerematen, the Ahafo District Officer Mr E.C. Kotey, the Goaso, Asutifi and Kukuom Council clerks, and the Goaso town Committee secretary Mr P.K. Owusu. I also use here quotations from tape-recorded interviews with the chiefs and people of Ahafo, to whom I am also very grateful. The translations are as simple and as accurate as I can make them.

I am grateful to the present editors, Mr John Dunn, Professor Meyer Fortes, Dr Jack Goody and Dr Malcolm Ruel for their useful comments on earlier drafts.

[2] Especially:

(a) A Committee on Constitutional Reform. Report to H.E. the Governor. Chairman J.H. Coussey. Colonial Office, London, 1949.

(b) Select Committee of the Legislative Council appointed to make Recommendation concerning Local Government in Ashanti. Chairman W.H. Beeton. Gold Coast government, Accra, 1951.

(c) Report of the Commissioner for Local Government Enquiries. Mr A.F. Greenwood. Accra, June 1957.

(d) Report of the Commission to examine the Native Courts System. Chairman Sir Arku Korsah. Gold Coast government, Accra, September 1951.

[3] Legislative Instrument no. 540, 1967. The Instrument made no mention of earlier instructions that former C.P.P. activists were to be excluded.

[4] The main recommendations which appear to have been accepted are as follows:

'It should be possible under our proposals for area or village committees to be established as desired.' (Proposals of the Constitutional Commission for a Constitution for Ghana – Memorandum. Section 668. Accra, 1968.)

'We recommend that the District Authorities should be enabled to create local or village committees within the District. These would be established in consultation with the traditional Authorities and would have specific delegated duties and powers. Their functions would consist mainly of minor environmental services conceived from local initiative and achievable mainly by communal effort not requiring major technological support. They would also be required to assist the District Authority generally in the locality in such matters as the collection of rates and taxes.' (Report of the Commission on the Structure and Remuneration of the Public Services in Ghana, Section 43, Accra 1967.)

'The law should... confer the right on every village or town to form a development committee. Village and town committees should not form a separate tier within the local government structure but should be voluntary associations catering for the welfare of their respective communities.' (Report of the Commission of Enquiry into Electoral and Local Government Reform, Section 17, Accra 1968.)

[5] Newspaper report; 'Daily Graphic' (Accra), 18 May 1970.

[6] I myself have adhered to the expression 'District Officer' throughout this essay to avoid unnecessary confusion. In this section I am particularly indebted to ideas and information supplied by Mr John Dunn.

[7] In 1952 Ahafo became one Local Council area. Rising population and electoral changes led to a division into two Council areas, Asutifi and Asunafo ('upstream' and 'downstream' on the Tano river) in 1962, and in 1966 Asunafo was further divided into Kukuom and Goaso Local Council areas (see Fig.1).

[8] In March 1960 the 'Chief, Elders and Town Committee' of Ayumso wrote to the clerk of Goaso Local Council complaining that they felt ill-represented:

'We, the Citizens of Ayumso feel we are like orphans, for, we know definitely that we have no representative on the Council through whom we can pass our requests. We are the sons and daughters of the Council and we believe that the Council will not neglect us as our representative is doing now.

Can a councillor claim to be the true representative of a certain people without knowing them and their needs? One may like to know whether this is the situation between Ayumso people and their councillor. Yes, indeed. Our Councillor passes through Ayumso either from Goaso to Fawohoyeden or from Fawohoyeden to Goaso daily. Let us ask on how many occasions he has ever stopped to greet either our chief, his elders or the common person in Ayumso? Not a day. Is that not a sure indication of our being neglected?' (Goaso Local Council records.)

[9] Goaso, Akrodie, Mim, Ntotroso, Ayumso, Sankoe, Kukuom, Dantano and Fawohoyeden (see Fig.1).

[10] In October 1957 the secretary of the Mim branch of the C.P.P. complained to the Council clerk and the District Officer that National Liberation Movement leaders in the town had 'met indoors and elected their own choice' for the town Committee, rather than holding a public meeting:

'We feel such election or representation is undemocratic and unconstitutional and as such should be regarded as null and void. People as members serving in a Committee or working for the best interest of a town, should be elected above party politics.' (Goaso Local Council records.)

[11] Much the same lethargy affected the Local Councils: there were, for example, 8 Asunafo Council meetings in 1965-6, compared with 18 in 1956-7.

[12] *Asafoakye* is the most common usage in Ahafo. It seems that the 'more correct' Ashanti term would be *Asafohene,* or possible *Nkwankwahene.*

[13] This is another statutorily recognised right of the traditional authority, e.g.

'Local Authorities and "Gong-gong"

'Local authorities are reminded that the power to order the beating of "gong-gong" belongs by custom to the traditional authorities, i.e. to the State Councils and other traditional bodies. It will, however, often be convenient for local, urban and district councils, by arrangement with such traditional authorities, to arrange for notices and other government matters to be brought to the attention of the public by means of "gong-gong".

'In such cases the local authority should request traditional authorities for "gong-gong" to be beaten, on payment, if necessary, of the usual customary charges. In no circumstances, however, should any local, urban or district councils directly undertake the beating of "gong-gong".'

(Ministry of Local Government and Housing circular no. L.A.C. 5/55, 12 June 1953).

[14] Local Council and District Office files are full of letters and petitions from chiefs, written on behalf of their townspeople. Communications from officialdom are normally addressed to the 'Chief and People of...', regardless of subject matter.

[15] I was frequently made aware of this need for impartiality during my fieldwork; on a visit to Sienchem, for example, I recorded and photographed the 'Roman Catholic Singing Band' and the chief did not allow me to leave the town until the Methodists and the Seventh Day Adventists had been similarly favoured.

[16] During my interviews with the Ahafo chiefs, which took the form of a special meeting of the stool Council, the chief might withdraw with a group of senior elders to agree what they should tell me when a controversial historical point cropped up.

[17] Early Asutifi Local Council meetings were deadlocked on the issue of the siting on the Council headquarters; the towns of Kenyase no.1 and Hwidiem were competing for this honour. By walking out 'unceremoniously' five members obstructed decision-making by breaking the quorum. The Council chairman complained to the District Officer: 'You will see that the walk-out is an illegal strike, and their behaviour... impeaches the justice of the state. There have been a collapse in administration owing to these incidents.' (Goaso District Office records.) The action continued, however. The following month a councillor '.. .left the Council hall without a question and came in immediately after all about the headquarters had been finalised.' (Asutifi Local Council minutes, It. 33, 1962.)

[18] At one memorable meeting of the Kukuom Local Council (management committee) the members divided equally on two successive, contentious issues. On the first occasion the hapless chairman was taken to task for using his casting vote 'in a partisan fashion', and in the second he was accused of poor chairmanship by abstaining from voting.s,

Appendix A

Ahafo town and village Committees registered in October 1968

(1) Size of the Committees:

Committees with	4 members	1
	5 "	3
	6 "	2
	7 "	9
	8 "	8
	9 "	8
	10 "	4
	11 "	33
	12 "	1
		69

(2) Representatives on the Committees:

Committees with	0 zongo member	28
	1 " "	31
	2 " "	9
	3 " "	1
		69

Committees with	0 woman member	53
	1 " "	16
		69

Committees with 1 elder   30

2 ”   18

3 ”   3

4 ”   1

(On the records for seventeen Committees, elders are not distinguished from other members.)

ALL Committees except 2 have a registered secretary

14 Committees have treasurers

7 Committees have vice-chairmen

1 Committee has a vice-secretary

Appendix B

Ahafo stool Councils registered in January 1969 in accordance with the Chieftaincy (Destoolment Proceedings) regulation, 1963

Apart from the chief,

3 Councils have 3 registered elders

6 ”   ”   4 ”   ”

6 ”   ”   5 ”   ”

2 ”   ”   6 ”   ”

4 ”   ”   7 ”   ”

2 ”   ”   8 ”   ”

1 ”   ”   9 ”   ”

1 ”   ” 10 ”   ”

3 ”   ” 12 ”   ”

28

20 registered Councils have *obaapanin* 'queen mother'

17 ”   ”   ” *gyasehene* 'head of the royal household'

17 ”   ”   ” *okyeame** 'stool spokesman'

11 ”   ”   ” *nifahene* 'right wing chief'

9 ”   ”   ” *krontihene* 'army head/chief counsellor'

*5 Councils have 2 or more *akyeame*)

Meeting of the Goaso Town Committee – 22nd November 1968

Notification and agenda

Goaso Town Committee.
The Secretary,
Goaso.
20th November 1968

Sir/Madam,

Goaso TOWN COMMITTEE MEETING
22nd November 1968.

You are summoned to the next Committee meeting to be held on 22nd November 1968 at the usual meeting place – the local court house at 4.30 p.m. prompt.

May I remind you that there should be no failure in attendance like the previous meeting scheduled for the 13th November, 1968 when the few attendants had to return to their homes disappointed.

The agenda will be as follows:

1. Approval of minutes.

2. Cocoa surtax.

3. Reorganisation of communal work.

4. Construction of street drains.

5. Other relevant matters.

Yours faithfully,

SECRETARY
(P.K. Owusu)

TO ALL MEMBERS
GOASO TOWN COMMITTEE
c.c.: The Dist. Adm. Officer, Goaso
      The Clerk of Council, Goaso
      The Ag. Health Supt., Goaso
      The Comm. Dev. Officer, Goaso
      The District Auditor. Goaso

Brief account of meeting of Goaso town Committee, at Goaso courthouse, 22 November 1968.

Chief absent: meeting chaired by his senior elder.

4.37 p.m.: Chairman asks member to lead meeting in prayer.

Complaints about previous poor attendance: one member complains of inadequate notification. Secretary requests a vote for stationery.

New Community Development Officer interrupts argument to introduce himself.

Previous minutes read, approved without question, and signed by chairman. They are written in English and interpreted in Twi.

Cocoa surtax: Member states that all tenants on Goaso stool land should pay tax; others apparently agree. Same member says a letter should be written to the Local Council complaining of increased market tax.

Secretary reports recruitment of 4 collectors: describes difficulties of ensuring that there is no evasion.

Committee members express indignation at subject villages' refusal to contribute cocoa surtax for Goaso school building and press chief to demand co-operation. Secretary, health Supt. and Community Development Officer all explain Committee has no right to demand co-operation. Decision made (no vote) to write final demand to three tax defaulters.

Criticism of lax attitude of tax collectors.

5.40 p.m.: meeting interrupted by arrival of District Officer, who sits centrally beside chairman.

Secretary announces government plans to install pipe-borne water in town: need for communal labour, but present 'foreman' *[asafoakye]* is not proving effective, must be replaced. One member says only the chief may appoint a new *asafoakye,* but the District Officer and the other officials overrule this.

Communal labour: argument develops over the division of the townspeople into work groups and the role of *asafoakye.* Community Development Officer intervenes, suggests a plan which the members accept.

Zongo member (first contribution) asks secretary's permission to speak: suggests division of *zongo* work force on a tribal basis. District Officer says he will hold public meeting in *zongo* with the Committee to explain the need for labour, and seek the people's approval.

District Officer, speaking in English and interpreted by the Community Development Officer, makes a formal speech about need for communal efforts in development, and for the suppression of conflicting interests in the Committee in the cause of community progress.

Secretary calls for a vote of thanks for the D.O.

Chairman obliges.

Drains: Secretary announces 2 contractors have tendered. Member asks Community

Development officer to help them decide, but he points out the tenders are incomplete. No decision.

Letter from Health Supt. read, calling for whitewashing of buildings and cleaning up of the market. Complaints of lack of co-operation in his efforts to persuade townspeople to keep their houses habitable. Committee agrees (no vote) to instruct the people to co-operate.

Meeting closes, well after nightfall, at 7.05 p.m., with a prayer from a member.

The meeting was run by the secretary, including calls for order, etc. Twice he was involved in a heated exchange with a member, and on each occasion threatened to resign. In a meeting which was more passionate than most, the Officials exerted considerable restraint. It was rumoured that the chief had discreetly absented himself to minimise the friction between the leadership factions in the face of quite complicated coming and going; although various decisions were minuted briefly there was no voting.

Appendix D

Methodological note

The town Committees provided the most intractable problems of my twelve months' field work in Ahafo. Foremost were difficulties with language; local Council business was conducted in English, and with extensive use of tape-recorders I was able to make reasonable progress with traditional political affiars, but attempting to understand the hurly-burly of Committee meetings was often frustrating. I was anxious not to confine my attention to Goaso, but an under-standing of proceedings implied a detailed knowledge of local circumstances in other communities which was difficult to acquire in the time at my disposal. Distances between communities and problems of communications severely reduced the number of meetings I could attend; adding to the problem was the fact that meetings could be called at hours notice, and despite assurances that I would be informed in time I was frequently too late. It was particularly frustrating to return to Goaso after a visit to another town to discover that a meeting had been held in my absence. I was also afraid, perhaps not very justifiably, that my attendance caused malaise and affected the processes which I hoped to examine objectively. So much depended upon my own observations and discussions with participants; written records were few, and it is regrettable that an enormous amount of valuable material was destroyed in the apprehensive days after the February 1966 coup d'etat.

I attempted to adapt my methods to these problems as best as I could. My greatest advantage was the freedom accorded me by the Ghana government and the District Officer; the latter had encyclopaedic knowledge of the District and its problems and in our regular discussions he provided me with invaluable insights into the affairs of the various communities. The District Officer and the Goaso Council clerk, Mr R.F. Ampah, took considerable interest in my work, not only allowing me access to local government records but also advising and assisting in the collection of current information. The national atmosphere of frankness and self-criticism prevalent during the years of National Liberation Council rule was an added advantage.

Most of my research on the Committees was carried out in the final four months of fieldwork. By then I was acquiring some knowledge of the organisation of the various Ahafo communities. I became most familiar with the Goaso Committee, benefitting from my residence in the town, and managed to interview in detail most of the eleven members. I visited, and interviewed the chiefs of all the Ahafo towns, and cultivated an interest in an assortment of five committees, whose affairs I followed as closely as I could. For various reasons a tape recorder was unsuitable for meetings; instead, my two assistants accompanied me and we took separate detailed notes. As soon as possible after the meeting we sat together and reconstructed it minute by minute. Latterly our proficiency increased, and we learned unequivocal ways of indentifying participants and methods of keeping pace with the rapid flow of contributions. Casual conversation immediately before and after the meetings often provided much illuminating information, and wherever possible I consulted the Committee secretary in advance about the issues which would arise and the interests which were likely to be expressed. Latterly I found it rewarding to invite members to a local bar after meetings for refreshments, as this often led to an informative and strangely detached *post mortem* on the proceedings.

I included questions about the Committees in the interviews I had with the chiefs and people of Ahafo. These were guided by a questionnaire and tape-recorded, and were later painstakingly transcribed/translated. I believe this process helped to compensate for my deficiencies in Twi, and also improved my learning of the language. As far as my studies of the Committees are concerned it is regrettable that I had to leave Ahafo just when my understanding was gaining ground.

PARTY POLITICS AND THE PROCESSES OF LOCAL DEMOCRACY IN AN ENGLISH TOWN COUNCIL

By Paul Spencer

Since the advent of the industrial revolution early in the nineteenth century, the role of local councils in the social life of English towns has changed considerably. With immigration from the more rural areas, an increasing proportion of the total population has become concentrated in the towns. Voting rights have been extended from local (all male) elites to all adult men and women. At one time, councils tended to be at the centre of local community life, playing a crucial part in the maintenance of law and order and in resolving matters of local concern. This is no longer so. The magistracy and direct control over police activities are now quite separate from the local councils. As society has become increasingly differentiated and means of communication have improved, so they have lost much of their local significance. New spheres of influence, often with more coherent regional and national ties have emerged. One now has commercial, industrial, professional and trade union interests that are quite independent of local government; and political parties are more readily identifiable at a national than a local level. These have opened up the range of opportunities for the individual aspirant.

It would be misleading, however, to imply that town councils have lost all their local importance. The last one hundred years have seen a sharp increase in public services in general and it is the local councils that are responsible for providing many of these services. In economic terms they account for 13·3% of the Gross National Product today, as compared with 3·3% in 1890. For the local communities, the principal significance of their.councils is in the running of these services.

It would also be misleading to imply that councils have no relevance for the other local interests that have developed more recently. Quite apart from the fact that the council members will also normally be personally involved in these (as employees, proprietors, members of local professional bodies or trade unions), there are also other features. Councils, for instance, are responsible for planning control and hence the development of any local enterprise must depend on their approval for any new plans; local employment problems will be seriously affected by the councils' policies towards the provision of new housing, traffic congestion will be affected by their policies towards the local road network, and so on.

Political parties, which are often associated with the activities of local councils, cut across all these interests and this chapter is concerned with the effects on the local democratic processes of a specific town council due to the unofficial presence of two opposed political parties, the Labour and the Conservative party, vying for power over the council.

Certain features and responsibilities apply to all English local councils. In the first place, as already noted, the bulk of council work concerns the administration of a wide variety of public services, and in many respects they are not matters over which there can be political controversy.[1]

Secondly, there is a well established constitutional framework for English local government. This does not specifically recognise the existence of political parties as such, but rather lays down the limits within which local councils are free or obliged to provide certain public services and specifies certain safeguards so that these limits are not infringed and so that control over any council can only be gained by legitimate means. Within the constitutional framework governing the whole country, each council has its own 'Standing Orders', specifying rules of procedure in debate, the delegation of council responsibilities for running its services to various committees, methods for choosing chairmen for these committees, or for choosing the mayor. For politicians or political parties interested in influencing the council in any way, the constitution and the Standing Orders provide a set of rules within which they can operate. Power cannot be achieved by ignoring these rules, but rather by manipulating them more successfully than one's opponents.

The basic structure of any town council is summarised in Fig.1. It should be noted that each link from the electorate of the community (all local residents over the age of 18 years). through the council, to the provision of public services may be expressed both in terms of appointment in one direction and of a corresponding accountability in the other. A councillor is appointed by the electorate through an election, and he is accountable to this electorate who may refuse to endorse a further period of office when he is due for re-election. Elections are held annually in each ward (or electoral district) of the town, and the winning candidate represents this ward on the town council for a period of three years – if he has no rivals for the seat then no elections are held and he is returned to the council unopposed. Thus, for any one ward there are always three councillors, each elected in successive years.

The appointment of aldermen is rather more complex. The present 'aldermanic system' was introduced into English local government in the last century to provide a certain stability. It was thought that if there were always a residue of older men on any council then it would be less vulnerable to any sudden intake of younger and less experienced men. For this reason, aldermen are elected for periods of six years and once again the method of election is staggered so that half of the aldermen are elected every third year. There is one alderman to every three councillors – in other words there are as many aldermen as wards. It is the coun-

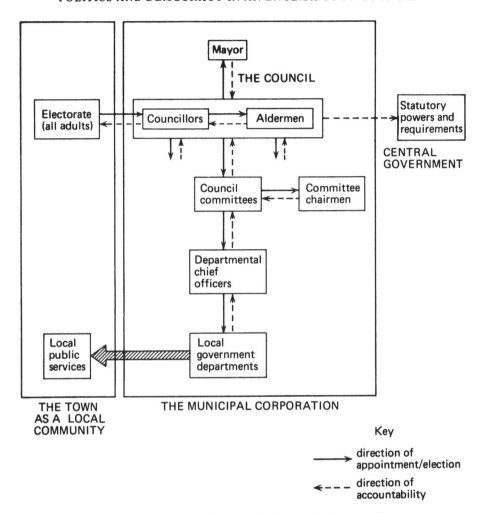

Fig. 1   The basic constitution of an English municipal corporation

cillors as a whole (and not the electorate) who elect the aldermen, and hence in the last resort aldermen are accountable to the councillors if they are to merit reappointment. The councillors and the aldermen together constitute the council, and meet in public in the council chamber under the chairmanship of the mayor. The mayor is chosen by the council members (i.e. councillors and aldermen) from among their number every year. The precise nature of his accountability to the council is discussed in a later section.

The committees of the council are the organs through which the various local government services are administered on behalf of the council. Individual council members are appointed every year to serve on these committees, and in certain

173

instances other members of the public may be co-opted to serve on them or may be appointed by some other relevant public body or trust as their representatives on a committee. However, regardless of outside participation on these committees, they remain as committees of the council and accountable to it. This not only entails the accountability of individual members at the end of their year of service who may or may not be reappointed – it also entails the committee as a whole whose decisions in major matters are not decisions as such, but recommendations to the council who have the right to accept, question, modify or reverse the committee proposals. This is especially important in matters of expenditure. It is the individual committees who appoint their own chairmen every year, and the accountability of each chairman to retain the confidence of his committee is no different here than on committees elsewhere.

The number and composition of committees, their relationship to the council and to one another is laid down in the Standing Orders of each council, and there is generally a regular cycle of meetings at various levels. In the town council considered later in this paper, for instance, there is a regular monthly cycle for the more important committees culminating with the monthly meeting of the full council at which their recommendations are considered. Altogether eighteen major committees are responsible for running the council's services and because this is often a matter of allocating expenditure, they are sometimes referred to as *spending committees*. There are in addition two other committees: the *finance committee* which has to endorse any proposals for expenditure before these are submitted to the council, and the policy committee which gives guidance to the spending committees on major questions of council policy and resolves any disputes between them.

Unlike the council meetings which are held in public, the committee meetings are held in private. It is at this level that the council members as voluntary part-time representatives come into direct contact with the full-time salaried officials in charge of the day-to-day running of the services: the chief officers and their assistants. It is in this context that the committee meeting emerges as a focal point in the decision-making process: the success of the system will hinge on the rapport built up between the council members and the officers. While there is an explicit 'master-servant' relationship maintained between them and any issue is finally decided solely by the council members, the latter depend on the officers for technical advice and guidance and the pressures towards certain decisions are by no means one-sided.

Further links in the chain are not strictly relevant to this chapter. But beyond the committee, it is worth noting an abrupt change in the method of appointment and mode of accountability. A councillor, as a local representative of his ward, as a council or a committee member, or as a committee chairman, is elected for a term of office and is only broadly accountable for his conduct. Any lapse of judgment may be overlooked by his colleagues or offset by excelling himself in other ways;

the accountability is essentially diffuse and unspecific. The chief officer of any department providing a service, on the other hand, having once been appointed by his respective committee (on behalf of the council) holds a permanent appointment under them and his accountability to them is relatively well defined and in the last resort unquestionable. Similarly, within his department the pattern is repeated at all levels from the chief officer and his deputy to the most junior member. The organisation at this point is overtly hierarchical and accountability is explicit and specific.

The council at Aberton

The present analysis is specifically of the local council of Aberton, an industrial town in the north of England. In many respects it is quite typical of a considerable number of local councils in the larger English towns and cities, and where there are differences, they are often matters of detail and degree rather than of substance. In 1964 the majority of councillors in Aberton were also members of the Labour party, and hence this party was effectively in control of council affairs and had been so for an extended period during which political power at a national level had changed hands three times. Only the fact that the Conservative party was locally well organised and had a considerable popular support in certain sectors of the town – including the tacit support of the local press – prevented local politics from sinking to complete obscurity as year after year, the Labour party retained its majority on the council. This situation came to a sudden almost completely unpredicted end in 1967 when a prolonged economic crisis had brought widespread unpopularity to the national Labour government. The Conservatives gained control of local councils up and down the country, and in Aberton, for the first time in more than twenty-five years, they gained control.

No such dramatic change, however, was envisaged during the period that this study was made. The Conservatives (and to a very minor extent other political parties) would challenge the Labour majority at each annual election with little success. It is worth paying closer attention to the activities at an election at this point, since it brings two features of local government into sharp relief. The elections of May 1964 were the last of a long series of uneventful elections when the initiative remained firmly with the Labour party. In theory, the balance of power was at stake, but still, the Labour party had a comfortable majority and would have had to lose seven of the ten seats they expected to win in order to lose control over the council. This possibility was so remote as not to be worth entertaining.

The results of fifteen wards of the town were counted at fifteen different tables in one large hall. These tables were linked by lengths of rope at knee height which served to divide the hall into two separate halves and ensured the strict segregation between the candidates and their political confederates in one half and the official local government organisation entrusted with the task of counting the ballot papers in the other. At each table the ballot papers for one ward were sorted, counted and stacked by volunteers (mostly local government officers) with an alderman presiding in a strictly non-political role. On one side of the division, senior local government officers supervised the general organisation of the count, while porters delivered the boxes of ballot papers to their respective tables as soon as these arrived from the different wards of the city. After ballot papers had been counted and stacked, they were removed from the tables to make further space available. The whole activity on this side of the division was one of smooth organisation and cool appraisal.

The scene on the other side of the division was rather different. Here the candidates were allowed to watch the proceedings but could not assist in any way. Each candidate was allowed a limited number of scrutineers to help him check that the vote counting was conducted entirely fairly. Altogether fifty-four candidates of four different political parties and about 170 scrutineers were crowded into one half of the hall. The atmosphere in this half was essentially a political one. Party emblems were worn and most conversation was earnest and between members of the same party. One or two instances of mild joking occurred between members of different parties, but for the most part activity ranged from intent concentration on the counting to a considerable amount of visible anxiety. The impression was that some candidates with relatively safe seats were as concerned with the precise state of their electoral majority as others in marginal seats were with their whole future as councillors.

In this instance, two very different types of involvement were clearly seen. On the one hand, the local government officers, whatever their private opinions and aspirations, were involved in a purely professional, impersonal and non-political sense with the routine workings of a system. On the other hand, the candidates and their confederates (many of them already councillors) were involved in a highly personal and wholly political sense in the outcome of the occasion. The physical barriers that divided the room into two halves served to emphasise the social distance that separated the two types of involvement in local government. It is hardly coincidental that it was an occasion where both the redistribution of power within the local authority and the democratic processes on which it was based were at stake. It was these factors which gave the occasion its colour and crystallised certain aspects of the structure of local government, reflected in the behaviour of all the participants. The local organisation of the two political parties in Aberton was as follows. Within the town, members of the Labour party belonged to the Aberton Borough Labour Party and members of the Conservative party to the Aberton Conservative Association. It was these two bodies who sponsored their respective candidates in the municipal elections, and, if they wished, either could effectively refuse to renominate a councillor of their own party with whom they were dissatisfied when he was due for re-election after a three-year term of office. This would not preclude such a man from standing again as an independent candidate, but without his party's support and with a rival candidate supported by them, he would have only a slender chance of succeeding, while the other party's candidate, benefiting from the split vote, would have an enhanced chance.

The control of these borough political associations over council affairs, however, stopped at this point. Their members who were on the town council as councillors or aldermen formed themselves into two autonomous groups: the Labour Group who among themselves formulated council policies, and the Conservative Group who devised their own strategies of opposition. The accountability of these groups to the borough associations at times of municipal elections was essentially a derivative of the accountability of the council as a whole to the electorate at this time; and just as councillors (and not the electorate) formally appointed aldermen, so it was the two groups (and not the borough associations) who decided who should be promoted to the aldermanic bench.

It is outside the scope of this paper to consider this relationship further. The discussion could be extended to the relationship of the borough associations with the local political organisation for each ward who officially sponsor their candidates (and indeed for each parliamentary constituency). Suffice it to say here that, while differences of opinion might arise over local policies or candidature, these did not dominate the meetings of either group. One outstanding reason for this was that most local politicians of ability and influence sooner or later became members of the council and hence of one group or the other. From that point, they might either assert their influence within their group to resolve differences with the borough association; or, more likely, their active interest in the borough association would begin to wane as they became more involved in council affairs and aware of the practical difficulties facing the council.

At first sight, the electoral advantage of the Labour party in Aberton was small: a mere 1·4% lead over the Conservatives over the years 1957 to 1966. However this did not take account of the number of potential Labour supporters who did not

Table 1. The consolidation of political power by the two competing
political parties at Aberton

Aspect of local government	Party advantage expressed as a percentage:	
	Labour party 1964	Conservative party 1967
Total votes cast in Aberton local elections	52	59
Number of councillors on Aberton Council	65	57
Total number of council members (including aldermen)	69	58
Number of places on standing committees	77	65
Number of chairmen and vice-chairmen of standing committees	100	100
Number of places on policy committee	100	100

* because only one-half of the aldermen were due to retire in 1967, the Conservatives were not able to press their advantage beyond this figure when they gained power in that year.

bother to vote in areas where the party held safe seats.

It may not be altogether fortuitous then that a small majority in the local elections should have given the Aberton Labour party effective control over a far larger proportion of the electoral wards – in fact 63% – but it was a matter of political expediencey that the Labour group should have enhanced their control through the election of a larger proportion of Labour aldermen. From 1945 until 1967, they consistently nominated Labour members of the council to all but three of the aldermanic seats, which were left to the Conservatives to fill.

The control of the Labour group was extended yet further by their control over the standing committees of the council. According to the Standing Orders, the council as a whole had the final power of electing each of its members to serve on two, three or four of these committees. But again, out of expediency, the Labour group reserved the bulk of seats on each committee for their own members ensuring that they each served on three or four committees. This left the Conservative minority with only enough vacancies to serve on two or occasionally three committees each.

Two final measures demonstrating the firm Labour control over council activities were that all chairmen and vice-chairmen of committees and *all* members of the policy committee were Labour members. In these respects, the Labour group increased their effective control to a maximum.

Control over the Aberton council passed to the Conservatives when they gained a majority of seats in 1967. The balance of power was now reversed, and almost inevitably the Conservatives used precisely the same tactics to consolidate their majority as the Labour group had done previously when they had been in power. Table 1 shows how the consolidation of Labour control (in 1964) and then of Conservative control (in 1967) was achieved through these successive measures.

The Labour group and the processes of policy making

It has already been noted that the majority formed by the Labour group on the Aberton Council prior to 1967 gave them effective control over council affairs. As Table 1 shows quite clearly, the Labour group's control over the various committees – where so much of the important work of the council was carried out – was even more firm. At first sight, it might seem that their substantial numerical superiority on all committees culminating in an absolute control over the policy committee and chairmanships would have given this group the necessary power to implement their policies, and this was certainly so in the major portion of their committee work. But this does assume that 'Labour policies' in local government were precisely defined and that there were no divergences of views between party members when faced with a particular decision in committee. Obviously, there could be no complete concord on all issues, however desirable this might have been. No set of policies based on some social ideal could hope to achieve a compromise with reality in an entirely unequivocal way. There had to be a constant dialogue as new factors emerged and established ideals were implicitly modified. In this respect 'policy' and its application to current problems had much in common with a judicial process where a body of law (as a social ideal) has to be applied to specific court cases and is modified in the process[2]

This fact has two corollaries. The first is that the process of arriving at some consensus of opinion at a committee meeting could involve a dispute between Labour members which might lay bare the rifts within the party in the presence of the Conservative members and local governmental officers. This would be politically inexpedient to say the least. The second is that in a committee with (typically) seven or eight Labour members of whom (typically) five were present at any meeting, it was by no means certain that the decision they might arrive at on some vexed issue would necessarily be consistent with the views of the majority of the Labour group. If this situation was to be avoided, some opportunity was required for the whole Labour group to achieve a consensus and instruct their committee members accordingly.

In this process, the chairman of any committee played a key role. Frequently, he was expected to speak on its behalf in council and at meetings of the Labour group or to make statements to the local press. So long as he was chosen for his ability and his active interest in his committee, and so long as he was in closer and more frequent touch with the departmental officers, he was better placed to know the relevant facts of any issue and to steer the meetings through controversial issues. When, as sometimes happened, he was chosen out of loyalty or political expediency rather than for his ability, there might be an opportunity lost by the Labour group to control the situation by appointing a more able person.

It is hardly surprising, then, in the first place, that chairmen were *not* freely elected by their committees but rather by the Labour group; secondly that all

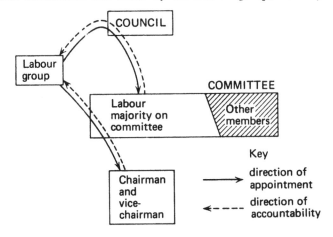

Fig. 2. Unofficial elaboration of the basic constitution in Aberton

chairmen (and vice-chairmen) were members of the Labour group; and thirdly that their active role in policy-making did not ultimately hinge on their relationship with their committees, but rather on their relationship with the Labour group, and any decision by that group was in effect an instruction to the chairman and other Labour members of his committee as to the policies they were expected to adopt.

Fig.2 shows schematically the elaboration of the formal appointment and accountability of committee members that followed from their adherence to a political party. Formally, it was the council who nominated members to the various committees and each committee who elected its own chairman and vice-chairmen. In reality the Labour majority of any committee was elected by the Labour group (by way of a formal resolution in council), and the chairman and vice-chairman were also elected by the Labour group (by way of a formal resolution in the committee when it met shortly after the annual elections). So far as the pursuit of Labour policies were concerned, the effective accountability of both chairman and committee was not to the council, but to the Labour group.

As was noted earlier, the committee system of the council was based on a monthly cycle. In superimposing its control over committee and council affairs, the Labour group logically accommodated itself to this cycle by meeting in a monthly cycle of its own. This involved the group in two sorts of activity: screening the decisions already made in the various committees before they were ratified by the council on the one hand; and arriving at an agreed group policy towards certain more general issues on the other (Fig. 3).

The screening was carried out on the evening before the council meeting. The agenda for this meeting was available several days in advance, and at the Labour group's pre-council meeting each member had the opportunity of raising any point related to the agenda which he felt should be given further consideration by the group. Any suggestion to reverse a committee decision could be debated in the group and settled by a free vote. In this way, by the time that the council met, the Labour group had had a chance to determine its strategy, both with regard to the negative aspects of withdrawing or modifying controversial items on the agenda and to the more positive aspects of presenting certain items of 'council' (i.e. Labour) policy in a way that would attract public approval or at least minimise criticism.

The process of arriving at an agreed group policy on any matter of less immediate concern was largely achieved at the meetings of the Labour group that were held halfway through the monthly cycle: these were known as the interim meetings of the group. At these meetings any individual members, and particularly the chairmen of the various committees, could raise items for discussion which entailed some future committee decision or policy.

If some issue was particularly complex requiring lengthy consideration, or if its policy implications were far-reaching, then it would normally be referred to a smaller group consisting of some of the more influential Labour members known as the Labour policy group. In a normal month, the policy group meeting was held a

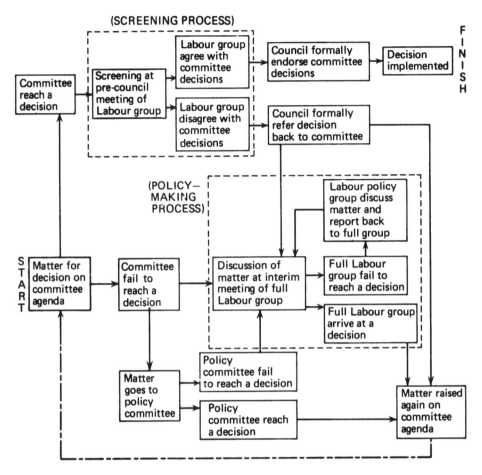

Fig. 3   The strategic position of the Labour group in the policy and decision-making process at Aberton

week after the pre-council group meeting.

A Labour policy group meeting was typically attended by some ten members as opposed to thirty or forty at a full group meeting. The limited size of the policy group alone was conducive to more sustained policy consideration, whereas the full group could only too easily be diverted by any number of extraneous issues. Before the recommendations of the policy group were adopted as agreed Labour policy, they could be debated by the full group and any decision became a decision of that group. Thus the nomination of members to committees and chairmanships would be first discussed annually after the local municipal elections by the policy group. Their proposed allocation was then presented at the annual general meeting of the full Labour group who could suggest modifications. It was not so much that control of committee membership and chairmanships was in the last resort in the hands of the Labour policy group as that the task of allocating these was more easily achieved in the first place in the more intimate atmosphere of that group.

There were, then, certain parallels between the policy committee and the Labour policy group; both were elected each year by the full Labour group, both were concerned with policy formation, and both comprised some of the more influential members of the Labour group (and no Conservatives). The main differences were that the policy committee was a formally constituted committee of the council attended by a number of key chief officers, whereas the Labour policy group was a wholly unconstitutional body and was not attended by any officers. If, therefore, a policy decision had important and complex technical considerations to which the officers could contribute, it was more appropriately discussed at the policy committee, while if it had more purely political implications, it was more appropriately discussed at the Labour policy group meeting.

It frequently happened that the full policy and political implications of an issue were only apparent once it had been discussed at the policy committee level with the officers contributing their own expertise to the general discussion. At such times, any decision could be deferred, giving the Labour group a chance to consider the matter further.

The Labour group, as a purely unofficial body, inevitably had to adopt indirect means to interfere with the official flow of council business. It would never be possible for a committee to refer a matter formally to the Labour group: both Conservative members and officers would point out that this was unconstitutional. On the other hand, it was a relatively straightforward matter for some (Labour) member of the committee to propose that some particularly vexed issue should be left with the (Labour) chairman and (Labour) vice-chairman, or that it should be deferred for further (Labour) consideration or should be referred to the (all Labour) policy committee.

The control of the Labour group did not stop at the point where an item had been formally agreed by a committee and then placed on the council agenda for its next meeting: if members of the group at their pre-council meeting disagreed with the decision, there could be no constitutional objection when the council met if the (Labour) chairman of this committee asked for the matter to be referred back to his committee for further consideration. It was only necessary for these proposals to have the majority (Labour) support either in committee or in council in order to give the Labour group a chance to re-discuss the whole matter at length.

There could never be any question as to the prime allegiance of any member of the group. If as a committee member he was inclined to view an issue in a different light from his Labour colleagues, then the correct place to argue his case was at the meetings of the Labour group and not in the committee or in council. If he failed to persuade them to change their views then he was obliged to withhold his opposition or face disciplinary action which could entail exclusion from the meetings of the Labour group, leaving him in political isolation.

This did not necessarily resolve the problems facing the Labour group among themselves, but at least it ensured that in the face of public attention elsewhere they presented a unified front and adopted the image of a political group who intended to govern.

Fig. 3 summarises the network through which any matter passed in the course of forming and confirming a decision. It will be noted that no major committee decision could be formally ratified as a council decision without first passing through the unofficial screening of the full Labour group, and that, where it was referred back for further consideration, it might pass through the hands of this group on several occasions.

Fig.4 has been included to draw attention at this point to the roles of the chief officer and the chairman of any committee in this process. Thus, typically, it will be the chief officer who first becomes aware of a problem to be raised with his committee. If he feels that the issues raised are largely routine with no political or policy content (A), then he may present it with his own recommendations. If he feels that there *is* a policy content (B) then he may discuss it with his chairman.

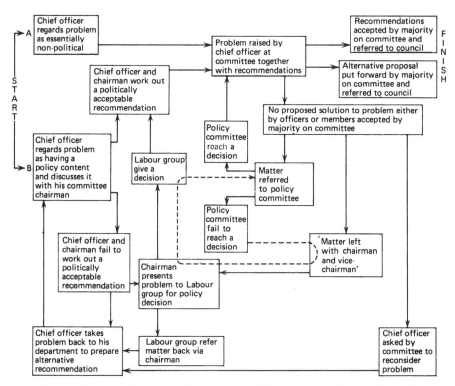

Fig. 4   The roles of the chief officer and committee chairman in the decision-making process at Aberton

The diagram shows how in either case the matter may ultimately be referred to the policy committee or (unofficially) to the Labour group.

The Conservative group and the strategy of opposition

By using their political majority to retain a firm control over the affairs of the council the Labour group were effectively denying the Conservatives in opposition a proportionate share in the running of the local authority. The Conservatives formed a minority on the council and on its committees, and they were powerless to take any direct action to modify Labour policies. The election of Labour members to the majority of aldermanic vacancies, to the majority of committee places and to all the chairmanships could be carried out quite legitimately, and matters decided in private by the Labour group could be made official council policy at the next meeting of the council.

At the same time, a degree of accommodation existed between the two parties. The Labour group could, if they wished, have gone much further; they could have reduced the number of Conservative aldermen from three to none, and the number of spending committee places allocated to Conservatives (in 1964) from forty-five to thirty-eight (leaving them with their minimum by right of two apiece). They could have dictated which committees each Conservative member should serve on, and could have altogether refused the party seats on any of the more powerful committees such as finance. In the last resort they could, through the policy committee, have drastically revised the Standing Orders in many ways so as to allow a ruthless exploitation of their majority on the council.

However, it was not in the best interests of the Labour group to create an image of an all powerful, ruthless party with no regard for the wishes of any minority sector of the public. Quite apart from the purely practical fact that the extrusion of Conservatives from the committees would increase the committee burden for individual Labour members, there was a sound tactical reason. By bringing the Conservatives into the various committees (except the policy committee), the Labour group could take some of the sting out of their opposition. They could argue that it was not in their own interests to have an unnecessary opposition to proposals which might otherwise have been essentially non-political if matters had been handled differently. In other words, issues could easily become political simply because the opposition had been excluded from discussion in the earlier stages.

This argument was not extended to the policy committee. Here the Labour group felt that the advantages of having sole possession of such a committee outweighed the disadvantages of increasing allegations against them. So long as they had one committee to which any matter with far-reaching policy and political implications could be referred from other committees, the advantages of maintaining sole possession over any of these other committees rapidly diminished.

The degree of accommodation was essentially a matter of political expedience, and it varied over time. Thus, it was not until 1952 that the Labour group deprived the Conservatives of their only place on the policy committee. Or again, in 1965 the Labour group decided to allow the Conservatives a block allocation of seats on the various committees and no longer insisted on a right to blackball specific members from specific committees. These phases of apparent hardening and softening of attitudes were not related to the potential threat posed by the Conservatives in their bids to regain power locally: this was seen as utterly remote throughout this period.

Inevitably, the Conservatives also formed themselves into a group, and, while they could not reverse the decisions of the Labour group, they could at least hope to expose and exploit various weaknesses in the Labour control. This called for a carefully considered strategy and concerted action. The two principal arenas into which they could carry their opposition were the meetings of the full council and the meetings of the various committees.

To this end, committee meetings were the less promising of the two. In the first place, the bulk of committee work was essentially non-political and the Conservative members would be open to allegations from the Labour members if they tried to infuse a political content into these matters; they might in addition find less support from those of their own Conservative colleagues who wished to play a useful non-political role in matters that did not directly concern their party. And secondly, all important committee work was carried out in private; the only audience to political controversy between the elected members would be the officers present who, first and foremost, were expected not to be involved in political matters, and in any case had heard all the political arguments between the two parties ad nauseam.

The positive value of committee work for the Conservatives was that it provided basic information on current matters and policies which they might find useful elsewhere. Moreover, in their capacity as the opposition on the council, it was necessary for them to attend these meetings to register formally their disagreement with contentious issues. Politically speaking, their role was essentially a passive one, but at least their presence acted as a check on Labour activities and their formal opposition at this stage protected them from any future accusations that their behaviour in committee was inconsistent with their public policies. It was not simply that the Conservatives as a group had little incentive for playing a major part in committees, but also that to take their opposition further at this level could give the Labour members a better chance to prepare for the defence of their policies when the two parties confronted each other in public.

The full council meeting, on the other hand, provided the Conservatives with an ideal arena for mustering their forces. It was a public occasion when the two parties met on rather more equal terms than elsewhere. Neither party took the poor public attendance at some of these meetings at its face value. They knew only too well that when a sector of the local population was seriously affected by the proposals they were debating, it would be well represented in the public gallery. Moreover, they were also fully aware of the presence of the local press whose reports on the meeting would be widely read the following day.

Of the various newspapers represented at these Council meetings, the one that gave the fullest and most regular account of the various debates was *The Aberton Echo*. The relevance of this from the Conservative point of view was far-reaching, since this newspaper was prepared to make independent comments on the Labour policies of the council, and at times of election allied itself to the Conservative cause.

The political stance of the local press went some way towards redressing the balance of power between the two parties. The Labour group could control council policies, but they could not prevent the Conservatives from having their full share of any debate in the council meetings, they could not prevent the local press from interpreting these debates in any way it chose, and in the last resort they could not alter their ultimate accountability as the de facto policy making group on the council to the electorate at every local election. On the face of it, the council meeting was an occasion when Labour policies were confirmed and every Conservative motion or amendment was resolutely out-voted. But implicitly, the debates and the voting were inconclusive; the proceedings reported to the public through the press were unlikely to tarnish the Conservative image, and often sought to enhance it. It was to the council meetings that the Conservatives could bring their insights and their knowledge gathered at committee meetings. They were still out-voted, but at least they had a golden opportunity to present their case to the public via the press and the gallery, and to emphasise the extent to which they dissociated themselves from the decisions made by the committees of the council.

The usefulness of the press to the Conservative cause was enhanced by the extent to which one failure was more likely to become prominent news in the local press than a number of successes. A sample of newspaper cuttings taken over one month indicated that of sixty-nine articles concerning corporation activities, thirty-three were in some way critical or associated with current difficulties, whereas only eleven concerned positive achievements. Of the thirty-three items of 'bad' news, twenty-four were displayed on the front or middle pages as compared with only eight items of 'good' news.

From the Conservative viewpoint, then, there was a political opportunity to be gained out of council meetings that was normally absent from committee meetings. That it was the presence of the local press that made this difference, was borne out by the behaviour of councillors at the meetings of the local education committee. Here, too, the occasion tended to become essentially a political one with the Conservatives playing an aggressive role. But this was the one committee that the press was allowed to attend (by law) and the meeting in effect became a 'little council'. So far as the routine constructive work of this committee was concerned, it was carried out in private by its various sub-committees, and in this respect these were similar to the other committees of the council from which the press was excluded.

In order to prepare their strategy for the council meeting, the Conservatives held two meetings of their own. The first was held a week earlier and was attended by a few of the more influential members who formed the Conservative policy group. At this stage, there was only an incomplete knowledge of what would be on the agenda for the council meeting. However, some of the committee minutes were available, and, in addition, the finance committee would have met on the same morning. This gave the group some scope for devising a basic strategy which could be elaborated a week later when the full Conservative group met and the council agenda was available. Because the Conservatives were in opposition, their activities as a group were very largely confined to this rather negative role of screening the council agenda rather than to formulating positive policies.

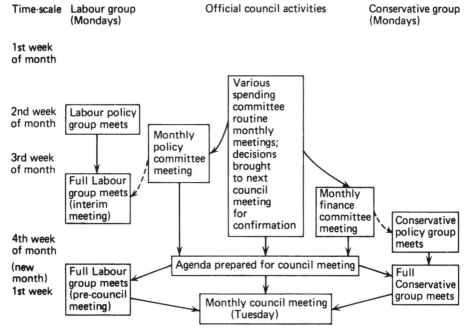

Fig. 5 The monthly cycle of party group, committee and council meetings at Aberton

Thus, on the evening preceding the council meeting, the groups of both parties separately considered the formal agenda and decided on their tactics. Neither knew precisely what the other intended to do, but they had faced one another often enough to make certain shrewd guesses. They both knew where they themselves and where the other party were most vulnerable, and when they had a point which deserved publicity.

Fig.5 shows the more important meetings of a typical monthly cycle and the general direction of flow of information in the decision-making process, especially in so far as it entailed the two party groups. The time-scale shown on the left of the diagram refers to the weeks of the calendar month.

The council meeting

The foregoing sections have outlined the relationships of the Aberton Council with the electorate (which it served), the committees (to which it delegated), and the party groups (for which it provided a political arena). Fig.6 shows the modification of the official constitution (in capitals). What was seen in Fig.1 as an official pattern of accountability, is now more aptly shown as a flow of information, with the party groups and the press acting as agents which controlled and to some extent modified this flow. The pattern of appointment was also modified since it was the Labour group rather than the council as a whole who ultimately determined the

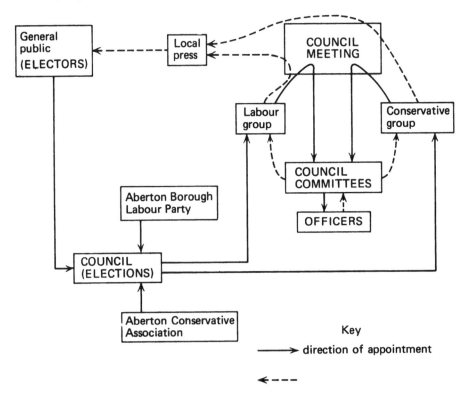

Fig. 6 The council, local press and political groups at Aberton

membership of the committees. The control of the Conservative group over their own membership of committees was somewhat tenuous, since they only retained what little strength they had by tacit consent of the Labour group. The diagram also draws attention to the fact that candidates for council seats are initially *selected* by the local political party associations before they can be *elected* by the electorate as a whole.

More can be said about the council meetings. These were made open to the public through an Act of 1835 in order to introduce a wider measure of public accountability than had existed previously. Certainly, the system still ensured that any council member could freely express his own personal opinion on council policy in public, and that no important decision could be officially confirmed in private; to this extent there was direct public accountability and a free flow of information. But even without the emergence of party politics in local government, it would have been impractical to conduct all the council's affairs in public. In the first place, the growing volume of work made some form of delegation essential, and the committee system was well adapted to this. And secondly, a public occasion was not the best one for agreeing to a large number of technical and often rather delicate matters; the council's legal and financial position would have been untenable if all its affairs and intentions (however philanthropic) were made known prematurely to an opportunist public.

Implicitly over the years, as more and more work became better suited to the committee table and as party politics increasingly influenced the scene, the council meetings ceased to be decision-making occasions in the normal sense of the word. In the view of many of the cynics, they are now little more than an anachronous rubber stamp to the local government machine.

In such towns as Aberton, this view tends to overlook the political importance of the occasion. While it may be true that no issue was immediately at stake, since the outcome was almost invariably the endorsement of committee decisions and Labour policies, the extent to which the occasion would tarnish or enhance the image of either party in the eyes of the press, and ultimately of the wider public, was something over which there was less control. As noted previously, the Conservative group had no feasible alternative but to make the council chamber the arena for party strife. Any suggestion that this battle was dragged down to the level of a farce does not explain the highly charged atmosphere that could sometimes be created by a debate on some explosive issue.

It is in this context that one should view the behaviour of the council members which varied from utter silence to uproar, from joking to exaggerated allegation, and from rapt attention to irrelevant interjections: all these were reactions to the public nature of the occasion. The outcome of the formal proposals on the council agenda were not seriously in question, but the score in the political struggle was less certain and each party (not to say each councillor) assumed that this would be reflected in their (or his) majority at the next local election.

The key figures in any council debate tended to be those with a useful experience of council affairs and a mental dexterity to be able to grasp opportunities as they arose. Such qualities were needed to discern at once the irrelevances and the implicit contradictions of an opponent's argument, and to put forward persuasive counter arguments that drew attention to previous council decisions from which relevant lessons could now be learned. The issues under debate had, of course, been discussed in private on the previous evening by the two party groups in devising their strategies for the present public occasion. However, the manner of debate contrasted in some ways. Disagreement within the party was less important when meeting in private, and individual council members could afford themselves the luxury of questioning their own party policy, of thinking aloud and of changing their point of view. At the council meeting, however, party policy had to be pursued in what purported to be a consistent and unanimous way, and it was the politicians who could think on their feet and argue consistently and coherently who dominated the scene. This is not to suggest that influence within the party group and in the council chamber necessarily came from different types of personality. Anyone who could put up an impressive performance in the council chamber was always in a sound position to influence his colleagues in the party group; and, moreover, an aspect of an orator's mental dexterity was his ability to adapt himself and his style to the occasion.

The cynic's view that council meetings were no more than a farcical rubber stamp, then, leaves much unaccounted for. A more perceptive cynic would regard the official constitution and the Standing Orders of the council as the basic rules of a game which individuals and groups manipulated for their own private ends. But, we should note that these same rules limited the extent to which this political battle could get out of hand. What was constitutionally intended as an aid to democracy in local government became through convention both a weapon and a restriction in party warfare. The rules demanded respect, but permitted exploitation; it required skill to turn a question into a political point, and it required a considerable knowledge of procedure to raise some point of order which would silence an opponent.

The rules for council debating were printed in the Standing Orders and were broadly as follows. The minutes from the various committees that had met in the course of the month were divided into two principle categories: The Part I Minutes which required confirmation from the full council, and the Part II Minutes which concerned delegated matters which the committees had been empowered to handle without requiring confirmation from the council. The Part I Minutes of each committee were presented to the council by its chairman, either as individual recommendations which he outlined to the council, or as series of resolutions which he presented en bloc. Any council member could propose some amendment to any recommendation or resolution of Part I Minutes, or he could propose that the matter should be referred back to its committee for further consideration. Each proposal and further amendments would be debated by the council and put to the vote. No member proposing a motion could speak for more than ten minutes and no other speaker for more than five unless the council (by vote) agreed to an extension of time. A Part II Minute was only on the council agenda as an item of information: members could raise questions relating to it for the committee chairman to answer, but they could not use it as a pretext for initiating a debate. At each stage of the meeting, which typically lasted for two to three hours, the mayor presiding in effect as chairman of the meeting had to determine whether contributions were irrelevant to the debate or in some other respect not in order. When a number of members were pressing to speak, he would invite them in an order of his own choosing to do so, and he could with the tacit consent of the council draw the debate to a close at an appropriate point.

Thus, the Standing Orders permitted any council member to initiate a debate on any matter that required confirmation by the council. It is this that provided the Conservatives with their cue for publicising their opposition to Labour policies. However, just as it was against the ultimate interests of the Labour group to make every issue a political one, so it was to some extent against those of the Conservative group. Where the latter felt that they had some really potent political points to make in a debate, they would not wish to lose the full effect of these by swamping their arguments with a host of minor far-fetched points. Indeed, one could go a step further and say that there were certain topics which both parties preferred should remain non-political. Welfare services were a case in point. Anything associated with an under-privileged sector of the general public was a matter for serious concern. It was not simply that as councillors they may have felt themselves responsible for the under-privileged, but also that as politicians they could not afford to be thought unconcerned. Both parties were aware of the dangers involved in opposing some welfare proposal, and of the ease with which their opponents could make political capital out of even a minor stand on some related point.

Political issues over which there was open conflict tended to focus on three recurrent themes. The first concerned the struggle between political ideologies: the Conservative defence of private enterprise as against the Labour group's defence of public enterprise and welfare subsidies. The second recurrent theme concerned the under-representation of the Conservatives on the various council committees, especially the policy committee. And the third concerned their self-appointed role as watch-dogs over the various activities of the corporation. It is worth noting that the second and third of these themes were courses which any minority group in opposition could be expected to follow regardless of party affiliations. Since 1967, when the Conservatives gained control of the council, the Labour group have been forced to follow a similar line.

In practice, these three themes tended to merge so as to appear to lend support to one another. Thus, in a proposal to acquire land for corporation development made by the policy committee, the Conservatives would point out in council that *they* were not included in the deliberations of this committee (theme 2), that the cost to the ratepayers was an unnecessary burden (theme 3), and that the development should be left to private enterprise (theme 1). Or again, in an attack on the delays in building a corporation development, they would upbraid the Labour group for permitting these delays (theme 3), while at the same time drawing certain conclusions: that private enterprise would not permit these delays (theme 1) and that in private hands the extra expenses involved would not have to be paid for by the public as ratepayers (theme 3). The annual debate when the new rate charges (i.e. the local taxation on property) were set also tended to combine themes 1 and 3: as public watch-dogs, the Conservatives were critical of any unnecessary increase in the rates, while as Conservatives they were critical of the extent to which this increase was due to the council's Labour policies. They could also argue that as public watch-dogs (theme 3) they should be entitled to full committee representation (theme 2); their exclusion from the policy committee could be used to discredit the intentions of the Labour group.

The defence of the Labour group to these attacks followed a very similar pattern, and again the three themes tended to be used to reinforce one another. Thus, the Conservatives, they would say, were excluded from the policy committee (theme 2) because of the unsoundness of their political ideologies (theme 1), and the uninformed and ineffectual way in which they criticised corporation undertakings (theme 3); and again they could point out that admitted shortcomings in the performance of the corporation (theme 3) at least compared favourably with the shortcomings of private enterprise where the extra costs were still met by the public in their capacity as exploited customers and clients (theme 1).

It is through tactics such as these that strong points could be made to appear to reinforce weak points. Both parties were aware that unsupported political ideologies (theme 1) were on the whole a weak point: the majority of the electorate had heard the same arguments many times before and had relatively fixed views about them. So it was that the extent to which the Conservatives could act as effective watch-dogs (a strong point) and could make capital out of being excluded from the policy committee, might be usefully used by them to propagate their political ideologies and their claim to greater representation on committees. While the extent to which the Labour group could succeed in discrediting the attacks of the Conservatives on corporation performance was also the extent to which they could reinforce their own socialist ideologies and their refusal to allow the Conservatives a greater share of the committee work.

This can be expressed in another way. The two party groups faced one another as adherents of opposed political ideologies. But in the context of the council chamber, their arguments inevitably tended to focus on the performance of the corporation's undertakings, especially in those respects in which Labour policies were seen to stand or fall. By generalising the theme, any activity to the credit or to the discredit of the council, regardless of its true political content, could be used by the two sides to bring credit or discredit to the Labour group and, by implication, to its policies.

There is one further point of interest in the monthly meetings of the council. In addition to providing the two political parties with an arena for debate, it was also an occasion when any determined sector of the public could make known their views on some issue. The most forcible way in which they could do this was to present a petition to the council which was read out at the next meeting by the Town Clerk.

The number of signatories to a petition tended often to be as much an indication of the amount of energy and organisation that had gone into preparing it as of the importance of its content. Councillors were quick to point out how easy it was to obtain signatures from people who were not always directly concerned with the issue at stake. However, neither political party could afford to ignore a petition, especially when it concerned some aspect of community welfare. The petition was another important event which reminded the Labour group of their accountability to the public. Very often it might imply some dissatisfaction with local government decisions and thereby put them on the defensive. They could not altogether ignore it and it would be inexpedient to try to fight it unnecessarily. The best they could hope to do was to capture it, and to associate themselves with it in council. For the Conservatives, a petition that voiced some dissatisfaction with Labour policies was powerful ammunition for opposition and an opportunity not to be lost. They too had good reason for wanting to capture a petition.

By tacit convention, each councillor had a right to present to the council any petition that originated in his ward. By speaking on behalf of the petitioners, he implicitly associated his party with their cause. This raised the interesting case of petitions that arose in those marginal wards that happened to be represented by *both* Labour and Conservative councillors. Both parties would want to capture these petitions and neither could claim a prior right to them. Much would depend on the tactics of the individual councillors at the earlier stage when signatures were still being collected. Between May 1965 and May 1967 there were altogether four marginal wards represented by both parties, and during this period forty-one petitions were handed in to the council. Table 2 analysing these petitions and the councillors who presented them is of considerable interest.

This table shows quite clearly the extent to which petitions originated in the four marginal wards with mixed representation, and the extent to which Conservative councillors managed to capture in a very real sense petitions originating in Labour wards. Analysis of the content of the petitions indicated that only eight (marked with asterisks) were actually critical of Labour policies of which the Conservatives presented all but two. No Labour councillor could have presented these without the Labour group losing face. Among those petitions presented by Labour councillors were several critical of specific council decisions but not of

Table 2 Analysis of petitions presented to Aberton council
(May 1965 – May 1967)

| Petitions prepared by residents of a ward with: | Petitions presented to Council by: | | | Proportion of electorate voting in these wards in the 1966 local elections (in per cent) |
	a Labour councillor	a Conservative councillor	Town Clerk (i.e. no councillor)	
Labour councillors only (8 wards)	10	6**	1	27.3
Conservative councillors only (6 wards)	–	2*	3*	38.5
Both Labour and Conservative councillors (4 wards)	9	4**	2	38.1
City as a whole (i.e. no specific wards	1	2*	1*	–

*Each asterisk indicates a petition critical in some way of council policies.

Labour policies as such; these could be presented without loss of face. The table seems to indicate that both parties missed opportunities of capturing petitions originating in their wards and compatible with their policies.

Because the Labour group tended to find themselves somewhat on the defensive when a petition was presented, they would urge their members to seek advice from the group on how to handle a petition rather than try to manage it on their own without party support. There was in addition another reason why the Labour group should want to be consulted in these matters. Potentially, the petition was a means whereby any individual member of the Labour group could curry favour with his ward or seek to pursue some individualist policy within the council. For the Conservatives to muster a petition and obtain full support from their group could in the right circumstances be excellent tactics on behalf of the party. For the Labour members to do this could amount to a challenge to the unity of the group and its policies.

Thus the council meeting was an occasion when each political party was concerned with maximising its own gain in terms of capturing any petitions that happened to be mobilised, of catching the headlines in the press with suitably coined phrases, and of wooing those members of the public present in the gallery. Skilled and influential members on both sides would try and use it as an occasion when they could score off their opponents without unnecessarily infringing the limits set by Standing Orders on matters of relevance or content. The monthly meeting of the Aberton council developed often into an arena for public debate between the two major political parties. It may not have been a decision-making occasion in the normally accepted sense, but it was still of strategic value in the dissemination of highly relevant information to the public at large, and this was closely linked to the accountability of the council to the electorate.

The role of the council meeting in the total decision-making process, though different from its constitutional role, was still very important. The precautions taken by the Labour group beforehand took much of the initiative out of the hands of the Conservative members and led frequently to rather dull debates in the council chamber, but they are at least evidence of the respect that the Labour group had for the damage that Conservatives could inflict on its policies through these debates. The knowledge of an imminent council meeting and of Conservative attempts to wrest the initiative acted as a public conscience that was ever present at the pre-council meetings of the Labour group.

It is now possible to appreciate why the mayor, for all that he was chairman of the council at these monthly meetings, was not in a position of influence in the decision-making process. Regardless of the statutory provisions, the hub of this process was the meetings of the Labour group and not of the council. As chairman of the council, the mayor was in a key position to regulate the extent to which one party or the other might wrest the initiative and openly woo the press. But this placed him in the invidious position of having to reassure his own party of his ultimate loyalty while appearing to the other party, the public, and the press to be above politics. If he was suspected of too much or too little loyalty by either side, he might find that they responded less to his attempts at keeping the political debates within bounds. He might welcome the dignity, the ceremonial prestige and the active social life as Aberton's first citizen: but few men with political interests and aspirations would want to serve as mayor for more than one year (preceded by a year as deputy mayor). In political terms, at best he could regard his period in office as a very indirect service to his party group and at worst he might feel himself walking a thankless tightrope, especially during council meetings. When afterwards he returned to his party group, he was very much at their mercy as to which committees he would serve on and this was one of the implicit sanctions in his accountability.

Local and national politics in Aberton

The Labour and Conservative parties who were contending for control over Aberton town council were also the two major parties involved in the struggle for power nationally at Westminster. The intrusion of national into local politics was evident in the council debates where from time to time the national dialogue on current issues was pursued at a local level also as part of a wider campaign to harry the government of the day or vehemently to defend it. This was a fourth recurrent theme in council debating which was constantly woven in with theme 1 in particular. It was, however, a theme that could easily become irrelevant to the debate and each group would appeal to the mayor on a point of order if they felt that some member of the other party was carrying his argument too far. The change in political power nationally in 1964 was followed by an abrupt change in the nature of council debating at Aberton where the Labour members were no longer concerned with harrying the government of the day but rather with defending it against Conservative attacks.

Indeed, it may be more than mere coincidence that the concessions conferred on the Conservatives by the Aberton Labour group varied with the fortunes of their party at Westminster. The Conservatives gained control at Westminster in 1951 and lost it again to the Labour party in 1964. At Aberton, the Labour group denied the Conservatives any seats on the policy committee for the first time in 1952; and in 1965 for the first time in many years they relaxed their control over the committee system by allowing the Conservatives a block allocation of seats instead of blackballing certain Conservative members from certain committees. It was as if the changes in power at the national level had led at first to a lesser and then a greater degree of accommodation on the local scene.

The intrusion of national politics into the local political scene had far-reaching consequences. National issues were generally more serious, more dramatic, and altogether more widely and well reported in the press, radio and television. In the final analysis, popular concern for party politics was focused on the battles fought in Parliament, and not on the minor skirmishes that occurred from time to time in the local council chamber. When they voted (or abstained from voting) in the local elections, therefore, the Aberton electors were often expressing their support for or their criticism of the government nationally.

That this occurred regularly was borne out by the extent to which political swings in the local Aberton elections from year to year followed the same course as swings in local government elections up and down the country, and local political groups found themselves allied to their party's national fortunes.[3] This recurrent feature in Aberton and elsewhere undermined the democratic safeguards built into their constitution. In the last resort the political groups in power were not held fully accountable for their degree of success in managing local affairs, but were held implicitly accountable for the current popularity of their party nationally. In Aberton these swings did not normally alter the balance of political power (1967 was an exceptional year) but they did encourage the Labour group to modify their policies, avoiding unpopular measures in times of Labour unpopularity and risking them in times of Labour popularity. In other towns where political power was more finely balanced, it led to the periodic change in control from one party to the other. The problem was not so much that it was necessarily a bad thing for political power to change hands periodically, but that it was liable to change hands at the wrong times and for the wrong reasons. When finally the Conservatives gained control of Aberton town council in 1967, they could claim that they deserved a period in power; but they could not claim that it was due to any recent fault of the Labour group or to any merit of their own that they were put in this position at this point in time.

It is in this respect that the basic model of accountability is weak and the whole logical basis on which the system rests can be seriously questioned. It is important therefore to note certain features in Aberton which seemed to indicate that the basic model did at least persist in a somewhat curtailed form.

A number of these features have already been noted. The behaviour of individual councillors at times of election seemed to indicate a real concern for their council seats, even at a time when no changes were expected. The Labour group before each council meeting were especially concerned that their performance should appear at least credible to the press and the public, even though there was never any doubt of their ability to force through any matter by their sheer voting strength. Petitions and public attendances at these council meetings served to remind Labour councillors of popular concern for essentially local affairs. Again, in the marginal wards where the loss of a few hundred votes could cost the Labour group a council seat, they were very aware of their vulnerability and of the effect of such a loss on their morale and popular esteem even if it did not seriously affect their strength within the council. Labour councillors for these wards were of course personally concerned in this delicate balance and they would be given considerable sympathy and support by their Labour colleagues on any local issue. Each of these features indicated the extent to which an accountability of sorts existed between the Labour group as the ruling body on the council, and the general public.

There is, in addition, indirect statistical evidence revealed by an analysis of national and local electoral swings between the two parties. A crude analysis showed the extent to which a national swing in voting from one year to the next corresponded to a local swing in a similar direction in Aberton. However, further analysis indicated an altogether more complex relationship whereby if the electoral swing in Aberton towards one of the parties in one year was less than the national average, then it would tend to be greater than the national average in the next year, and vice versa. Nothing obvious could be found to account for this, except to infer that if the electoral fortunes of the local Labour party in Aberton were worse than those of other Labour parties, then the Labour group would modify its policies and improve its *relative* popularity in the next year. It does not necessarily follow that the Labour group undertook this type of statistical analysis of the voting figures for themselves. It would only have been necessary for them to be sensitive to subtle changes in local popularity (reflected in voting figures) for this effect to occur.

This apparent contradiction in the evidence can be summarised as follows.

Voting trends indicated quite clearly that the electorate as a whole (including those who abstained from voting) tended to hold the Aberton Labour group accountable for the activities and fortunes of the Labour party nationally. However, while the Labour group were well aware of this and reacted to it, they also sensed a degree to which they were held accountable for local issues and assumed (correctly) that this would affect the local elections to an extent that they could not afford to ignore. To this extent, the Labour group accepted a public accountability and the system could be seen to retain a certain marginal validity.

Politics and local democracy
This outline of the political processes infusing one broadly typical town council provides a useful point from which to consider more general implications.

The existence of party politics in English local government is an issue with which many commentators have taken exception. The arguments against it have been that local government activities are basically not of a political nature; that it is not necessary for a local councillor to be a member of a party group in order to make himself known to the electors; that local elections are used to keep the party machinery in working order; that some candidates are chosen solely because of their party membership irrespective of personal ability; that where a ward has a clear majority one way or the other the selection of a councillor is virtually in the hands of the committee of the majority party; that the 'group system' has a harmful effect on the working of local councils by making debates in the council chamber meaningless; that the regular stirring up of a political feeling in small communities is harmful; and that decisions taken on party political grounds discourage officers who see their unbiased advice (in committee) disregarded. Each of these arguments was put forward recently in evidence to a government sponsored committee on the management of local government. The reply was quite simply that 'party politics are an inescapable part of public life and their influence is likely to grow in local government if re-organisation results in fewer and generally larger authorities'[4]

There is other evidence available which suggests that the *absence* of a keen political rivalry in local councils is also harmful. Thus, it has been noted that in certain councils in the London area where there was a substantial control by one party, there was a relatively large number of uncontested seats, opposition to the controlling party was nominal and the turn-out at elections low. In such boroughs an 'air of unreality seems to pervade the public affairs of the council, particularly the council meetings. They are largely a hollow ritual and consequently seldom receive adequate press coverage: in this way the one important link with the general public is weakened. In these conditions, it is probable that the rudimentary knowledge of local government affairs possessed by the public declines and its attitude towards local government elections becomes increasingly apathetic'.[5]

That the public is generally unconcerned with local government is borne out by the findings of two recent surveys where it was found that only 18% of the electorate could remember having been taught about local government at school, only 17% had ever been in touch with a local councillor on some local government matter, only 9% had ever held any position or sat on a committee for *any* kind of public service, and only 6% had ever been interested in taking an active part in the running of local government. Even when one considers the more fortunate one-quarter of the electorate whose education had gone beyond the primary school level, these proportions were still only increased to 29%, 18%, 17% and 12% respectively.[6]

From the point of view of degrees of active interest in local government, it is possible to envisage local elites emerging from the community having greater or lesser involvement in local affairs. That this is equally true within the political parties has been well brought out in a study of another English town where the authors have demonstrated that the class structure (measured by occupational status) is reflected in an implicit hierarchy in both the Conservative and the Labour parties. Table 3 shows the extent to which there is a progressive rise in status as one progresses from voters for either party (the more passive supporters), to party members, to council members, to party stalwarts (defined as those who play an active part in controlling their party's affairs locally).[7]

Table 3 Occupational status and political involvement in Newcastle-under-Lyme

Occupational status		Conservatives				Labour party		
	Voters	party members	council members	stalwarts	Voters	party members	council members	Stalwarts
	%	%	%	%	%	%	%	%
Business proprietors	16	32	43	74	2	2	12	0
Professional and managerial	21	25	57	26	4	9	10	22
Clerical	11	24	0	0	4	9	20	53
Skilled manual	36	14	0	0	27	43	27	25
Unskilled manual	16	5	0	0	53	37	31	0

In the present paper, the standpoint has essentially been that of a local council and political processes within it. No attempt has been made to complete Fig.6 by examining the processes whereby the Aberton Borough Labour Party or the Aberton Conservative Association were in a sense self-selected from electors of the local community, or of the processes whereby specific members of these political associations emerged to be nominated as candidates for vacancies on the local council. It is clear, however, that such processes must have existed and have played an important role in relating the political parties and their policies to local issues.

In 1835, the problem facing English local government reform was the extent to which town councils were not fully accountable for their activities. The measures taken to counteract this have been largely successful, but only to the extent that local electorates are sensitive to these activities. The major problem posed by English local government in the mid twentieth century is that while local government has taken on an increasing responsibility for public services, this has not apparently been matched by any increasing public concern for the running of these services. The evidence from Aberton and elsewhere suggests that while party politics may introduce extraneous issues into council debates, the vying for headlines in the local press also serves to increase public awareness (the role of the party in opposition). Or again, while decisions made by unofficial political groups may interfere with the normal channels of accountability, their need to present a favourable image can lead to more positive and consistent policies in running the services than would be so if each issue were decided by the more purely personal preferences of individual councillors; it is the formulation and the interpretation of these policies which is the role of the majority party on any council.

The view put forward by some commentators of the English local government scene is not that party politics are wholly undesirable, but rather that they may play a greater part in increasing public awareness and ultimate accountability. In this context the current trend of extending local government boundaries, in London (recent) and elsewhere (proposed) can be seen as potentially beneficial. The principal reason for these changes has been because the services can be better co-ordinated by fewer and larger councils than exist at present. As a by-product, however, this will also result in more heterogeneous council areas as industrial towns become linked with their more dispersed hinterlands, and as the richer and the poorer districts of various conurbations become merged into one authority.[8] It is the basic homogeneity existing in many present council areas that has led to the absence of political rivalry there. A by-product of the current reforms in English local government may not be the stifling of party politics but their cultivation.

Certainly, there has been considerable change in the processes entailed in local democracy since the Municipal Commissioners made a report on Aberton in the 1830s and described the corporation as

'a permanent and self-constituted body – powerful from their position and possession of magisterial authority – influential from the considerable revenues over which they exercise an irresponsible control, and from the distribution of extensive charities, which they assume a right to dispose as a matter of personal patronage – presiding over a commercial city, subject to the influence of no individual patron – it became the leading object of the corporation to secure to themselves the nomination of the members of Parliament for the city:'

They also reported that elections in Aberton were frequently accompanied by tumults and riots, and that mob fighting between the political parties of rival candidates were frequently headed by members of the magistracy (aldermen) and on one occasion apparently by the mayor himself. One could hardly apply such melodramatic terms to describe the democratic processes of Aberton in 1964.

Notes

[1] Services for which these councils are responsible include local education, local highways, planning and planning control, public transport, domestic water supplies, refuse collection and disposal, sewerage, the emergency services (fire, police and ambulance), public health services, the welfare of the aged and handicapped, child care, public lighting, traffic control, public libraries, parks, swimming baths and a wide range of lesser services. The extent to which a council may (or must) provide these services and the limits to which they may (or should) go are constantly revised with every Parliamentary Act relating to these services.

[2] For a fuller discussion of this topic in relation to law, see B.N. Cardozo, 1921, and M. Gluckman, 1955.

[3] It is generally assumed that this is due largely to fluctuations in the degree to which supporters of either party are prepared to vote in the local elections rather than the extent to which they actually switch their vote from one party ot the other;: it is not so much a matter of changing loyalties as of flagging enthusiasm by supporters of each party.

[4] *Management of Local Government, vol.1,* Report of the Maud Committee, H.M.S.O. 1967, paras. 374 and 389.

[5] L.J. Sharpe, 1960: 169-70.

[6] *Management of Local Government, vol.3, The Local Government Elector,* H.M.S.O. 1967; *Community Attitudes Survey (England)* H.M.S.O., 1969 *(Research Report to the Royal Commission on Local Government in England).*

[7] Bealey, Blondel and McCann, *Constituency Politics, a study of Newcastle-under-Lyme,* 1965, p.404 (table derived from the chart).

[8] C.f. Sharpe, 1960. op. cit.

REACHING AN AGREEMENT OVER BRIDEWEALTH IN LABWOR, NORTHERN UGANDA: A CASE STUDY

By R.G. Abrahams

I

My purpose in this paper is to examine some of the processes of inter-group decision-making which formed part of a particular marriage in late 1967 among the Labwor people of Karamoja, northern Uganda.[1] The material which I discuss is, in its fundamentals, typical of most bridewealth negotiations in Labwor, though certain elements of opposition and conflict between the parties concerned were unusually strongly developed in it. Despite the differences between such bridewealth negotiations and some of the more formally constituted council systems discussed elsewhere in this volume, I consider that both sets of institutions also have important attributes in common. For both serve as media for discussion and for reaching consensus on matters of common concern between two or more parties whose interests and advantage only partially coincide.

In his book *Social Control in an African Society* Gulliver has suggested that two polar types of decision-making and dispute-settling process can be usefully identified. At one extreme there is a 'judicial' system in which an authoritative, impartial judge decides the issue in accordance with a body of accepted norms. At the other pole, there is a 'political' process of settlement through direct violent or peaceful confrontation of the parties. As M.G. Smith has recognized, both sorts of process are likely to be present in any society, though the contexts in which they operate and the extent to which one form predominates will vary from one social system to another. The existence of intermediary forms on a continuum between the poles has also been explicitly asserted, and it would appear that many types of deliberative council can be usefully considered as lying on such a continuum and combining certain tendencies towards each polar type.[2]

The negotiations and decision-making which I describe in this paper, with their sometimes acrimonious discussion between different clans, clearly lie towards the 'political' pole which Gulliver delineates, and this is also broadly true of most of the other traditional Labwor forms of deliberative and dispute-settling process which survive today. Most important of these are the series of annual *ameto* gatherings which are held in a number of different parts of Labwor and which are closely associated with age-organization. At these gatherings a range of matters is dealt with, such as the opening and closing of age-group recruitment, and the meting out of punishment for various moral offences, especially those involving strongly insolent behaviour by a person to his parents or to other senior members of the community. I was unfortunately unable to attend *ameto* since the customary season for holding it did not coincide with the period of my stay in the area, but it is clear from a number of accounts I have collected that 'segmentary' opposition between proximal age-groups and alliance between alternate ones form an important element in the proceedings.

In some contrast, modern innovations since the 1920s, such as the Local Government courts and a system of Local Government chiefs and headmen, are predictably much more hierarchically structured and approximate more closely to the 'judicial' and 'administrative' poles. It should be noted, however, that such newer institutions and structures have been externally established and imposed largely in place of a traditional system, in which agreement or opposition between clan groups, comparable to that discussed in this paper and occasionally mediated by incumbents of an embryonic form of ritual chiefship, was the customary means of handling most major issues, including homicide, and, of course, marriage and related matters involving members of different clans. For these reasons, it seems fair to say that the material which I present in this paper is reasonably representative and illustrative of processes and general principles of organization which are and have traditionally been operative in a wide range of Labwor dispute-settling and deliberative contexts.

I have noted earlier that there are differences as well as similarities between the system of negotiations I describe, and a more formally structured council system; and I have suggested that one such difference is the closer proximity of my own material to a 'political' as opposed to an 'administrative' polar type. Another point of some importance here is the relatively ad hoc, and contextually defined nature of the recruitment to and organization of the meetings I describe. This of course is in some contrast to the well-defined and lasting constitution, and to the special meeting place and highly formalized procedural conventions which are possessed by many councils, and other corporate bodies also. But this too is a matter of degree. For in the type of situation I describe there exist clear rules about the rights and obligations of persons to participate in the negotiations, and the main features of their roles vis-a-vis each other are well defined. There are also clearly understood conventions about the correct places in which the various stages of the negotiations should be held, and the fact that different stages are recognized is also in itself significant here. Similarly there are, as I shall describe, customary patterns of procedure which form part of and are quite special to the occasion, such as the driving out of the cattle from the kraal of the groom's family, and their assignment to different sections of the bride's assembled kin.

II

The Labwor people, who call themselves Jo Abwor, number about 9,000 and live in a well-watered hilly area, known as the Labwor Hills, in the far west of Karamoja District. Culturally, the people are in many respects more closely linked to their western neighbours outside Karamoja, the Acholi and the Lango, than to the major tribes who live within the District. Thus in contrast to their Jie and Karimojong neighbours to the east, the Labwor are a Luo-speaking group whose main economic activities are agriculture including cash-cropping, and iron-working, although some cattle and other livestock are kept. Despite these differences, however, and indeed to some extent because of them, there are a number of important economic and other ties between the Labwor and these pastoral tribes, especially the Jie. In times of food shortage the pastoralists may seek grain and even long-term refuge in Labwor, and the area has for a long time been the pastoralists' main source of supply of spears and other iron goods. Return payments for such goods and services are often in the form of livestock including cattle. In addition, the Labwor have at some time in the past apparently borrowed their system of age and generation grouping from these pastoral neighbours, though they have since modified it.

This system of age and generation grouping has for long formed one of three main frameworks of social organization in Labwor. The others are, today, the relatively recently introduced system of Local Government administration and the system of kinship and marriage. It is certain features of this last system which are mainly relevant in the present context, and I shall try to outline them before moving on to the discussion of the case I wish to deal with.

III

The Labwor people are divided among a number of named, exogamous, patrilineal descent groups which I shall call clans and which the people themselves call *kaka* or *ateker*. [3] I collected the names of about thirty of these groups but it is possible that several smaller clans are not included in my list. There is considerable variation in the size of clans and, to some extent concomitantly, in the patterns of segmentation which are found within them. Since the case I shall examine concerns the marriage of a man of one of the smaller clans in the area to a woman of one of the larger clans, a brief discussion of the form of these two groups may serve as an example of the various arrangements which occur, in addition to providing background information on the parties to the marriage.

The husband's clan is called Jo k'Atik and contains a hundred and fifty or so men, women and children. In addition to forming an exogamous unit, the members of the clan take a lively interest in each other's marriages and claim the right to participate in the feasts and beer drinks which may accompany different stages of these. Clan members stress, however, that the group does not act as a unit with respect to actually paying or receiving bridewealth. In this context, two major sub-divisions of the clan, known respectively as Jo k'Obura and Jo k'Olum, are usually mentioned as acting separately from one another, and it is in fact further sub-divisions of these units which have the ultimate responsibility for these matters. Moreover, the clansfolk who are held to have a right to share in bride-wealth which is paid into the group are typically more numerous than those who are by right expected to contribute to the bridewealth of male members. There is some flexibility in these matters but it is fair to say, for this clan and in general, that whereas it is fundamentally the responsibility of a man himself or of his father or other jural guardian to find the wherewithal for his marriage, a girl's father and his full siblings plus some of their dependants tend to form the minimal group of clansmen who may share by right in bridewealth paid for her. This is not to say, however, that clansfolk and others will not help a man to pay bridewealth if they can and want to, as is often the case. I should also add, as will be clear later, that participation in negotiations over bridewealth is not restricted to those who are either contributing to it or receiving a share of it.

The woman's clan is called Jo Epanyamenya and has several hundred members. Like Jo k'Atik, it contains two major named sub-divisions and these are known as Jo k'Obol and Jo k'Agole. With the exception of exogamy, however, which is still clan-wide, each of these major divisions acts more or less as a separate clan, and people talk about the possibility of intermarriage taking place between them in the not too distant future. Beer drinks and feasts which would be clan events for Jo k'Atik are thus affairs for Jo k'Obol and Jo k'Agole separately in this larger clan, and each division has its own segments of varying depth and span which are comparable to those of Jo k'Atik.

Like many other clans in Labwor, the two clans in question are to a considerable extent localized in the sense that many, though by no means all, senior male members have their homesteads within easy walking or, in certain cases, calling distance of each other. Thus, many Jo Epanyamenya homesteads are sited in a locality known as Areng'epua and in the neighbouring locality of Oring'obita where, significantly in the present context, many Jo k'Atik clan members also have their home. Marriages between members of such neighbouring and inter-settled clans are common, though the form which they can take is limited by certain rules. These forbid a person to marry a member of their mother's or their father's mother's clan, and it is also forbidden to marry certain other cognates including mother's sister's children.

As such rules to some extent imply, matrilateral links form an important part of the system of kinship and marriage in the area, and this is especially true of a younger person's tie to his close senior matrikin. Like certain agnates, these kin have a right to share in a girl's bridewealth, and it is not uncommon for a mother's brother to provide a beast to help a young man marry. It should, however, be remembered in this context that it is their senior agnates, rather than the young couple themselves, who are mainly in charge of the formal arrangements for their marriage; and for such senior persons, in these and many other matters, it is not so much their own matrilateral kinsfolk as their agnates and affines, including of course the children's matrilateral kin, who are of main significance to them. In addition, I may mention that such senior persons often have one or two close friends with whom they are involved in the reciprocal exchange of goods and services at marriages and in other contexts.

Labwor marriage is polygynous and there is a house-property complex associated with this. Most marriages take quite a long time to arrange and they are very rarely broken once arrangements are well under way. All marriages involve transfer of bridewealth. The actual procedure of a marriage varies in accordance with a range of factors including the age and jural status of the husband and the amount of bridewealth available for more or less immediate transfer. Bridewealth nowadays typically consists of an agreed amount of money, which usually goes to the bride's father himself, and an agreed number of cattle which are distributed among the bride's kin according to a fairly clear-cut customary pattern. Agreement over these matters is reached during a series of negotiations such as those which I shall go on to consider.

IV

I turn now to the particular case I wish to discuss. Before examining the actual negotiations in some detail it will be useful to provide a brief account of some of the events preceding them.

Arrangements for the marriage in question had begun some five or six years earlier, and relations between the parties had gradually deteriorated since that time. For reasons which are not wholly clear, the marriage became less attractive to the young man, Peter, and his father, William, who were not, however, willing to abandon it completely.[4] No bridewealth was transferred beyond a preliminary earnest of 500 shillings to the girl's father, George. Nonetheless, Peter cohabited with the girl, Mary, from time to time on the basis of the understanding that they would be married in due course, and she bore him two children. Meanwhile, to make matters worse, William entered into and completed new arrangements for Peter to marry a fellow-clanswoman of Mary, thus making Mary merely his prospective second wife.[5] William still, however, proclaimed his intention of completing his son's marriage to Mary, and successfully used this as an argument to keep off various rival suitors.

Matters finally began to come to a head in September 1967. It was clear that Mary's family's patience was by this time near exhaustion, and William, apparently in fear of reprisal, told one of Mary's mother's co-wives that he believed her husband, George, was trying to find medicine to kill him. On hearing this from his wife, George brought a case of slander against William before the Local Government headman. At the hearing, William apologized for uttering the slander, and went on to stress his desire to bring the affair to an amicable conclusion by paying bride-

206

wealth to complete the marriage. George, however, said he was no longer interested in the marriage. The headman closed the the hearing by asking the pair to see if they could come to some agreement since it would be a most serious step for George to take the case of slander forward to a magistrate's court hearing as he was in theory entitled to do.

During the next few weeks William made a number of visits to George's home to try to persuade him to go on with the marriage and, on one of these occasions early in November, George eventually assented to this with the agreement of his two younger full brothers whom he had insisted upon calling to the discussion. Although bridewealth was not discussed in detail at this meeting, William was warned that a large amount would be demanded, and that he would have to pay it quickly.

William in due course issued an invitation for George and his people to come to his homestead on 25 November to 'see' the bridewealth cattle, which he had assembled in the kraal there. This was the occasion for the main negotiations. Before going, George and his younger brother – with the secretarial help of a close clansman schoolteacher – drew up a written list of bridewealth demands which would be made. These were divided, as is customary, into three main parts – family, clan, and mother's kin – and were as given in table 1.

Table 1.

Demands (head of cattle)			Notes
A.	Family		Literally 'compound'. (Luo term *dyekal)*
1.	Girl's father	5	He would actually be in charge of all *dyekal* cattle.
2.	Girl's mother	5	
3.	Girl's oldest full brother	6	The girl was older than all her brothers, the
4.	Girl's second full brother	4	oldest of them being about 20 years of age and
5.	Girl's third full brother	3	already married.
6.	Girl's fourth full brother	1	
			No claim was made in the name of the girl's fifth and youngest full brother.
7.	Mother's most senior co-wife	2	The mother was herself the most senior wife of
8.	Mother's second co-wife	2	the family.
9.	Mother's third co-wife	1	Demands in the name of co-wives are for their 'houses' rather than for the women themselves.
B.	Clan		Luo term *kaka.*
			As will be seen only close agnates among clanfolk are involved. The list also contains two friends of the father.
10.	Alfred	10	Father's eldest brother. He lived and worked outside Labwor and did not attend the negotiations, but his agreement to go on with the marriage was obtained by the bride's father.

Table 1. *(continued)*

Demands (head of cattle)		Notes
11.	James	7	Father's younger brother.
12.	Jacob	6	Father's youngest brother.
13.	Herbert	2	Father's senior paternal halfbrother.
14.	Stephen	1	Father's junior paternal halfbrother
15.	Rupert	1	Father's father's full brother's son.
16.	Roland	1	Father's father's full brother's son.
17.	Thomas	1	Father's father's paternal half-brother's son.
18.	Andrew	1	Father's close friend and maternal kinsman.
19.	County chief	1	Longstanding close friend of father
20.	Father's eldest full sister	1	
21.	Father's younger full sister	1	
22.	Father's youngest full sister	1	

C.	Maternal kin		Luo term, *neo.*
23.	Mother's brothers	5	These were not listed separately but it emerged
24.	Mother's senior full sister, Emma	1	that the mother's 2 full brothers were involved.
25.	Mother's second full sister, Natalie	1	
26.	Mother's third full sister, Rose	1	
27.	Mother's paternal half sister, Teresa	1	
28.	Mother's paternal half sister, Jane	1	

| | Total cattle demanded | 73 | |

When the list had been prepared, George and a party of about thirty men, consisting of close fellow clansmen and others, including his two friends, set off on the few hundred yard journey to William's homestead. A female contingent, consisting largely of the wives of these men, followed shortly afterwards. On arrival they were greeted by William and the various members of his homestead, and also by a number of his clanfolk and affines who had assembled there. After a short time George and his male companions were invited over to the cattle kraal to see the cattle.

Seating and other arrangements were roughly as in Fig.1. The women mostly watched from the verandahs of the nearby huts. As far as I could ascertain the cattle were all William's own. He himself was in sole charge of their distribution. As will be seen, some additional cattle and money were also offered by others to supplement William's contribution in the course of the negotiations.

When things were ready to start, William was given the prepared list of demands which he first read over to himself. He then began to talk about the 500 shillings which had originally been paid and he suggested that, with the addition of a further

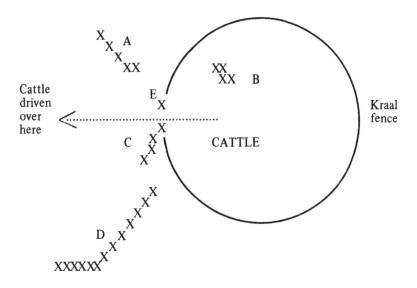

Key.

A   Small group of William's clansfolk and affines watching proceedings.
B   William's elder brother and a few other close clansmen helping William to drive out the cattle.
C   William's wives.
D   George and his male party.
E   William generally directing proceedings, driving out the cattle and announcing their recipients.

100 shillings, these should count as four head of cattle. After some discussion this point was accepted, and George told William to start bringing out the cattle which were in the kraal. This William did, driving out one person's share at a time in front of George's group and naming the proposed recipient as he did so. He began as follows with the cattle for the members of the family *(dyekal)*. (Table 2) The numbers in brackets refer to those in Table 1.[6]

	Recipient	Table 2.		Offer
1. (1)	Girl's father	(5)	A cow and its calf. These count as two head and two of the four head paid in shillings were added to them.
2. (2)	Girl's mother	(5)	A cow and its calf. The other two head paid in shillings were added to these, and it was known that a bell-ox would also be given.
3. (3)	Girl's oldest full brother	(6)	A cow and its calf. The brother complained when this was announced and a large bull was driven out in addition for him.
4. (7)	Mother's most senior co-wife	(2)	A cow and its calf.
5. (8)	Mother's second co-wife	(2)	A heifer.

209

Little argument was raised about the distribution at this stage. It may be noted that it fell particulary short with regard to the girl's full brothers (numbers 3-6 in Table 1) for whom a total of fourteen head of cattle were demanded. William next began to drive out cattle for the clansfolk *(kaka)* of the girl as in Table 3.

	Recipient	Table 3.	Offer
6. (10)	Alfred	(10)	A cow and its calf. A heifer was added when one of Alfred's wives who was staying in Labwor complained.
7. (11)	James	(7)	A cow and its calf.
8. (12)	Jacob	(6)	A heifer. Jacob said he refused to have this since it fell so far short of the demanded figure, but this refusal did not stop the proceedings.
9. (13)	Herbert	(2)	A small ox. Herbert complained bitterly about this and a sum of 200 shillings was offered instead by the father of one of William's sons-in-law.
10. (14)	Stephen	(1)	One cow.
11. (15)	Rupert	(1)	He was told there was a cow for him at William's sister's home.
12. (19)	Chief	(1)	William's full brother announced he had a cow for him in another village.
13. (20)	Father's eldest full sister	(1)	One cow.
14. (22)	Father's youngest full sister	(1)	One ox.

William then moved on to the cattle for the girl's maternal kin *(neo)* and drove out the following:

15. (23)	Mother's brothers	(5)	A cow and its calf.

16. (24)	Mother's senior full sister, Emma	(1)	A heifer.

He also promised a heifer to the girl's mother's half-sister Teresa, and this brought him to the end of the list. The girl's mother complained very strongly that her other sisters had not been allotted cattle since, she said, there were obligations to them for cattle which she had been given at their daughters' marriages. However, nothing more was done about this for the moment. A variety of dissatisfactions were then voiced about other claims and an effort was made to meet some of these.

	Recipient	Table 4.	Offer
1. (4)	Girl's second full brother	(4)	A cow and a calf were driven out for him.
2. (5)	Girl's third full brother	(3)	A cow was promised for him*.
3. (23)	Girl's mother's brothers	(5)	Some money was promised for one of these by the father of another of William's sons-in-law who is also a fellow clansman of the recipient.
4. (18)	Andrew	(1)	The small ox originally offered to (13) Herbert was now offered to him.

*I am not sure who made this offer.

Finally an ox with a bell tied round its neck was driven out. This ox, known as *otem,* is a customary payment to the bride's mother, and its appearance marks an important stage in the proceedings since it is the last beast actually to be driven out of the kraal. There were still some cattle in the kraal after this bell-ox had been driven out, and I was told that this too was customary since it would be shameful for a man's kraal to be left completely empty by bridewealth demands.

The proceedings at the kraal itself were now over having lasted about one and a half hours. Their general form may be summarized as the relatively formal presentation of a series of demands for cattle by one party followed by a series of offers (and non-offers) in response to them by the other party. Complaints about some of these responses resulted in the making of supplementary offers, but not all complaints were successful in this. Overall, some 73 cattle had been demanded and 38 (with due translations of money contributions) had been driven out or promised, these figures breaking down as follows.

	Demanded	Offered
Family	29	18
Clan	34	15
Maternal kin	10	5
Total	73	38

It is perhaps worth noting explicitly that, with the main exception of the father's elder brother Alfred, most of the adult recipients and claimants *had* been present at the distribution and a number of them who were close clans folk – the girl's eldest full brother, her father's brother Jacob, and her father's senior paternal half-brother Herbert – voiced complaints on their own behalf. Other complaints were made by persons on behalf of others, for example, by the girl's father and eldest brother for her younger brothers who were not yet adult, by the girl's father on behalf of his friend Andrew who, though present, has no formal right to demand a beast, and by the girl's mother on behalf of her sisters to whom she felt a debt. Although no further business was conducted at the kraal, the negotiations were by no means over. The girl's group was invited to continue the discussion in the hut of the groom's mother, and this invitation was accepted. George's party in the hut mainly consisted of himself, his brothers, the girl's eldest full brother, her mother and her mother's brother, and various of her own and of her mother's clansmen plus some of their wives. On William's side were himself, his brother and some other clansmen with their wives including the groom's mother, the groom's mother's brother and also some of William's other affines.

As we have seen in the case of William's son-in-law, who was also a fellow clansman of the girl's mother, the less closely linked categories of persons on either side were not necessarily nor actually mutually exclusive of each other, and indeed the combination of the rules of exogamy with the frequency of marriages between members of neighbouring inter-settled clans will clearly tend to produce much overlapping of this sort.

Discussion in the hut was rather less formally organized than had been the case at the kraal and it was also, at least in its earlier stages, rather more acrimonious. William tried to instill more order into the proceedings by insisting that demands should be addressed to him personally and that people on his side should also make their comments to him. He was, however, only partially successful in this attempt to establish himself as a sort of chairman of the meeting. William's brother handed round tobacco at an early stage and a pot of beer was brought into the hut after about an hour. This served to lubricate the discussion, but by the time it was brought in there already seemed more chance than at first that an agreement would be reached between the parties.

A number of claims were raised and discussed in the hut including those of George's full brothers, his second sister, his two clansmen Roland and Thomas, his friend Andrew and the girl's mother's sisters. For the first half-hour or so it appeared that no progress would be made, since neither side seemed willing to yield on any point of consequence, and hard bargaining appeared to be the order of the day. George's younger brother Jacob was particulary angry and obdurate in the pursuit of his claim for all of the six cattle originally demanded for him. During the early stages of discussion the only positive move for an agreement came from one or two senior clansmen on both sides who counselled acceptance of the offered cattle on the general grounds that marriage was a good thing, and because, as one of them put it, 'A girl (i.e. a bride) joins people together' *(Nyako en aye dribo jo)*. The position of these particular elders is perhaps worth further comment. As clansmen of the parties they were entitled to be present at and speak at the negotiations, and as senior clansmen their opinions carried extra weight. Additionally, none of them was closely enough related to either George or William to be personally involved in either the receipt or payment of the bridewealth, and this enabled them to play almost a mediating role in the proceedings. It should be noted that the attribution of differential roles to the clan on the one hand and to its various constituent segments on the other, tends to guarantee that this useful sort of participant will be on hand on such occasions.[7]

After a while, when deadlock seemed to have been reached, a variety of participants on both sides began to make a series of more practical gestures, and these eventually resulted in a change of tone in the proceedings. With the exception of Jacob's continued adamant demands for his six cattle, the atmosphere in the hut became gradually friendlier and more co-operative, and when I left, after some two and a half hours of discussion there, it was clear that a basic agreement had been reached and that only small details needed to be ironed out. By this time the beer had also done its work and the gathering had begun to turn into a jovial beer party, with much singing and shouting which went on for several hours more.

The practical gestures which I mentioned were as follows:

(1) 100 shillings was given to George for the women of his party. Such a payment is called *me buko tyello,* i.e. to fan the (hot) feet (of the visitors after their journey).

(2) A cow was offered to George's second sister. The offer was made by the brother and guardian of the groom's first wife, who is a fellow clansman of the recipient.

(3) George's friend Andrew said he would do without his part of the bridewealth in order to help. George was very reluctant to let him do this but at last agreed. The beast in question went to Alfred.

(4) Thomas announced that he and Roland were willing to do without their share and this was accepted. (Roland was in debt to George and this may have influenced his decision.)

(5) Rupert, who was himself promised a cow as George's fellow clansman, offered to contribute 100 shillings to Alfred's share. He did this in his capacity as William's affine, since he is married to William's daughter.

(6) William's son-in-law who belongs to the bride's mother's clan offered 100 shillings for James. His father had already offered money for his fellow clansman, the bride's mother's brother.

(7) The bride's mother's brothers announced that they were satisfied with what they had been given.

(8) William's brother promised a further cow for James.

(9) William offered a third cow to Jacob who still tried to insist upon his full portion.

(10) George himself eventually announced that he was in favour of the marriage and said that if Jacob wished to continue to make an issue over his cows, he could have George's own portion. This left Jacob in an untenable position and he eventually accepted the three head of cattle offered to him. George also said that he was not deterred from supporting the marriage by his recognition that yet other dissatisfied persons might come to obtain redress from himself after the marriage.

(11) Just before I left some small extra payments were offered including two goats for the bride's mother, a sheep and a lamb for Alfred's wife, 5 shillings for one of the bride's senior clansmen who was her classificatory grandfather, and a chicken for myself.

As I have mentioned, the making of this series of offers proved to be a major turning point in the proceedings. Partly, of course, the offers showed that the participants had realized that they had reached the limits of advantage to be gained by hard negotiations. But it is true too, I think, that some at least of those involved were also moved at this stage by a genuine desire to be helpful. [8]

It may be noted that numbers (2), (5) and (6) at least, of these last offers were made by interstitial persons with ties to both parties, and I have already pointed out that the system itself tends to guarantee the presence of such persons. It remains to add that George's offer is also significant in this context, since it reflects the development of ties between him and his new affines, which complement and may even conflict with those between him and his agnates and other kin. Labwor people explicitly recognize the fact that fathers-in-law may wish to give help of this sort to their sons-in-law during the period of bridewealth negotiations, and they speak of it as *Konyo kor or* (literally 'helping the breast of the son-in-law').[9] They are also fully aware that a man's kin may well ultimately be the worse off for such help, as Jacob was as a result of George's ultimatum to him. It may be added that it is perhaps in this light that we should understand the better initial response at the kraal to 'family' *(dyekal)* demands as opposed to those for clansfolk and others.

The next morning I was brought a written list of the agreed payments. This included a few extra items in addition to those mentioned, the most important being a goat for George's friend Andrew. The total payments amounted to forty-three cows and seven sheep and goats, the various monetary payments having been translated into livestock equivalents. Later I heard that a couple more goats had since been added and I was told that such additional payments were likely to be made from time to time.

V

I have set out in this paper to describe a particular set of bridewealth negotiations, and I have tried to bring out some of the main features of the negotiating machinery involved. Among these the more or less structurally guaranteed presence of senior clansmen who will not themselves be making or receiving bridewealth payments, and the similar presence of a variety of interstitial persons seem to be important, as does the tendency of the bride's father to develop his own rather special ties with the groom's people. In this context, the extraordinary degree of conflict which existed between the parties in question seems to me to be a matter of particular interest. For although this conflict in some ways makes the material which I discuss somewhat atypical, the fact that it did not prevent the reaching of agreement between the parties is, in part at least, a testimony to the efficiency of the negotiating system which may be more easily overlooked or taken for granted when it is not working under strain.[10]

Notes

[1] The fieldwork, upon which this essay is based, was carried out in Labwor during the greater part of 1967. I am extremely grateful to the British Academy, the Makerere Institute of Social Research, and the University of Cambridge for generous financial and other help in support of this work.

[2] Cf. Gulliver (1963: 297-8) and Smith (1956: 47-9 and *passim*).

[3] The term *ateker* is a Central Nilo-Hamitic one found among such peoples as the Jie, Turkana and Karimojong, and also among the Luo-speaking Lango. Both *kaka* and *ateker* may be used occasionally to describe lower order segments than the clan.

[4] I have not used the real names of the persons concerned in this case.

[5] This fellow-clanswoman was married in the Local Roman Catholic Mission Church in addition to the traditional marriage procedure. A Church wedding, which is only possible for a first wife, is a source of some pride and prestige to the bride, and this added to the tensions of the situation.

[6] Bracketed numbers before the name or other designation of a person refer to his place in the list in Table 1. Numbers following refer to the number of cattle demanded for him.

[7] Evans Pritchard, (1940: 153) has noted the comparable presence and participation of such persons in his insightful discussion of Nuer bloodwealth negotiations.

[8] It is perhaps worth noting here that my material points very clearly to the co-existence and importance of both 'economic' and 'social' factors in bridewealth payments rather than a simple predominance of either.

[9] Gulliver (1955: 238-9) discusses similar behaviour by fathers-in-law among the Jie and Turkana.

[10] A tragic testimony to the reality and strength of the conflicts in this case was the suicide of the bride, after a quarrel apparently involving her husband and his first wife, in the latter half of 1968. As is customary, she was buried in her husband's father's compound where she had been living since the transfer of bridewealth. Prior to this she had been mainly living at her father's home.

BIBLIOGRAPHY

Andriamanzato, R. 1957 *Le Tsiny et le Tody dans la Pensée Malgache*, Paris.

Apter, David E. 1963, *Ghana in Transition*, New York.

Arbrousset, F. 1950, *Le Fokon'olona a Madagascar*, Paris.

Ashton, E. H. 1952, *The Basuto*, Oxford.

Bailey, F. G. 1965,'Decisions by Consensus in Councils and Committees' in A.S.A. Monographs no.2, *Political Systems and the Distribution of Power*, London.

Barnes, J. A. 1954, 'Class and Committees in a Norwegian Island Parish' *Human Relations*, VII, 1.

Bealey, F., Blondel J. and McCann W. P. 1965, *Constituency Politics, a study of Newcastle-under-Lyme*, London.

Bloch, M. 1967a, 'L'extension de la notion de "Havana" dans la societe Merina rurale,' in *Bulletin de l'Academie Malgache*, (N.S.) XL111, 2, 1965.

1967b, 'Notes sur l'organisation sociale de l'Imerina avant le regne de Radama 1', in *Annales de L'Universite de Madagascar*, no.7.

1968a, 'Tombs and Conservatism among the Merina of Madagascar', *Man* (N.S.) 3, no.1.

1968b, 'Astrology and Writing in Madagascar', in J. Goody (ed.), *Literacy in Traditional Societies*, London.

1971, *Placing the Dead*, London and New York.

Bohannan, Laura 1958, 'Political Aspects of Tiv Social Organization' in John Middleton and David Tait (eds.), *Tribes Without Rulers*, London.

Bohannan, Paul 1957, *Justice and Judgment among the Tiv*, London.

Bradbury, R. E. 1969, 'Patrimonialism and Gerontocracy' in Mary Douglas and P. M. Kaberry (eds.), *Man in Africa*, London.

Busia, K. A. 1951, *The Position of the Chief in the Modern Political System of Ashanti*, London.

Caldwell, J. C. 1967, 'Population: General Characteristics' in Birmingham, Neustadt and Omaboe (eds.), *A Study of Contemporary Ghana*, vol.II, London.

Cardozo, B. N. 1921, *The Nature of the Judicial Process*, Yale.

Casalis, E. 1861, *The Basutos* (1st English ed.), London.

Chapus, G. S. and Ratsimba, E. 1953, *Histoire des Rois; traduction du Tantaran'ny Adriana du R. P. Callet*, Tananarive.

Condominas, G. 1960, *Fokon'olona et Collectivités Rurales en Imerina*, Paris.

Delteil, P. 1931, *Le Fokon'olona et les Conventions de Fokon'olona*, Paris.

Deschamps, H. 1961, *Histoire de Madagascar*, Paris.

Ellis, W. 1938, *History of Madagascar*, London.

Evans Pritchard, E. E. 1940, *The Nuer*, Oxford.

Fallers, Lloyd A. 1969, *Law Without Precedent*, Chicago.

Forde, C. D. and Jones, G. I. 1950, *The Ibo and Ibibio Speaking Peoples of South-eastern Nigeria*, London.

Fortes, Meyer 1948,'The Ashanti Social Survey – a Preliminary Report', *Human Problems in British Central Africa*, no.6.

1953, 'The Structure of Unilineal Descent Groups', *American Anthropologist*, vol.55.

Frankenberg, Ronald 1957, *Village on the Border*, London.

Gann, L. H. 1958, *Birth of a Plural Society; Development of Northern Rhodesia under the British South Africa Company 1894–1914*, Manchester.

Gluckman, Max 1955, *The Judicial Process among the Barotse of Northern Rhodesia*, Manchester.

Grandidier, A. 1892, 4 vols. in *Histoire Physique, Naturelle et Politique de Madagascar*, Paris.

Grandidier, A. and Grandidier, G. 1908, 'Ethnographie' in *Histoire Physique, Naturelle et Politique de Madagascar*, Paris, 1892.

Green, M. M. 1947, *Ibo Village Affairs*, London.

Gulliver, P. H. 1955, *The Family Herds*, London.

1963, *Social Control in an African Society*, London.

Hailey, Lord 1953, *Native Administration in the British Africa Territories, Part Five* H.M.S.O. London.

Hunter, M. 1936, *Reaction to Conquest*, Oxford.

Isnard, H. 1953, 'Les Bases Geographiques de la Monarchie Hova', in *Evantail de l'Histoire Vivante, Hommage a Lucien Febvre*, Paris.

Julien, G. 1908, *Institutions Politiques et Sociales de Madagascar*, Paris.

Kagwa, A.1952, *Ekitabo Kye Mpisa za Baganda* (3rd ed.), Kampala and London.

Kuper, Adam 1969, 'The Kinship Factor in Ngologa Politics', *Cahiers D'Etudes Africaines*, IX, 34.

1970, *Kalahari Village Politics: An African Democracy*, London.

Leach, E. R. 1961, *Pul Eliya*, London.

Legamble, 1963, *Le Fokon'olona et le Pouvoir*, Tananarive.

Mair, Lucy 1962, *Primitive Government*, London.

Maud Committee, 1967, *Report of the Committee on the Management of Local Government*, vol.1 H.M.S.O., London.

Meek, C. K. 1937, *Law and Authority in a Nigerian Tribe*, London.

Mitchell, G. Duncan, 1952,'The Parish Council and the Rural Community', *Journal of African Administration*, IV, 3.

Naipaul, V. S. 1967, *The Mimic Men*, London.

Nsarkoh, J. K. 1964, *Local Government in Ghana*, Accra.

O'Brien, Conor C. 1962, *To Katanga and Back: A U.N. Case History*, London.

Pain, L. 1910, *De l'Institution de Fokon'olona a Madagascar*, Poitiers.

Raharijaona, H. 1965,'Le droit Malgache et les Conventions de Fokon'olona' in J. Poirer (ed.), *Etudes de Droit Africain et de Droit Malgache*, Tananarive.

Rattray, R. S. 1929, *Ashanti Law and Constitution*, Oxford.

Razafindraibe, *Fokon'olona* (occasional newspaper).

Research Report to the Royal Commission on Local Government in England, H.M.S.O. London.

Richards, A. I. 1935, 'Tribal Government in Transition', Supplement to *Journal of the Royal African Society*, XXXIV, 3.

1939, *Land, Labour and Diet in Northern Rhodesia*, Oxford.

1969 , 'Keeping the King Divine', *Proceedings of the Royal Anthropological Institute for 1968*.

Schapera, I. 1943, 'The Work of Tribal Courts in the Bechuanaland Protectorate', *African Studies*, vol.2.

1947, *The Political Annals of a Tswana Tribe*, Cape Town.

1956, *Government and Politics in Tribal Societies*, London.

1966, 'Tswana Legal Maxims', *Africa*, XXXVI,2.

1970, *Tribal innovators: Tswana chiefs and Social Change 1795–1940*, London.

Sharpe, L. J. 1960, 'The Politics of Local Government in Greater London', *Public Administration*, vol.38, London.

Silberbauer, G. B. and Kuper, A. J. 1966, 'Kgalagari Masters and Bushman Serfs: Some Observations', *African Studies*, 25 no.4.

Smith, M. G. 1956, 'On Segmentary Lineage Systems', *Journal of the Royal Anthropoligical Institute*, vol.86, London.

1960, *Government in Zazzau*, London.